Input-based Tasks in Foreign Language Instruction for Young Learners

Task-Based Language Teaching: Issues, Research and Practice (TBLT)

ISSN 1877-346X

Task-Based Language Teaching (TBLT) is an educational framework for the theory and practice of teaching second or foreign languages. The TBLT book series is devoted to the dissemination of TBLT issues and practices, and to fostering improved understanding and communication across the various clines of TBLT work.

For an overview of all books published in this series, please see
http://benjamins.com/catalog/tblt

Volume 9

Input-based Tasks in Foreign Language Instruction for Young Learners
by Natsuko Shintani

Input-based Tasks in Foreign Language Instruction for Young Learners

Natsuko Shintani
University of Auckland

John Benjamins Publishing Company
Amsterdam / Philadelphia

The paper used in this publication meets the minimum requirements of the American National Standard for Information Sciences – Permanence of Paper for Printed Library Materials, ANSI Z39.48-1984.

DOI 10.1075/tblt.9

Cataloging-in-Publication Data available from Library of Congress:
LCCN 2015050476 (PRINT) / 2016006656 (E-BOOK)

ISBN 978 90 272 0733 3 (HB)
ISBN 978 90 272 0734 0 (PB)
ISBN 978 90 272 6730 6 (E-BOOK)

John Benjamins Publishing Company · https://benjamins.com

Table of contents

Acknowledgement

I thank the three series editors, Martin Bygate, John Norris, and Kris Van den Branden for their professional and thoughtful editorship of this book. I received enormous support and encouragement as well as detailed feedback from Martin Bygate, in particular. I owe thanks to many people who supported my PhD research project which this book is based on. I would like to thank Scott Tordoff, who provided me the support I needed when conducting the classroom study. I am especially grateful to the Japanese children for their time and enthusiastic participation in my research project. Perhaps more than anyone else, I am indebted to Rod Ellis for his support throughout the process of my PhD and the assembling of this book.

Series Editors' Preface

Since its inception, the series *Task-Based Language Teaching: Issues, Research and Practice* has seen 'issues' as focal, and their relationship to both research and practice as fundamental. Although all our volumes are inevitably articulated around issues that authors see as critical, it is equally inevitable that the weight they each attach to the dimensions of research and of practice will vary. With this in mind, it is a special pleasure to welcome Natsuko Shintani's volume to the series.

As the reader will see from its opening chapter, the entire volume is rooted in a practical classroom issue, as it was experienced at first hand by the author, namely how to teach English to young, absolute beginning learners. In order to find potential solutions, practical challenges (e.g., based on cultural and institutional traditions of language education) first had to be conceptualised, in order to enable the formulation of alternative approaches that might prove effective. This in turn led to relevant background research, trial and error, and subsequently to the planning and implementation of a carefully thought-through and reflectively implemented classroom-based innovation as well as its empirical investigation. The result is a volume which we are delighted to include in this series. Indeed, this work represents the kind of "researched pedagogy" that we have hoped to encourage through the series, and which we believe to be the ultimate justification for a task-based approach to education.

This volume has a number of distinctive qualities, above all combining a range of elements that might be considered key for a genuinely applied linguistic and researched pedagogic publication: firstly, it starts from a personal narrative, including sensitive description and careful documentation of the immediate and wider educational context, as well as associated challenges for educational innovation. Next, the theoretical backgrounding it provides is motivated both theoretically and practically, leading to a statement of probable best practice under the given teaching and learning circumstances. The design and implementation of the investigation are systematic from both practical and epistemological perspectives, and clearly explained. Qualitative and quantitative data are used to complement each other, leading to a triangulated set of findings that offer deep insights into the process and product of the task-based innovation at hand. Finally, the book is written in a way that is accessible throughout to researchers and practitioners alike.

Thus we believe that the resulting publication is an important and cutting-edge contribution, not just to the series and to the field of TBLT, but to applied linguistics in general.

Martin Bygate, John Norris, Kris van den Branden
Series Editors

CHAPTER 1

Getting started with task-based teaching

This book is an account of my experience of task-based language teaching (TBLT) with very young, beginner learners in a small private language school in Japan. My dissatisfaction with traditional approaches to teaching English involving presentation-practice-production (PPP) led me to experiment with TBLT to see whether it could be an effective way to promote second language learning in children in a so-called 'acquisition poor' context like Japan. My primary focus in this book is to report on a study that compared these two different approaches to language teaching, both in terms of instructional practices and learning outcomes. In this introductory chapter, however, I would like to provide a more personal account of my experience with the two approaches to show readers why I came to reject PPP and to switch to TBLT in my own teaching. My hope is that the 'story' I have to tell will provide a concrete context for the more academic chapters that follow and also provide a practical example of what TBLT can offer teachers such as myself.

The starting point – presentation, practice, production (PPP)

I started my new career as a language teacher in a large private language institution where I taught English to young children aged three to eleven years. However, after a while I became somewhat disillusioned, as students who had studied English at the school for several years still had very limited communicative proficiency in English (e.g., they were only able to provide brief answers to simple questions). I thought this was because the children only took lessons once or twice a week and the lessons themselves were of very short duration (i.e., 40 or 60 minutes). I believed that more frequent and longer lessons were needed to allow the students to practice more and this would help them to acquire communicative ability more rapidly. This made me decide to start my own school in Toyota city in Japan where I lived. The first job at my school was to design a curriculum. I decided to provide longer lessons than other language schools and so offered the students one 90-minute lesson per week.

I devised a format for lessons partly based on my teaching experience and partly based on the teacher's guide attached to the ready-made course book I employed in my school. The course book was the *Let's Go* series (Nakata, Frazier, Hoskins, & Graham, 2007), one of the bestselling books at that time in Japan. It consisted of a set of six books for children of primary school age (about 6 to 12 years old). As in many course books for young learners, the six books introduced vocabulary and grammar points roughly sequenced from easy to difficult. A typical book had eight units, each of which presented and engaged learners in the practice of some target words and one or two grammatical structures. The Teacher's Book for this series emphasized three basic steps: (1) teach the target words first in isolation (e.g., "pencil"), (2) practise them in sentences (e.g., "It's a pencil"), and finally (3) practise them in question-and-answer sequences (e.g., "What's this?" → "It's a pencil"). The course book also recommended teaching the question ("What's this?") and the answer ("It's a pencil") separately before combining them into a 'conversation'. My teaching was based on the recommended methodology for this book but also introduced a number of innovations. I will first describe a typical 90-minute lesson in my school and then outline the additional activities I devised.

Unit 2 in *Let's Go Book 1* introduced 11 colour adjectives and two target sentences: "What colour is this?" and "It's (colour)". The lesson began with a warm-up session where I greeted the students and asked their names in English. Then I instructed the students to open the page of the text book to the day's lesson. The page first showed the 11 different colours on a colour palette. I modeled the oral form of each colour word followed by a production exercise requesting the students to repeat each word after the teacher. At this stage, the target words were produced in isolation. Then I introduced each target word in the first target sentence (e.g., "It's green"), translating the sentence into Japanese. This was followed by a substitution exercise where I pointed to each colour and asked the students to make sentences such as "It's green". Then I introduced the other target sentence, "What colour is this?" using the pictures in the text book which depicted a number of colour paint jars on shelves. First, the students repeated chorally after the teacher's model (e.g., "what colour is this? It's orange"). Then, they took part in teacher-led choral production practice of a simple two-part dialogue:

> Teacher: What colour is this?
> Class: It's green.

Finally they worked in pairs to practice the same dialogue. This part of the lesson concluded with a simple listening activity where the students listened to audio-recorded sentences, such as "What colour is this? It's green" and circled the correct colour in their book.

The additional activities I devised were intended to enable further practice of the target items and structures in the 90-minute lesson. My idea was to provide the students with an opportunity for using the target features more extensively and more communicatively. One of the activities that was popular in my school was called "Stepping Game". This was a competitive game that involved the students in naming the objects shown in pictures or making a sentence containing the target word. I arranged colour flash cards on the floor of the classroom and then asked two students to step onto one of the cards. One student said "What colour is this?" and the other replied by naming the colour (e.g., "It's blue"). They scored points if they could successfully complete this mini dialogue. The students competed in teams, and the team that scored the most points was declared the winner. The second activity was a "Tell-and-Do task", which I designed to provide a more communicative context for practicing the target items. The students worked in pairs. One student was given a sheet with just numbers written on it. The other student had a sheet with a colour next to each number. This student had to say the name of the colour next to each number so that his/her partner could draw in the colour next to the correct number on his/her sheet. I walked around the class helping out when a student was unable to name a colour correctly.

Although I did not realize it at the time, the lesson format I followed involved the traditional presentation-practice-production (PPP) sequence (Byrnes, 1986; Ur, 1996). It started with the presentation of a language feature, followed by controlled practice exercises using the materials in the text book. My additional activities then encouraged freer production of the target items and structures. By providing opportunities for the students to produce the target words and sentences in both mechanical drills and more communicative activities I hoped that the students would learn and remember what they had been taught and would develop the ability to communicate in English.

However, as time passed I became more and more doubtful about the efficacy of the approach I had adopted. As the students who had first enrolled in my school got older, I recognized the same problem I had experienced earlier. Their communicative abilities still failed to develop. I noted that although they were able to produce the structures they had learned in the context in which they had learned them, they were still not able to use them in real communication (i.e., outside of the classroom activities). One of the typical questions I received from parents was, "When is my child going to start speaking English?" I found myself asking: "If the students can only use the structures they practice intensively and repeatedly in the lessons in which they were taught, how many lessons would be needed to teach sufficient structures thoroughly enough for them to be able to communicate freely?" In fact, many of the students stopped coming to the school before they had acquired any real communicative skills. As a result, I came to the conclusion that PPP was not very effective for developing communicative ability in young, beginner learners in Japan.

Moving forward – task-based language teaching

As a consequence of this experience, I started to look for a radically different approach – one that was more compatible with how learners learn a second language (L2) and one that would be well-suited to my young children. The second language acquisition (SLA) literature (Long, 1985; Skehan, 1998; Ellis, 2003) pointed me in a potentially interesting direction – task-based language teaching. I was also encouraged by the work of Willis (1996) that provided a clear framework for conducting a task-based lesson.

The essential difference between PPP and TBLT lies in how language is viewed and consequently what happens in the classroom. In the case of PPP, language is dissected into bits which are then treated as 'objects' to be taught one at a time. In the case of TBLT, language is treated as a tool for 'doing things', that is, activities are primary. Such an approach accorded well with how children naturally orientate to language and how they had learned their first language (L1). I also noted that TBLT does not just aim to foster communicative skills; it also aims to assist learners to acquire linguistic features incidentally through engaging them in focus-on-form activities embedded within meaningful communication.

The central construct in TBLT is 'task'. Lessons are built around tasks. I began, therefore, by ensuring that I had a clear grasp of what a 'task' was. Ellis (2003) proposed that a 'task' must satisfy four basic criteria:

1. The primary focus should be on 'meaning' (i.e., learners should be <u>mainly</u> concerned with encoding and decoding messages not with focusing on linguistic form).
2. There should be some kind of 'gap' (i.e., a need to convey information, to express an opinion or to infer meaning).
3. Learners should largely rely on their own resources (linguistic and non-linguistic) in order to complete the activity. That is, learners are not told what language forms they should use to perform a task although they may be able to 'borrow' from the input the task provided to help them perform it and in some cases limited pre-teaching of language can take place.
4. There is a clearly defined outcome other than the use of language (i.e., the language serves as the means for achieving the outcome, not as an end in its own right). Thus, when performing a task, learners are not primarily concerned with using language correctly but rather with achieving the goal stipulated by the task.

I also needed to consider how to construct a whole task-based lesson. I noted that many TBLT researchers had suggested the use of three principal phases; a pre-task phase, a main-task phase, and a post-task phase (e.g., Estaire & Zanon 1994; Willis 1996). Ellis (2003) suggested ways in which teachers can adjust the difficulty of a task-based lesson in each of these phases (see Table 1.1). For example, the pre-task options listed in Table 1.1 can make the task easier while time pressure in the main task phase can make it more difficult. There were a number of options for focusing on form in all the three phases (e.g., pre-teaching language in the pre-task phase, providing contextual support in the main task, and 'language work' in the post-task phase). The pre-teaching language aims at helping students learn other aspects of language during the task by equipping them with some language to perform the task comfortably, but without aiming to proceduralise it through practice, as in the first phase of PPP (i.e. presentation). I decided to use some of these options to make the tasks suitable for my students.

Table 1.1. Implementation options in the different phases of a task-based lesson (based on Ellis, 2003)

Phase	Options	Description
Pre-task phase	1. Modelling performance of the task	1. Students listen or watch the task being performed by 'experts'.
	2. Pre-teaching language	2. The teacher presents language that will be useful for performing the task.
	3. Schema-building	3. The teacher elicits and extends students' knowledge of the topic of the task.
	4. Strategic planning	4. The students are given time to prepare to perform the task before they actually perform it.
Main-task phase	1. Time pressure	1. Students are given only a limited amount of time to perform the task.
	2. Contextual support	2. Students are allowed access to the input data when they perform the task.
	3. Explicit instruction	3. The teacher takes time out from the performance of the task to explicitly teach a linguistic feature that is useful for performing the task.
	4. Surprise element	4. Additional information relevant to the task is provided after the students have started to perform the task.
Post-task phase	1. Repeat performance	1. Students are asked to repeat the task.
	2. Report	2. Students are asked to report the outcome of the task to the whole class.
	3. Language work	3. Students complete language exercises related to linguistic problems that they experienced when performing the task.

I first tried out TBLT with older children (aged 10 to 12), as it seemed easier to do so with students who already had some English knowledge and the ability to produce some English. In one lesson I used a task I called the Map Task. This involved the students working in pairs. Each member of a pair was given the same map but only one of them had a starting point, a goal, and the route marked on the map. In accordance with Ellis' definition, this task required a primary focus on meaning, there was a gap (only one student had the route marked on it), the learners had to rely on their own linguistic resources (although I did provide some help with the language needed to describe the route), and there was a clearly defined outcome (the student had to draw the route that his/her partner described on his/her map).

The lesson proceeded like this. I began by asking the students to name shops or facilities in their own neighbourhood in English. I wrote the words on the board; if the students did not know the English word, I told it to them. This served a double purpose – 'pre-teaching' the key words and 'schema-building' in the above table. The list of words was also available to the students as they performed the task so they could refer to it anytime they needed to (i.e., it provided some linguistic support for the main task). I then performed a version of the task with all the students, illustrating how to describe the route on the map while the students drew it in on their individual maps. I encouraged the students to ask me questions. In this way I 'modelled' how to undertake the task as suggested by Prabhu (1987), and at the same time I provided the students with input containing the expressions they could use when they performed the task in pairs.

In the main task phase, the students worked on similar Map Tasks in pairs. They repeated the task twice with a different route each time. Then they performed the task a third time but I introduced a "surprise element". This time the two maps were not identical, and so the students also needed to solve the referential problems that arose as they worked through the task. When they realized there were differences in their maps, I told them that one of the maps was an older version.

For the post-task phase, I asked the students to make their own Map Task in pairs. I gave them two blank sheets and asked them to draw the maps making sure that there were some differences in the location of different building on the two maps. Finally, the students exchanged their maps with other students and performed the task again. Throughout the lesson, I helped the students by answering questions and providing feedback on their production. When necessary, I also provided some model sentences to help them give directions. However, the students' primary focus was always on the task outcome rather than accurate production of English. It required them to treat language as a tool, not as an object to be learned. The students had to work together to collaboratively exchange information and, as in real-life communication, deal with any communication problems that arose.

What impressed me was how the students were prepared to struggle to cope with the problems the Map Task posed for them. This was particularly evident when the students realized that their maps contained some referential problems. They did their best to use their limited English knowledge to deal with these. When making their own Map Task in pairs, they mostly used Japanese but code-switched into English at times. However, when they started to work on the Map Task created by a different pair, they only used English. From watching the students perform this task I discovered a number of important points about task-based teaching. First, the task created a context where the students felt it was comfortable and natural to use English. Second, it was not necessary to insist on the use of English all the time. Third, I recognized the benefits of asking them to perform the same kind of task several times (see Bygate, 2015, on task repetition). These understandings informed the approach I adopted in the study reported later in this book.

Input-based TBLT

The Map task – like most of the tasks discussed in the TBLT literature – requires productive ability on the part of students and thus was clearly not suited to another group of students in my school – six year olds who were complete beginners. These were to be the participants in the study I later designed. For such learners, it was essential that I found a way of adapting tasks. I decided to use input-based tasks. These are tasks that require only a non-verbal response from students, while not prohibiting them from attempting to produce language if they so wish. Input-based tasks must still satisfy the four criteria for tasks listed above. In the case of the third criterion (i.e., learners use their own resources) learners need to use both their linguistic and non-linguistic resources (i.e., context and world knowledge) to process the input they are exposed to as part of the task.

I looked first for an example of an input-based task in the SLA research literature and found one in Ellis, Tanaka, and Yamazaki's (1994) study. This seemed especially relevant as it also involved Japanese learners of English, albeit much older than the learners I planned to work with. This study was conducted in a whole-class context. The task – called the Kitchen Task – involved the students listening to the teacher's instructions about where to place various objects in a kitchen. The students were given numbered pictures of these objects and a matrix picture of a kitchen. To show they had understood an instruction they had to locate the correct picture of the object and then write its number in the correct position in the picture of the kitchen. Ellis, Tanaka, and Yamazaki (1994) used this task to investigate the effects of different kinds of input on learners' comprehension and their acquisition of new words, which they used to label the kitchen objects. I was especially interested in one of the conditions they investigated – what the authors called 'interactionally modified input' – as this also involved the students requesting clarification if they could not understand one of the teacher's instructions. I planned to allow my six year olds to also interact if they wanted to.

The kind of input-based task that Ellis et al. investigated was a 'listen-and-do task' (i.e., the students had to listen to the teacher's instruction and respond by performing the appropriate action). Listen-and-do tasks seemed ideal for young children, as they created an interactional context very similar to what they must have experienced when learning their L1. Later in Chapter 5, I provide a full description of the tasks I developed. Here I offer a brief description of one of them. For the "Zoo and Supermarket Task" I designed a number of flash cards depicting different animals and foods. I also designed a three-sided board with pictures of the 'zoo' and the 'supermarket' and small pockets to hold the flash cards. The task worked in this way: I told the students that the purpose of the task was to help the zoo or the supermarket by finding the right cards and placing them in a pocket in the holder. Then I gave instructions which required the students to select the correct card and hold it up. Those students who had chosen the correct card placed it in the pocket on the board. Those students who displayed the wrong card were told to put it in their individual 'incorrect' box. The student with the most cards in the folder was announced as the winner. Of course, as they were complete beginners, initially the children could not understand the instructions. This led to attempts on their part – using their L1 – to address their non-understanding, and interactional work on my part to help them achieve understanding.

As will become clear when I report the study, these listen-and-do tasks resulted in interactions that were very different from those that occurred in my traditional PPP classes. They also involved fundamental differences in the students' attitudes to learning English (i.e., a shift from seeing English as 'study' requiring the memorization of words and patterns to viewing it as a tool for achieving a communicative outcome). The tasks, of course, involved the students in a constant struggle to understand the instructions. I realized that this struggle was an essential element of task-based teaching. In Chapter 3, I will consider why this is so.

Conclusion

In this chapter I have given a personal account of my experience of teaching Japanese children. This experience was the foundation of the research that I report later in the book. I discovered that it was not necessary to narrowly determine which specific items were to be taught in order to plan a lesson and that an alternative approach was to select tasks that could create a context for both pedagogic and communicative work with the students. I realized the limitations of an approach that sought to present discrete language items and practice them in isolation in mechanical type drills, and that even when these were complemented with more communicative activities it did not seem to enable the learners to use what they had been taught in real communication. This led me to experiment with a radically different approach based on tasks and to try to find ways in which I could assist my learners to perform them. I observed that the learners were not flustered when they found they did not possess the English they needed to perform a task but were prepared to struggle, using their L1 and the support

I provided them, to try to complete the task. I saw how the children's attitudes changed from viewing English as an object to be 'learned' to treating it as a tool for purposeful communication, and how this created a context in which English could be acquired naturally. Finally, I understood the importance of my own role as a teacher in TBLT. I was no longer a provider of knowledge but a co-participant who could guide the learners in their struggle to complete a task.

An obvious question, however, is the extent to which the task-based approach I adopted is feasible in an educational system such as that found in Japan. It does not necessarily follow that, because I was able to introduce TBLT in my own school, where the classes were small and where I had complete control over the curriculum, it would also be possible to introduce it more broadly for teaching young learners in the Japanese elementary school system. In the next chapter I consider the problems of achieving this and how they might be overcome, before moving on to a fuller treatment of my own efforts at implementing TBLT for young learners.

CHAPTER 2

Task-based language teaching in "difficult" contexts

Pedagogical issues

In the previous chapter I described how I experimented with task-based language teaching (TBLT) in my own private language school in Japan. I described how the change from PPP to TBLT brought about a fundamental change in the classroom behavior of the children. I observed how young learners of two different age groups with different proficiency levels engaged enthusiastically in performing the tasks I designed. Whereas previously they had treated English as an object to be learned, they now began to use it as a tool to communicate to achieve the outcomes of the tasks. In this chapter, I will turn our attention to various issues in implementing TBLT in teaching context in Japan.

One of the main reasons for the reluctance to embrace TBLT is the strongly held belief that TBLT is not a suitable approach for Asian learners. For example, Swan (2005) argued that TBLT might be suited for "acquisition-rich" environments (e.g., where learners have access to the target language in the wider community) but not for "acquisition-poor" environments (such as many "foreign" teaching contexts) where a more structured approach is required to ensure that learners develop the grammatical resources needed for communicating. Carless (2007) questioned the value of TBLT in a "Confucian-heritage culture context where task-based teaching may prove to be in conflict with traditional educational norms" (p. 596). Hu (2002) and Jing (2006) pointed out that a major obstacle to communicative language teaching in many Asian countries is the examination-oriented educational system. However, Asian contexts are not monolithic. Tsui and Tollefson (2007), for example, noted that English is viewed differently in different countries in Asia. For example, it is linked with economic competiveness in Singapore but it is more closely associated with individual opportunity in Bangladesh.

In general, however, PPP remains the dominant approach in Japan and elsewhere. Surveys of existing teaching materials (Ellis, 2002; Nitta & Gardner, 2005) show just how dominant PPP has been. The text book I used – *Let's Go* – is a good example of this approach. By contrast, TBLT has made only limited inroads in Japan and in most other contexts. There are reports of the implementation of TBLT for young learners in Flanders (Van den Branden, 2006) and in Hong Kong (Carless, 2002), but otherwise

PPP remains the preferred approach even with young learners. There are very few, if any, published course books for beginner learners of English based on task-based language teaching. The dominance of PPP is undoubtedly the result of 'tradition' – it is passed down from one generation of teachers to the next through teacher guides (e.g., Ur, 1996) and through the text books produced and reproduced by major publishers. There is also a pervasive ignorance to TBLT among teachers and teacher educators (see Ellis, 2009 for a review). This situation is particularly the case in Asia (see Adams & Newton, 2009) but also worldwide.

This chapter focuses on the English education of young learners in Japan. It starts by outlining the recent historical background of English education in Japan. The focus is on the policy for foreign language education in public elementary schools, but the role of private language schools will also be considered. The chapter then explores a number of key contextual issues that impact on the successful implementation of TBLT for young learners. I will draw on both the published literature and on personal communication with English teachers. The chapter concludes with suggestions for implementing TBLT in elementary schools in Japan.

Background: "Communicative English ability" in Japan

English education in Asia has been developed under the influence of "economic globalization" – the increasing economic interdependence of national economies across the world through the rapid increase in the cross-border movement of goods, service, technology, and capital (Joshi, 2009). This is the background for the formation of language education policy in Japan.

The "development of communicative language ability" has been a major theme of pronouncements by the Japanese government since the 1980s (Kubota, 1998). In the most recent report, for example, the Ministry of Education, Culture, Sports, Science, and Technology's (MEXT) emphasised that "English is a means of international communication" (MEXT, 2011) and suggested a number of actions needed to achieve this goal. However, this was a view not shared by everyone. Kubota (1998) observed that, in Japan, discourses related to English language often focus on non-Western or anti-Western cultural identities. According to Kubota, Japan's socio-political history is characterised by its power struggle with the West, resulting in contradictory social discourses representing both resistance and accommodation to Western hegemony. Anti-West critics purport that the dominance of English influences the Japanese language as well as people's views of language, culture, race, ethnicity and identity, which are affected by the world view of native English speakers. Seargeant (2009) argued that language instruction directed at communication skills requires 'adopting' Western cultural attitudes and behaviours, leading to a persistent unwillingness to learn English in Japan because of its closed cultural history and its strong essentialist view of its national language. Hu and McKay (2012) pointed out that Japan has "a love/hate relationship with the learning of English" (p. 355). They stated:

> At least in its public rhetoric and school policies, the Japanese appear to have an ambivalent attitude towards the teaching of English: on the one hand, the value of English is recognised as important for Westernisation, globalisation and trade; on the other hand, both Westernisation and globalisation seem to threaten the Japanese people's sense of identity and the uniqueness of their culture and traditions. (p. 355)

In a similar vein, Ortega (2012) pointed to the gap between external value ('globalization') and hidden agenda ('nationalism'). In short, the attitude of Japanese people to English is complex and contradictory. Tsui and Tollefson (2007) reported that, in Japan, English is treated as "a mechanism for rejuvenating the study of local languages as part of nation-building and nation-preserving processes" (Tsui & Tollefson, 2007, p. 261). This ambivalent attitude towards "communicative English ability" has directly or indirectly resulted in a number of practical difficulties in implementing TBLT in Japan.

English education in the elementary school in Japan

In the late 1980s, the Central Council for Education, an advisory body to the Minister of Education, began to discuss the possibility of introducing foreign language education into elementary schools. However, the introduction of English education in elementary schools was hindered by substantial disagreement. There was opposition based on the ideological conviction that elementary schools should focus on Japanese language education in order to establish a distinct identity in students as Japanese nationals (e.g., Otsu & Torikai, 2002). It was also pointed out that introducing English education in elementary schools would result in less time being allocated to other important subjects such as the Japanese language, science, and mathematics. There was a further concern, namely that the inappropriate, exam-oriented, grammar translation methods common in secondary schools would be transferred to elementary schools.

These objections resulted in the Ministry of Education, Culture, Sports, Science, & Technology (MEXT) delaying the introduction of English as a school subject in elementary schools. This reluctance contrasted with other neighbouring East Asian countries such as South Korea and China, which moved rapidly to implement English education at the elementary level. In 2002, MEXT finally authorized the New Course of Study, which allowed individual schools to introduce foreign language activities as part of the "Period for Integrated Study" programme, though not as an academic subject. As the teaching of a foreign language (which, in practice, meant English) was not mandatory for schools, the somewhat vague Ministry guidelines led to considerable diversity in how the policy was interpreted at both local government and school levels (Butler, 2007). Although by 2004 approximately 92.1% of all Japanese public elementary schools were offering some kind of English instruction (MEXT, 2005), the actual implementation varied widely – from a type of immersion programme to irregular activities held for less than ten hours per year. As English was widely viewed as a high stakes subject for students' future educational path and careers, the unequal access to English education in public elementary schools led to a sense of dissatisfaction among parents. Responding to this state of affairs, in 2006 MEXT published a further policy document that made "foreign language activities" a compulsory subject for 5th and 6th graders, but only for one lesson a week. This policy was finally implemented in 2011. In fact, Japan was the last Asian country to introduce English education into its elementary schools. Further, English was still not an academic subject; it continued to constitute "foreign language activity". The political attitude towards English in Japan was and still is uncertain compared to both those Asian countries that have endeavoured to introduce English as the medium of primary education (e.g., Malaysia and the Philippines) and to other countries that have introduced English as a school subject (e.g., China and Korea).

The *Five Proposals and Specific Measures for Developing English Proficiency* issued by MEXT in 2011 introduced a number of structural changes aimed at improving communicative ability of English at the junior and high school levels. However, in the case of elementary school, the goal of foreign language education was much vaguer – cultivating a "positive attitude to communication" (p. 3). None of the five proposals included any practical suggestions for teaching a foreign language in elementary schools.

In short, the official purpose of English education in elementary school has not been "language learning" but rather "attitude cultivation towards a foreign language culture". However, disappointing as this situation is, I would argue that it actually creates an opportunity for introducing TBLT in elementary schools. As I will discuss later, language instruction in elementary schools is not constrained by the linguistic syllabuses which direct the curriculum of junior and senior high school, which make it very difficult to implement TBLT. I would also argue that TBLT, particularly for young learners, is not just a means of developing "communicative language ability". It also has a general educational value, as it has the potential to facilitate creativity and identity construction and also foster the development of the critical and analytical thinking needed to perform opinion and reasoning gap tasks successfully (Prabhu, 1987).

While foreign language education in elementary school has made slow progress, the number of private English language schools for young children has been increasing (Benesse, 2009). This can be traced to two major factors (Koike & Tanaka, 1995). Firstly, due to the lack of clear policy and resources from the central government, public schools have relied on private organizations and individuals to help conduct English instruction. Secondly, the dissatisfaction with language teaching in the public schools has led to parents sending their children to private language schools. As a result, such schools have played an increasingly important role in English education for young learners in Japan.

Issues in implementing TBLT in Japan

Adams and Newton (2009) identified three sets of unique factors that have been found to lead to difficulty in implementing TBLT and other communicative language teaching approaches in Asian countries: institutional factors, classroom factors, and teacher factors. Accordingly, I will examine a number of issues relating to the introduction of communicative approaches in elementary schools in Japan in terms of these three sets of factors. I will also suggest possible solutions to each problem.

Institutional factors

Linguistic syllabus versus task-based syllabus

A linguistic syllabus specifies the content of a language course as a list of linguistic items in the order in which they are to be taught (Ellis, 1993). Linguistic syllabuses cannot be easily reconciled with task-based syllabuses, where the content is specified in terms of a sequence of tasks rather than itemized grammatical features. This has been considered a weakness in the eyes of some commentators (e.g., Swan, 2005), who argue that TBLT neglects the teaching of grammar. Teachers have also expressed doubts about how tasks can serve as an instrument for teaching grammar (Willis & Willis, 2007; Samuda & Bygate, 2008). However, grammar can be taught in various ways through TBLT. Some tasks are designed to direct attention to specific, pre-determined features of language, including grammatical ones, while still conforming to the criteria for a 'task' that I described in Chapter 1. Also, there are various methodological strategies to induce a focus on grammatical form in task-based lessons – for example, by providing opportunities for pre-task planning (i.e., allocating time for learners to plan before they begin to perform a task), allowing time for online planning while they perform the task, and by assisting learners to address their linguistic problems during performance of the task. I will examine these strategies and the theoretical rationale for them in the next chapter. Also, a task-based lesson can include a post-task phase where direct (and even traditional) teaching of linguistic features that were observed to be problematic for learners in the main-task phase can take place.

As in many other Asian countries, junior or senior high school teachers in Japan are required to follow the designated linguistic syllabus (Hu & McKay, 2012) but, as English has not been considered an academic subject in elementary schools, teachers are free to choose the type of syllabus. In practice, however, elementary schools have chosen to adhere to a linguistic syllabus. This is because the course books authorized by MEXT are based on a linguistic syllabus that specifies the formulaic expressions, vocabulary, and grammar to be taught (MEXT, 2012). Teachers are familiar with a syllabus that specifies the content to be learned in precise terms as most other academic subjects in the elementary school involve such syllabuses. Also, as learners of English they had all experienced a structural approach, and most elementary school teachers have no knowledge of task-based syllabuses. Hence teachers are unlikely to adopt a task-based approach until there are suitable course books available and until they receive training in the principles and techniques of task-based teaching. As these are unlikely to be immediately available, alternative solutions are needed.

Two alternatives have been suggested by TBLT advocates. The first is to adhere to a linguistic syllabus but to make use of focused tasks to implement it. This approach has been suggested by some teacher educators as a way of introducing tasks into an existing curriculum. For example, Willis and Willis (2007), drawing from Brumfit (1979), suggested "reversed PPP" where the last phase of PPP (i.e., free production activities) becomes the first phase, followed by grammar presentation and controlled practice as needed. Alternatively Carless (2007) suggested utilizing the post-task phase to teach pre-planned grammar. However, this approach does not address one of the fundamental problems of a linguistic syllabus, namely that learners have their own built-in syllabus and do not acquire grammar as a set of 'accumulated entities' (Rutherford, 1988). In the next chapter, I will consider how learners' acquire the grammar of an L2 and the difficulty this poses for a linguistic syllabus. Also, it is not really feasible to design focused tasks for every single grammatical feature that needs to be taught. As Loschky and Bley-Vroman (1993) pointed out, it is very difficult to design a task that makes the use of a specific grammatical feature essential, as learners are likely to avoid the use of structures they find difficult by finding other means for performing the task.

The second option is to employ a modular syllabus (Brumfit 1984; Ellis, 2003), where a linguistic syllabus and a task-based syllabus are used in parallel. The lessons in the linguistic syllabus can be taught with PPP. Ellis suggested that this would serve to develop learners' explicit knowledge of grammar. These lessons would be entirely separate from the task-based lessons that would provide a basis for developing the kind of knowledge needed to engage effectively in free communication. Ellis argued that the two syllabuses should exist as separate modules and no attempt made to establish links between them.[1] He pointed out the danger of tasks being treated as a means of practising linguistic features that had been explicitly taught, namely, that learners

1. Ellis' proposal for two separate modules echoes in Brumfit's (1984) earlier suggestion that 'accuracy' and 'fluency' be addressed separately in a language curriculum.

would revert to practising 'objects' rather than using language as a tool to achieve a communicative outcome. Ellis' proposal might serve as a practical way of introducing TBLT, as it would avoid confronting teachers with an approach that is entirely new to them. They would have the security of the linguistic syllabus for some of their lessons while the TBLT module would allow children to experience learning in the way they were most familiar with as a result of their experience of learning their mother tongue. However, to achieve this, teachers would still need to be familiar with the various strategies for implementing TBLT with young learners.

Examination system

Nunan (2003) pointed out the large gap between principle and practice in English teaching in Japan. He noted that while the curriculum emphasises the "implementation of communicative activities to enable students to communicate their feelings or thoughts", in actual classrooms "teachers emphasise the development of reading and writing skills to help learners pass entrance exams to senior high school and, later, university" (Nunan, 2003, p. 600). The problems that traditional examination systems pose for communicative language teaching in Asian countries have been frequently commented on (e.g., Carless, 2007; Hu, 2002; Jing, 2006; Kubota, 2011).

Although the elementary school child is still a long way from the university entrance examination, many young students are, in fact, still not free of the examination system. As English is considered to be an important academic subject in the junior/senior high school and at university, many parents encourage their children to "start early" in order to ensure their future academic success. There are large numbers of cram schools (i.e., private schools specializing in preparing students for the entrance examinations) that offer English classes for elementary school students. Consequently various commercialized English proficiency tests for elementary school students have seen the light of day in the last decade (e.g., ACET [Association of Children's English Testing] test, Test of English Communication Skills for Preteens [TECS], Cambridge Young Learners English Test, and JAPEC [The Japan Association for the Promotion of English for Children] test). An on-going concern in discussions of language education in Japan is how to link the instruction provided in elementary schools (i.e., as a non-academic subject directed at listening and speaking) with that provided in English classes in junior high schools (i.e., instruction that is examination oriented and focused on reading and writing; Butler, 2007). It was in response to this problem that the government decided to abandon the idea of language instruction as "foreign language activity" in favour of making it an "academic subject" (MEXT, 2012). Unfortunately, this makes it more likely that exam-oriented teaching will become the norm in elementary schools as well as high schools.

The solution, however, is not to abolish the examination system. As Chen, Warden, and Chang (2005) observed, examination-oriented motivation is of value in a context such as Japan where there is no opportunity to use the L2 outside the classroom for most learners. The real problem lies not in the idea of having an examination but in the kind of examination that is likely to be developed (i.e., an examination that focuses heavily on assessing learners' understanding of the linguistic rules that figure in a linguistic syllabus). Such an examination is likely to emphasize reading and writing rather than listening and speaking. Indeed, it was the danger of this happening that led MEXT to initially resist making English an academic subject. The solution, of course, is to ensure that the examination focuses on assessing communicative skills. This will encourage teachers and students to place the emphasis on developing those skills.

There is some sign that the government recognizes the need for this. The government report *Five Proposals and Specific Measures for Developing Proficiency in English for International Communication* (MEXT, 2011) acknowledged that the "Action Plan" for the New Course of Study had not been met in full and that "tasks and policies for English education in this country have to be revised in order to truly cultivate Japanese with English abilities" (p. 2). The five proposals were: (1) establishing national learning attainment targets; (2) ensuring that students "feel the necessity of English" through international exchange learning, school trips abroad, etc.; (3) hiring more Assistant Language Teachers (i.e., native speakers of English); (4) providing opportunity for teacher education and encouraging teachers to improve their English; and (5) encouraging universities to use more oral-oriented entrance examinations. These proposals might have an effect in the future – although top-down pronouncements by MEXT have typically had little impact on what goes on in most classrooms. Many of the commercialized English proficiency examinations developed for elementary students focus on writing and reading comprehension.

Some educators argue that actual change needs to start from the bottom – with individual teachers. Wedell (2009) noted "after all, if [the exam system were to change] before most teachers were at least beginning to teach for 'communication', most learners would fail, and they, together with teachers and teacher educators, would probably be the ones blamed by public and policy makers alike" (p. 631). I will examine this issue in detail later.

Classroom factors

Learners' ability

Some critics of TBLT have questioned the feasibility or appropriateness of TBLT for learners who have limited ability to produce L2 in free communication (e.g., Swan, 2005; Carless, 2007; see also Ellis, 2009 for review). A commonly held view of advocates of PPP (e.g., Swan, 2005) is that beginner learners need to be taught grammar because without it they will not be able to communicate. Swan (2005) argued that "holistic focus on form is valuable once learners are ready to integrate the language elements they know into realistic communicative exchanges, but this will often need to be preceded by discrete presentation and practice" (p. 394).

As English is not commonly used in daily life in Japan, most learners have almost zero competence when they start learning English at school. The school curriculum to date supports Swan's position by employing a linguistic syllabus. However, as I argued in Chapter 1, for young children the starting point should not be discrete points of grammar but rather the creating of contexts in which they can communicate with the limited linguistic resources at their disposal (including their L1). Also, as I have pointed out earlier, although tasks primarily focus on communication it is also possible to introduce a focus on grammar in various ways. In other words, TBLT can enable students to develop communicative and grammatical ability concurrently.

However, it is also true that using tasks with beginner learners requires additional skills on the part of teachers. Ortega (2012) suggested three possible ways of increasing the opportunity for young learners with limited L2 proficiency to attend to linguistic forms in TBLT: (1) guided planning, (2) task repetition, and (3) input-based tasks. Guided planning utilizes the pre-task phase to help learners prepare to perform the tasks and in the process becoming aware of the grammatical features they will need to use. For example, Mochizuki and Ortega (2008) investigated task-based learning among first-year high school students in Japan. The students were asked to complete an oral story-retelling task with a class partner under one of three conditions: without any prior planning (n = 17), after 5 minutes of unguided planning (n = 20), or after 5 minutes of planning with guidance in the form of a grammar handout about English relative clauses (n = 19). The guided planning group received L2 audio input and grammar guidance in their pre-task phase. This study also showed that high school students in Japan, who have little, if any, experience of communicative oral activities can successfully benefit from tasks. The second way, task repetition, has been shown to have a favourable effect on learners' performance of a task (e.g., Bygate, 2001; Lynch, 2000; Pinter, 2005). In the Japanese context, Hawkes (2012) investigated the effect of asking learners to repeat tasks, as a post-task activity, on the attention they paid to form. The results showed that the participants appeared to switch their attention from meaning towards form in the repeat performance. The third approach suggested by Ortega is input-based tasks. As we have seen in the example of an input-based task in Chapter 1, the children were able to perform the task even though they were complete beginners. Learners do not need grammar to perform simple 'start-up' tasks. Input-based tasks also provide an answer to another criticism of TBLT, namely that it fails to ensure adequate input. Swan (2005) claimed that TBLT "provides learners with substantially less new language than 'traditional' approaches" (p. 377). This view, however, is based on the faulty assumption (among other inaccurate interpretations about tasks in that article) that all tasks should be production-based. Input-based tasks and the interactions they foster are capable of providing learners with rich input. There are a number of studies (e.g., Ellis, Tanaka, & Yamazaki, 1994) that have shown that input-based tasks are effective in developing linguistic competence.

Further, the claim that learners have to be capable of using grammar before they can begin to communicate reflects a fundamental misunderstanding about the nature of language acquisition. Both L1 and naturalistic L2 acquisition do not begin with 'grammar' but with a 'pre-basic variety' that is essentially lexical in nature (Klein & Perdue, 1992, 1997). This evolves into a 'basic variety' when verbs start to appear in the learner's communicative speech and finally a 'post-basic variety' when verbs are now inflected for tense and aspect. In other words, grammaticalization takes place only very gradually. There is also clear evidence that this also happens in classroom learning with children (Ellis, 1984). This suggests that there is no need to delay task-based teaching until learners have been taught some grammar by means of PPP.

To sum up, I have suggested that TBLT is feasible with beginner learners if teachers make use of various teaching strategies such as guided planning, task repetition, and input-based tasks. TBLT is ideally suited to young children because it conforms to their understanding of what language is – a tool for making meaning. TBLT is also compatible with what is known about the gradual way in which L2 learners acquire the grammar of a language. These are points that will be explored more fully in the following chapter.

Shared L1

Sugita and Takeuchi (2009) claimed that "in Japan, as in other Asian countries, students learn English in the classroom and usually have little chance to speak English outside the classroom. It is thus very difficult for teachers to motivate their students to learn English for communication" (p. 21). Also, as Kubota (1998) pointed out, classroom harmony is important in Japan and communicating in their L1 (Japanese) serves as an important way of maintaining social cohesiveness. This has also been suggested for other contexts (e.g., Dornyei & Kormos 2000). In other words, it will be difficult to ensure that students make the effort to use English when performing tasks. Nor is it desirable to try to do so.

However, the very fact that students have little opportunity to speak English outside the classroom makes it even more important that such opportunity is available inside the classroom. It is natural for students to resort to their L1 when they face difficulty in communication but, as I observed in my own school, they tend to switch to the L2 once they recognize that the task goal can be achieved by communicating in it. Tasks can serve to motivate learners to use the L2 because their focus is not just on practising English but on using it to achieve the task outcome. Also, the use of English can be encouraged by the way the teacher implements a task. For example, allowing the learners to start in the L1 and then shift to the L2 once they have a grasp of the task procedures, as can occur when children are asked to repeat the same task (Pinter, 2006). Also, the problem of overuse of the L1 is reduced in the case of input-based tasks, as the students have no choice but to try to process the L2 input they are exposed to. Finally, the issue of a shared L1 is less problematic in teaching young children than adults or adolescents. Children naturally enjoy competition, and if they need to use the L2 to 'win', it will be natural for them to try to do so. The fact that one child tries to speak English will motivate the others to also try.

It should be noted, however, that L1 use is not necessarily a bad thing. Studies have reported that learners use the L1 as a mediating tool to complete tasks collaboratively when working in small groups (Alegria de la Colina & Del Pilar Garcia Mayo, 2009; Storch & Wigglesworth, 2003). Other studies have shown that learners can perform at a higher cognitive level when they use their L1 (Alegria de la Colina & Del Pilar Garcia Mayo, 2009; Antón & DiCamilla, 1998; Swain & Lapkin, 2000). Translation and code-switching help learners to access both L2 forms and their meanings (Antón & DiCamilla, 1998). They also help to reduce learner anxiety (Auerbach, 1993). Storch and Wigglesworth (2003) suggested that L1 use is a natural and necessary process and Cook (2001) argued that denying a learner the use of the L1 is like rejecting a part of the learner's linguistic repertoire and is neither feasible nor desirable. In other words, the use of the L1 is entirely appropriate, as long as it serves to achieve the L2 task outcomes.

Large, teacher-centred classrooms

Another criticism of TBLT is that it is not well-suited to large, teacher-centred classrooms, which are common in Japan. A classroom in the junior or senior high school typically holds 40 to 45 students. Butler argued that teacher-centeredness in Japan is culturally rooted in the strong emphasis on "classroom harmonization" (Butler, 2005). Butler explained that:

> [T]he art of harmonizing learning and teaching with context, encompasses various components: it includes both the arrangement of the physical conditions of a given classroom (e.g., the size of the class, seating arrangements, classroom cleanliness, the availability of various technologies) as well as the integration of various psychological variables pertaining to both students and teachers (e.g., the expected roles and behaviours of students and teachers, motivations, anxieties, self-images).
>
> (pp. 438–439)

Task-based teaching, however, is often seen as learner-centred. Swan (2005), for example, argued that task-based language teaching promotes learner-centredness at the expense of teacher-directed instruction. He commented: "the thrust of TBLT is to cast the teacher in the role of manager and facilitator of communicative activity rather than an important source of new language" (p. 391). From these perspectives, TBLT might be considered not well-suited to Japan.

Two issues are relevant here. The first is whether large, teacher-centred classrooms are in fact incompatible with TBLT. There are a number of problems with this position. It assumes that TBLT always involves particular kinds of tasks, specifically oral pair-work or group-work. Clearly, tasks performed in groups will only be effective if the students have sufficient communicative skills in the L2. If learners do not have these skills, they will resort to their mother tongue to complete the tasks without any use of the L2. Implementing tasks through group work, therefore, is of doubtful value for beginner learners. However, there has been some evidence that group-work tasks can be effectively used for low proficiency learners in a large class if appropriate guidance is offered (see Taguchi & Kim, 2014). Also as I pointed out in Chapter 1, tasks can also be input-based. There is plenty of evidence (see, e.g., Ellis, 1999 for a review of studies) to show that input-based tasks enable learners to develop not only the ability to comprehend input but also the grammatical resources they will need to speak and write. Thus, I would argue that whatever the approach, an appropriate teacher-class participatory structure is needed for beginner students. In such a classroom, there is no threat to "classroom harmonization". Also, it is possible to carry out input-based tasks with large classes. In short, TBLT is not incompatible with either teacher-centredness or large classes.

The second issue is whether TBLT degrades the role of teachers because they no longer serve as the source of new language (Swan, 2005). I would argue, however, that the teacher's role is just as important in TBLT as in PPP. A number of teacher educators have pointed out the important role that teachers play in TBLT. Prabhu (1987), for instance, argued that only the teacher is the source of the "good models" of English needed to promote interlanguage development. Van den Branden (2009) claimed that:

> [T]he teacher remains a crucial interactional partner in task-based language classrooms, by taking the role of motivator (i.e., launching the students into action by constructing joint projects), organizer (i.e., making sure that students know what they are expected to do and organizing temporal and spatial aspects of task performance), and, last but not least, conversational partner and supporter, as the more proficient, knowledgeable interlocutor who can feed the language-learning needs of different students in a wide variety of ways." (p. 284)[2]

In a later chapter, I will illustrate the various roles a teacher can adopt when performing input-based tasks with young beginner learners. However, even in production-based

2. Swan (2005), however, took a different view. He argued that that the roles teachers are required to adopt in TBLT are too demanding for many teachers. Adams and Newton (2009) also noted that many non-native teachers lack confidence in teaching "communicative" English.

tasks, the need to direct learners' attention to form during the performance of the task requires skill on the part of the teacher. Thus, I would reject Swan's argument that in TBLT the teacher functions just as a 'manager'. Far from degrading the role of the teacher, TBLT enhances it by requiring the teacher to function as a facilitator and, crucially, as a source of new language. In other words, the roles of the teacher in TBLT are different but no less important than those in traditional approaches.

Unmotivated students

Unmotivated learners are learners who lack motivation. Demotivated learners are learners who had motivation but lost it for one reason or another. Dörnyei (2001) defined demotivation as due to "specific external forces that reduce or diminish the motivational basis of a behavioral intention or an ongoing action" (p. 143). The problem in Japan is twofold. Learners often are unmotivated (i.e., they have no extrinsic or intrinsic reason to try to learn English), but they are also frequently "demotivated" possibly as a result of the traditional type of teacher-centred instruction involving excessive memorization and grammar translation they experience.

Kikuchi and Sakai (2009) examined the demotivating factors in Japanese public and private high schools by asking university students to reflect on their language learning experience in high school. They conducted interviews with five university students from three different colleges and administered a questionnaire with open-ended questions to 47 students in a public university in Japan. The results indicated the following five demotivating factors: (a) teachers' behaviour in the classroom, (b) the use of the grammar translation method, (c) the nature of the tests/university entrance examination, (d) the emphasis placed on memorization, and (e) the choice of learning materials. Out of these five factors, (b), (c), and (d) occur as a result of the traditional type of instruction that dominates in many Japanese classrooms. Kikuchi and Sakai concluded: (1) the nature of a grammar-translation approach does not generally allow students any chance to engage in genuine communication in the target language; (2) classes that focus entirely on university entrance exam preparation should be avoided; (3) teachers are blamed for being critical of their students' errors while their own pronunciation of English is very poor. Without necessarily addressing this last point, TBLT has the potential to prevent demotivation occurring. Tasks create opportunities for communication using the L2. Also, as suggested above, by employing a modular syllabus, it is possible to prepare students for the entrance exam but also to provide lessons that are enjoyable for students. TBLT, therefore, serves as a way of addressing points (1) and (2). Additionally, if students can see that the aim of the teacher is to communicate with them rather than to provide model sentences for them to memorize, the teacher's pronunciation might become less of an issue for students.

Carreira (2012) administered a questionnaire to 505 fifth and sixth grade elementary school children in Tokyo. Based on this investigation, Carreira concluded "students who regard English study as important or useful are likely to enjoy it, but students who feel forced to study English tend not to like it" (p. 197). She also identified three basic psychological needs – autonomy, competence, and relatedness – as important elements in motivation. She suggested that classrooms which increase students' involvement in task design, and which give students leadership roles and freedom in choosing the content, methods, and performance outcomes of learning, will foster a sense of ownership of the learning process and make them more responsible for their own learning. She also claimed that regular experience of success would enhance students' perceptions of competence. She suggested that teachers should provide multiple opportunities for success in the classroom and adjust the difficulty level of tasks to suit the students' abilities.

Carreira's study points to two ways of enhancing learners' motivation: (1) allowing learners to take more control in the classroom and (2) providing multiple opportunities for success. As for the first point, tasks allow the students to take control in the classroom in many ways. One of the criteria for a 'task' (see Chapter 1) is that learners are free to use their own linguistic resources. It is in this respect that TBLT is fundamentally different from PPP. As Cox (2005) put it, "in a PPP lesson learners are being unnaturally constrained when they should be experiencing the richness of meaning potential and practising normal conversational skills" (p. 179). In TBLT, however, learners choose the language for performing a task. Regarding the second point, a task has an outcome other than the display of correct language. For example, in the Map Task introduced in Chapter 1, learners were evaluated in terms of whether they achieved the task outcome (i.e., identified the correct route in the map). The whole aim of TBLT is to enable learners to experience success by helping them to achieve the outcomes of the tasks. Tasks are designed to create a linguistic challenge but also to ensure that students can successfully complete them. TBLT is success-oriented in this respect.

TBLT cannot guarantee motivated learners but it has a much better chance of preventing 'demotivation' than the kind of traditional language teaching found in many English classrooms in Japan.

Teacher factors

Teachers' knowledge and skills

Adams and Newton (2009) observed that teachers in Asian contexts are concerned about the demands that TBLT places on their own language proficiency. Many teachers feel that teaching 'communicative' English is "outside their domain and beyond their ability" (Adams & Newton, 2009, p. 10). Perhaps, this is the biggest problem facing communicative language teaching in Japan. To address this issue, it is important to distinguish teachers' English proficiency level and their ability to implement tasks.

In order to address the issue of teachers' English proficiency, we need to consider what type of L2 knowledge is required to teach communicatively. Krashen (1982) distinguished 'acquiring' a language and 'learning' a language. For Krashen, 'learning' language is a conscious process focused on the grammatical rules of a language, which results in explicit knowledge. 'Acquisition', on the other hand, is a subconscious process that allows for automatic use of language. PPP aims to develop learners' communicative ability but it is doubtful whether it facilitates 'acquisition'. While it may help learners to internalise formulaic chunks, it is more likely to result in learners developing explicit knowledge of grammatical rules. English education in Japan has focused on 'learning' rather than 'acquisition'. It is understandable, then, that most English teachers have failed to develop the kind of procedural knowledge needed to communicate easily and confidently in English. Thus, it is not surprising that teachers consider communicative language teaching "beyond their ability".

Surveys have shown that there is a serious lack of confidence about teaching communicative English among teachers. This problem is more serious among elementary school teachers than junior and senior high school teachers. The Benesse Corporation 2010 (cited in Sakamoto, 2012) reported the results of a survey conducted with 2326 primary school teachers. It reported that while 77% of teachers noted that English should be taught to develop students' communication skills, 68.1% of the teachers stated that they were not confident in teaching English. Similar results were reported by Fennelly and Luxton (2011) who conducted a survey research in a regional city in Japan. The results showed that out of 147 primary teachers they surveyed, only 9% said they were confident in their English teaching abilities, and 72% of respondents said that their English ability was insufficient to teach English. 69% of the teachers surveyed said that they did not have sufficient knowledge to teach English at all. Hu and McKay (2012) reported a survey by Yagi and Igawa (2010). Fifty-four elementary Japanese English teachers attending a professional development course at Shitennooji University expressed a high level of anxiety about teaching English. Almost 97% of the teachers reported a lack of confidence in their own English communication skills and were particularly concerned about their English pronunciation. Hu and McKay also reported a growing concern regarding the quality of team-teaching involving Japanese English teachers and assistant language teachers (ALTs). Over 30% of the elementary school teachers in the survey conducted in Fennelly and Luxton (2011) expressed concern that their team-teaching classes were ineffective because of their inability to communicate with the ALTs and the lack of time to prepare for the team-taught classes. These studies demonstrate that elementary school teachers are anxious, even fearful of teaching English because of their perceived lack of proficiency.

In Korea, primary school teachers receive a minimum of 120 hours of in-service teachers' training involving courses on English conversation, English language pedagogy, educational psychology, and educational philosophy. However, they report still feeling a lack of confidence about communicating in English in front of their students (Butler, 2004). Japan has also taken steps to improve teachers' English proficiency. In 2010, MEXT started the "Japan-US Training and Exchange Program for English Language Teachers", which provides an opportunity for young school teachers to go to the US for one or two years to improve their English ability. However, this opportunity was limited to 1,000 teachers in 2010 and to a smaller number in 2011, which is just a small portion of the total number of English teachers in junior high school (31,487) and senior high school (29,255) (MEXT, 2008). Thus, it is doubtful if such programmes can solve the problem and, in any case this programme does not extend to primary school teachers. It is not clear how much English training is needed to ensure that teachers have the language skills needed to teach communicative English (Butler, 2004), and clearly the training opportunities currently available are still insufficient.

Perhaps, then, it would be better to focus on developing teachers' methodological skills – to equip them with a better understanding of how to teach communicatively and to equip them with the strategies needed. Carless (2003) found that even when elementary school teachers in Hong Kong possessed the necessary English proficiency to implement task-based teaching, they still struggled to do so, in part because they were unclear of what a 'task' was and because they equated TBLT with group work. In other words, these teachers had not yet sufficiently mastered the strategies involved in a task-based approach. And there is another reason for focusing on teachers' methodological skills. Preparing teachers to teach lessons using tasks will create opportunities for teachers to use the L2 communicatively and thus help them to develop their own proficiency. I have argued earlier that teachers need to take on various roles in implementing tasks. I would add another role here – the teacher as a model learner for students. If students see their teacher making an effort to use English to communicate they will be more prepared to try to do the same themselves.

As I pointed out earlier, many of the apparent problems in implementing tasks in Japanese contexts are based either on misconceptions or on an overly narrow view of TBLT. One of the main goals of a training programme for TBLT should be to ensure that teachers have a clear idea of what constitutes a 'task' and understand the importance of treating English as a tool for communicating rather than as an object to be studied and 'learned'. Teachers also need to understand that TBLT is not monolithic and can be modified to suit different institutional contexts and learners of different levels of proficiency (Ellis, 2009). As Carless (2011) pointed out, teachers must be able to "gradually implement ideas of their own choice at a pace that suits them and in a way that matches with the exigencies of their context" (p. 201) but they need help in doing this. Pre-service and in-service teacher education courses should provide teachers with various strategies for implementing tasks in the contexts in which they work. One way in which this can be achieved is by familiarizing them with case studies of teachers who have attempted to introduce TBLT in different instructional contexts (e.g., Willis & Willis, 2007).

Thus, while I do not wish to dismiss programmes directed at improving teachers' English proficiency, I do not see this as the main solution to the problem of how to introduce TBLT into elementary schools in Japan (or elsewhere in Asia). Instead, I advocate programmes that concentrate on developing teachers' understanding of tasks and the methodology of TBLT. Teachers need to experience performing tasks both as a means of developing their own proficiency and as a means of learning how to use them in their own teaching. Perhaps, too, to overcome their lack of confidence in speaking in English, teachers could be provided with 'scripts' of the language needed to implement a particular task. Teaching scripts are already available for teaching PPP lessons in Japan. For example, the Aichi Prefectural Education Centre (2002) provides a list of 532 English sentences classified in 15 main categories (e.g., greeting, direction, evaluation, question, pair-work, group-work, and presentation) with some sub-categories (e.g., activities, dictionary, explanation, and homework) for teachers to use in the English classroom. Some examples for "Direction" are:

Category: *Direction* (sub-category: *Activity*)

1. Could you please read the passage slowly?
2. Please read this page aloud.
3. Please read this page silently
4. Let's take a look at our last/previous lesson.
5. We will perform the skit.
6. We will read the dialogue.
7. Now, let's go on to the next activity.
8. Let's start over.
9. Let's quickly review what we have learned so far.
10. Take a look at the reference book.
11. Let's play a gesture game.

(Aichi Prefectural Education Center, 2002, p. 5)

This is clearly not ideal for conducting task-based lessons, which require the teacher to be able to respond flexibly to communicative problems as they arise. However, they can have a role in input-based tasks performed by the teacher with the whole class, especially if the teacher scripts reflect the characteristics of spoken (not written) English (e.g., they should include pauses, repetitions, and paraphrases). These 'scripts' can help teachers to use English more confidently and accurately in the classroom and increase the students' exposure to the L2. Using scripts in teaching might also help the teacher to improve their teaching strategies. Reeves' (2010) reported a study that showed the benefits of teaching based on a scripted instruction programme (i.e., instruction based on standardized, written scripts) in a second language classroom in the US. Reeves commented "teaching by script opened insight into the English language and introduced the teachers to new pedagogical strategies" (p. 241).

Teachers' willingness to innovate

Karavas-Doukas (1998) pointed out "teachers are the instruments of change and without their willingness, co-operation and participation, there can be no change" (p. 31). Teachers have to accept the need for change, however, as they are in a rapidly changing environment, where many of their students have the opportunity to hear and use English via the Internet. To implement TBLT teachers need to be prepared to change both their attitude to teaching and their practice. However, my personal communication with English teachers and teacher educators in Japan has made it clear to me that many teachers in Japan are reluctant to change the way they teach. To understand why this is so, I will examine Ely's (1990) "Conditions of Change". Ely (1990, pp. 298–299) proposed eight conditions that influence the adoption and implementation of educational innovations by teachers. They are:

1. *Dissatisfaction with the status quo.* This is the first steps to initiate change in an education environment.
2. *Sufficient knowledge and skills.* In the case of TBLT the 'knowledge' that teachers need relates to their understanding of what a task is and the principles of task-based teaching while 'skills' relates to the strategies needed to implement tasks with students.
3. *Resources are available.* Resources refer to materials or tools that are accessible to assist learners to achieve learning objectives.
4. *Time is available.* In the process of educational change, time should be considered as a distinct condition that must be made available for implementation to occur.
5. *Rewards or incentives exist for participants.* There must be sufficient reason to consider change and that is where incentives play an important role.
6. *Participation is expected and encouraged.* Unless the individual who is expected to implement the change has some part in deciding what to do, it is unlikely that the innovation will be implemented with fidelity and enthusiasm.
7. *Commitment.* There must be visible evidence that there is endorsement and continuing support for implementation.
8. *Leadership is evident.* Leaders provide initial encouragement to consider new ideas; they ensure that the necessary training is given and that the materials to do the job are easily available; they are available for consultation when discouragement or failure occur; and they continually communicate their enthusiasm for the work at hand. They need to be acknowledged and respected by their peers.

I have already addressed the issue concerning teachers' language proficiency and teaching skills. I will now discuss two general factors – teachers' dissatisfaction with the status quo (Ely's point 1) and the need for systematic support for the change (Ely's points 3 to 8).

Dissatisfaction with the status quo

Even though Japanese teachers may be reluctant to change, they also experience dissatisfaction with the traditional way of teaching. They acknowledge limitations of the traditional approach and they are also under pressure from the school principal and from parents who want to see evidence of students' developing communicative ability. In Chapter 1, I described how my own "innovation" originated in my dissatisfaction with my teaching and also from the pressure from the children's parents, who expected their children to develop communicative ability in English. In other words, the impetus to change arose from both my own personal dissatisfaction and from external expectations. However, these external expectations may not have much influence on many teachers as parents also expect their children to do well in the junior or senior high school entrance examinations. In other words, they want to see evidence of their children's growing communicative ability but they also want them to succeed in the examinations. As I have already pointed out, the entrance examinations do not assess students' communicative ability. As a result, teachers prioritize teaching to the examination employing traditional approaches. Thus, ultimately, change is unlikely to occur unless teachers experience personal dissatisfaction with the way they are teaching and are prepared to resist teaching to the examination. Ultimately, change depends on whether teachers are prepared to accept that the goal of teaching is to develop students' communicative ability and acknowledge the inadequacy of traditional approaches for achieving this.

Support systems

It is the lack of support systems that poses the biggest obstacle to any change in Japan. Teachers play no part in determining what or how to teach, and there is an implicit assumption that they will teach in the same way as the other teachers in their school. In other words, there is an expectation that they will simply follow the conventional approach. Nor is there any system of rewards for teachers who would like to innovate. Further, as the junior and senior high-school curricula are based on linguistic syllabuses, there are no ready-made materials that teachers can use, and teachers are too busy (Hu & MacKay, 2012) to develop their own materials even if they possessed the expertise to do so. There are only limited opportunities for in-service training and there is no follow-up on these to help teachers implement new practices. There is no system for training leaders to support their peers in implementing a communicative approach.

Overall, then, the situation in Japan has not met any of the Ely's "conditions of change". This suggests that if TBLT is to establish itself in Japanese classrooms, it will only do so if individual teachers' are willing to innovate and to make the effort to overcome all the obstacles they face.

Conclusion

I have examined a number of problems concerning the implementation of TBLT in elementary school classrooms in Japan. Some of the problems reflect a misunderstanding of what TBLT involves and a misrepresentation of its goals. These can be addressed by ensuring that teachers have a clear understanding of what a 'task' is, by helping them to recognize that TBLT is not monolithic but can be implemented in various ways, and by equipping them with the teaching strategies needed to implement tasks in different contexts. However, there are also a number of obstacles rooted in the educational system in Japan, the teaching culture this system has given rise to, and the lack of support systems. These cannot easily be overcome.

Ultimately, then, the prognosis for the introduction of TBLT in Japanese elementary schools is not promising under the status quo. Nevertheless, there are some grounds for optimism. First, there is certainly more opportunity for innovation at the elementary level than at high-school level. Second, young children are more naturally inclined to view language as a 'tool' and thus more ready to accept an approach based on tasks rather than on structures. Third, although many teachers express doubts about their ability to teach communicatively, they recognize the limitations of the traditional approach to teaching young children and the need for communicative activities. Fourth, even though the examination system in Japan inhibits change, this has less impact at the elementary-school level, at least in the early years. In other words, there is space for change. Fifth, the need to develop communicative skills in Japanese students is now official policy and is also supported by the wishes of parents. Thus, while it is unlikely that TBLT will replace traditional approaches to the teaching of English in the near future, there is a real possibility that teachers will be prepared to experiment with task-based lessons.

An innovation can start from a small individual success when a teacher is willing to try something new. One way of encouraging innovation is to provide an example of its adoption and implementation. This is one of the purposes of this book. In a "difficult" context such as Japan, there are no published models of TBLT for teachers to follow. I hope that the study that I report in later chapters will provide an example of TBLT in practice and how it can not only foster communicative ability in children but also assist linguistic development.

CHAPTER 3

Theoretical foundation of task-based language teaching

In Chapter 1, I explained how my dissatisfaction with presentation-practice-production (PPP) led me to experiment with task-based language teaching (TBLT). I also discussed my attempts to introduce TBLT into my own language school by means of input-based tasks, which seemed best suited for beginner learners. In Chapter 2, I reviewed the issues surrounding the implementation of TBLT in Japan, a "difficult" context, and I concluded that it is likely to be more feasible to implement TBLT in primary schools there than in the junior- or senior-high school. These introductory chapters lead to an important question – Is TBLT more effective than PPP for teaching young, beginning second language (L2) learners? This question is of special significance given that current text books for such learners in Japan are based on PPP. Somewhat surprisingly, however, I found that there are no existing studies that have compared the effectiveness of TBLT and PPP for young, beginner learners (see p. 52 for discussion on studies comparing different approaches). This motivated the research project I report in later chapters of this book.

As discussed in Chapter 1, TBLT likely needs to be input-based for beginner learners as such learners lack the linguistic resources to engage with production-based tasks. PPP, however, is by definition production-based. An input-based approach thus addresses the problem of requiring such learners to produce from the start by pre-teaching the new linguistic feature(s) (i.e., a set of vocabulary items or a grammatical feature) and then eliciting production by means of carefully controlled activities involving picture labelling, substitution, blank filling, imitation, and the like. However, my personal communications with language teachers of young children has revealed that in general they are sceptical about input-based tasks. They feel that just waiting for the children to pick up language while doing comprehension-based activities is not enough to make them learn. They also are concerned that they would not be able to tell whether the students are learning if they are not expected to speak or write in the L2. Indeed perhaps one of the reasons for the continued popularity of PPP is that it meets teachers' need for feedback on whether learning is taking place.

In response to these concerns, I set about considering how best to carry out an effective comparison of TBLT and PPP for young, beginner learners, and arrived at the following decisions:

- The setting for the comparison should be a real classroom. While a laboratory setting makes it easier to control variables, the results from such a study would be unlikely to convince Japanese elementary school teachers.
- Ideally the children should have no prior experience of second language learning and no knowledge of English (the target language). If the children had already experienced learning English in a classroom they would have formed expectations about what classroom learning involved. I therefore chose to investigate input-based TBLT and PPP with six-year-old children. This is the age that children enrol in elementary schools in Japan, and these days many schools introduce some kind of English lessons as early as this age.
- In order to cater for such learners, the tasks in TBLT and the activities in PPP needed to be prepared with care. They had to be suitable for young, beginner learners of English and, importantly, enjoyable. It was relatively easy for me to design PPP activities for young learners based on my previous teaching experience. For TBLT, however, I needed to consult books on TBLT (e.g. Ellis, 2003), which led me to employ simple listen-and-do tasks.
- The comparative study would be experimental but needed to consist of much more than just one TBLT and one PPP lesson. I felt it essential to design a study that involved a series of lessons spanning several weeks. Again, my reasoning was that the results from such a study would be much more likely to be taken seriously by teachers.
- I also decided to repeat the same lessons several times because my experience as a teacher told me that young, beginner learners would need substantial repetition to become used to the lesson procedures and learn how to perform the different activities.

I then began to consider the design of my study in detail. I needed to think carefully about how to measure the learning that resulted from the two types of instruction to ensure that it was not biased in favour of either TBLT or PPP. In PPP the students are informed about what they are going to study at the beginning of the lesson, and thus are likely to learn the feature intentionally (if not performatively). In TBLT, students are not told what the linguistic targets of the lesson are. Instead they are asked to engage holistically with tasks to achieve non-linguistic outcomes. However, as explained in Chapter 1, tasks can be focused, where particular language features are (not overtly) targeted and the task requires the learners to process the features in order to achieve the outcomes. In this case, any learning that takes place is incidental. It was essential, therefore, that I chose target features that could be taught intentionally (in the case of PPP) and that also could be embedded in input-based tasks to create opportunities for incidental learning (in the case of TBLT). Given that the children were all absolute beginners I settled on a set of vocabulary items.

The design of the study was also motivated by another consideration. Irrespective of the type of instruction, the children would not just be exposed to the target items but also to the utterances in which the items were embedded. Presumably, young children have a natural ability to 'pick up' language from the interactions they participate in (as when they learn the L1). I wanted to investigate this possibility as well. Thus in both the TBLT and PPP classes there were opportunities for the incidental acquisition of language other than the target items. This meant designing the instructional materials in such a way that learners would be incidentally exposed frequently to two grammatical structures – plural *-s* and copula *be* – and to measure whether they had acquired these forms to any degree. In other words, in addition to comparing the intentional and incidental acquisition of the target vocabulary items, I would also investigate the incidental acquisition of these two grammatical structures.

Further, I gave a lot of thought to how to measure the learning of the vocabulary items and the grammatical structures. Language tests used in schools in Japan are typically of the discrete-point type, such as fill-in-the-blank and multiple choice questions. Such tests can be considered biased in favour of PPP as they are non-communicative and invite controlled use of the target language only. However, if I were to only use tests consisting of input tasks that are communicative and invite more automatic processing, I would be likewise biasing the assessment in favour of TBLT. Hence I decided that I needed tests of both types.

Finally, as my study was a comparative method study (i.e., a study that compared two teaching methods) and such studies have been criticized for failing to ascertain whether the types of instruction being compared did actually consist of distinctive classroom processes (see Ellis & Shintani, 2014; also Beretta, 1990, 1992), I knew that it was important to go inside the 'black box' of the classroom and obtain evidence of what took place in the actual lessons. I therefore decided to video-record all the TBLT and PPP lessons. I also had in mind that the resulting evidence might help to explain whatever learning did or did not take place.

Underlying all these decisions were some important theoretical issues concerning the difference between incidental and intentional learning and between input-based and production-based instruction, the role of interaction in language learning, and the effect of repeating instructional activities. Therefore, before turning to the study itself, I will consider these issues by addressing the following questions:

1. What is incidental and intentional learning and how does incidental/intentional language acquisition take place in PPP and TBLT?
2. How has incidental and intentional language acquisition been compared in previous studies?
3. What theoretical perspectives support language acquisition through input?
4. In what ways does interaction in the classroom create opportunities for L2 learning?

5. What does previous research tell us about task repetition?
6. What do we currently know about how young, beginner L2 learners acquire vocabulary and grammar?
7. What steps can be taken to improve the validity of a comparative method study?

In the following sections, I will consider each question in turn.

What is incidental and intentional learning and how does incidental/intentional language acquisition take place in PPP and TBLT?

A second language can be learnt intentionally (i.e., through deliberate, purposeful attempts by a learner to acquire specific language features) or incidentally (i.e., by leading learners to do something by using the L2 as a tool, rather than concentrating on the features). While language learning is mostly incidental in a naturalistic language learning context such as L1 learning or L2 learning in an immersion setting, L2 classroom teaching, such as PPP, generally focuses on intentional learning. TBLT is an approach that aims at providing the opportunity for primarily incidental learning in a L2 classroom context. Thus, the occurrence of incidental learning is a central focus of the study reported in this book. In this section, I will consider the difference between intentional and incidental learning and how these two types of learning can take place in PPP and TBLT.

Intentional L2 acquisition

Skill-Acquisition Theory (DeKeyser, 1998; 2015) provides the theoretical justification for intentional learning. DeKeyser claimed that a rule is first learned as a declarative fact (that is, expressed as a statement such as, "when referring to present habits use the present simple, and for third person use stem+*s*"). Then, following practice in the use of the rule in controlled and communicative activities, the declarative knowledge helps a production procedure, which eventually becomes automatic and so available for use in spontaneous communication. Thus, this type of learning is intentional (especially by adult learners) in the sense that it commences with conscious use of declarative knowledge to develop automatic procedural knowledge through practice.

Along similar lines, PPP involves intentional learning (i.e., deliberate, purposeful attempts by a learner to acquire some language feature). It explicitly presents a predetermined target feature in the 'presentation' stage. In the following two stages (practice and production), the learners are engaged in activities aimed at establishing procedural control over the use of the target feature. During the whole lesson, the learners are likely to be aware of the linguistic target and be focused on trying to use it correctly.

As discussed in Chapter 1, instructional materials in Japan, particularly for beginner learners, are typically based on this view of learning. However, as I also pointed out, in the case of most Japanese learners, years of explicit, intentional learning do not usually result in the ability to use English fluently. This may be because PPP is inherently limited or, as DeKeyser (2015) suggests, a typical production activity in a PPP classroom does not result in automatisation, which needs intensive, highly specific practice similar to what is experienced in an authentic conversation.

Intentional language learning can also take place through input-based approaches as, for example, in the structured input activities that are central to Processing Instruction (VanPatten, 2000). Structured input activities consist of exercises that require learners to process the form-meaning mapping of specific grammatical features in the sentences they are exposed to. It typically involves 'explicit instruction' (i.e., grammar explanation), which makes the linguistic focus of the exercises clear to the learners. However, arguably, even when there is no prior explicit instruction, the nature of the exercises is such that learners are still likely to engage in intentional learning. The exercises typically involve short, decontextualized sentences, and the structure of the exercises deliberately focuses learners' attention on the target feature.

A key question is whether the intentional learning that results from PPP or Processing Instruction is also evident in free production. A number of studies have shown that this can be found in the case of PPP. Explicit instruction together with practice has been shown to lead to gains in accuracy in communication-focused activities over time and to statistically significant differences when the experimental groups which received the instruction were compared to control groups that did not. PPP results in gains when the target features involve grammar (Harley, 1989; Housen, Pierrard, & van Daele, 2005), vocabulary (Shintani, 2011), pragma-linguistic features (Lyster, 2004), and pronunciation (Saito & Lyster, 2011). In the case of the studies that investigated grammatical features, the gains were evident in simple features and also in more complex features known to cause problems to L2 learners. Also, the effects of PPP are evident not just in discrete point tests but also in tasks eliciting free production.

The results of studies that have investigated Processing Instruction are less clear. In most of the studies there has been no attempt to measure the effect of the instruction on free production. Salaberry (1997) and VanPatten and Sanz (1995) were exceptions. These studies tested the acquisition of L2 Spanish clitic pronouns by an oral story telling task after the learners had received structured input with explicit instruction. In both studies the experimental groups failed to show significant gains compared with the control group. Erlam (2003), however, reported that both PPP and structured input activities resulted in the acquisition of the target feature when this was measured by a free oral production test. The explanation for the difference in these studies may simply lie in the length of the instruction; while Erlam provided three lessons, Salaberry, and VanPatten and Sanz provided only one. This is a general tendency in the whole body of the Processing Instruction studies (Shintani, 2015). Intentional learning might need intensive practice opportunities, including communicative ones. In the study reported in this book, I provided nine PPP lessons to the young learners, and measured their language development using both a relatively free oral production test as well as a discrete point test, to investigate whether intentional learning resulted in the use of new vocabulary items in a free production test.

Incidental L2 acquisition

Incidental acquisition is learning without intention. It is typically investigated by focusing learners' attention on some aspect of the input and then seeing whether they have acquired some *other* feature that was also present in the input. For example, learners might be asked to engage in listening-for-comprehension but then tested on whether they have learned any new vocabulary while listening. Incidental acquisition, then, occurs when learners are primarily focussed on meaning but they 'pick up' words or grammatical structures and remember them so that they can later show that learning has taken place. TBLT caters to incidental acquisition; the interactions that learners engage in when performing a task create contexts for picking-up new language which the learner had no particular intention to learn, and while the learner was thinking about the communication rather than about learning goals.

Incidental acquisition can take place with or without awareness. Learners may pick up items from the input they are exposed to without any awareness of doing so. In this case they engage in implicit learning. However, they may also momentarily pay conscious attention to specific items even while their primary attention is on comprehending the input. This 'noticing', as we will see later, is considered facilitative of learning.

The notion of incidental learning is central to a number of SLA theories. Cognitive-interactionist theories of L2 acquisition assume that learning occurs when learners are exposed to input and have opportunities for production in communication, and that such learning does not require them to make an initial deliberate effort to acquire specific grammatical features. Researchers working within this paradigm have sought to investigate a range of conditions that facilitate such incidental learning. For instance, research based on the Input Hypothesis (Krashen, 1985) has examined how simplified input that learners can comprehend assists learning. Other research based on the Interaction Hypothesis (long, 1983, 1996) has investigated how comprehensible input, feedback, and modified output promote learning when learners attempt to negotiate meaning in order to address a problem that has arisen in communication (Mackey, 1999; Pica, 1994). N. Ellis (2002) has argued that input is important because a primary determinant of acquisition is the frequency of exposure to grammatical forms contained in that input. Finally Schmidt (1994, 2001) has proposed that the conscious 'noticing' of exemplars of specific grammatical features in communicative input constitutes a key condition for the acquisition of those features. These various perspectives have in common a concern for incidental rather than intentional learning. Each of these theories will be discussed in detail later in this chapter.

Incidental learning is also of pedagogical importance. There are limits to any learner's capacity to learn a language intentionally and therefore limits on the extent to which grammatical competence or vocabulary knowledge can be directly taught. Krashen (1982) pointed out that even the best students will only be able to learn a small part of the language intentionally and thus must rely predominantly on 'incidental learning' – "picking up" language features from the input they are exposed to. In a naturalistic context, L2 acquisition, like L1 acquisition, is typically incidental rather than intentional.

As noted earlier, incidental learning can take place in PPP as well as TBLT. The study reported in this book investigated the occurrence of incidental acquisition in both teaching contexts. Thus I will now consider how incidental learning in these two teaching contexts can be investigated.

Incidental learning in TBLT

TBLT aims to provide opportunities for incidental learning through tasks that require a primary focus on meaning while also affording occasions for attending to form.

There are two ways of investigating whether performing tasks results in incidental acquisition. In the case of input-based tasks, learners are required to comprehend the input but then, without prior warning, they are tested on some of the linguistic features contained in the input to see if they have learned them. This is the approach used, for example, to investigate whether vocabulary learning takes place through extensive reading (Eckerth & Tavakoli, 2012; Krashen, 2013; Laufer, 2003). In the case of output-based tasks, learners first complete an oral task, as in Loewen (2005), and recordings are made of the interactions that result from the performance of the task. Then the learners are tested on the linguistic items that figure in the form-focused episodes that arose in the interactions. Any acquisition is assumed to have been incidental if it only took place through performing tasks that required the learners to process input and output for communicative purposes without engaging in deliberate learning.

Incidental learning in PPP

PPP is directed at intentional learning. However, incidental learning can also take place within PPP. Learners may 'pick up' linguistic forms other than those that were the target of the lesson by participating in the interactions which the instruction gives rise to. In other words, incidental learning can occur 'accidentally' while learners are focused on learning the forms that are the target of the lesson. Thus, one way of investigating incidental acquisition in PPP is to see if learners have acquired a specific feature that is not the target but is present in the interactions that take place. Or to put in another way, learners might be taught feature *x* but acquire feature *y* – either instead of *x* or in addition to it.

However, there have been very few studies that have examined incidental learning in PPP lessons. Slimani (1989) used self-report to investigate adult beginner learners' incidental acquisition of English. After receiving a two-hour, teacher-fronted, form-oriented lesson (i.e., presentation followed by practice exercises), the individual learners filled in an "Uptake Recall Chart" in which they reported the "completely new" language items that they had learned in the lesson. The lesson was also audio-recorded to identify whether these features were topicalized by the teacher in the classroom. The procedure was repeated in six lessons. Slimani reported that 11% of the language features that the learners claimed they had learned in the classroom were not topicalized in the lesson (i.e., there was no evidence that the classroom discourse drew attention to the feature). Although Slimani did not include any post-tests to measure learning, the results of her study indicate that the learners, at least to some extent, had incidentally acquired a number of linguistic features that had not been directly taught.

Loewen et al. (2009) investigated the incidental acquisition of 3rd person *-s*. In this study, the focus of the lesson was on the use of the indefinite article to express generic reference but the input also contained a high frequency of 3rd person *-s* in sentences like 'A cheetah <u>runs</u> fast' and 'Cheap transport <u>makes</u> life easy'. The learners were tested by means of an elicited oral imitation test and an untimed grammaticality judgement test, designed to measure implicit and explicit knowledge respectively (see Ellis, 2005). The results showed that the learners failed to demonstrate any gains in implicit knowledge. Loewen et al. suggested that this was this because the learners were unable to dual-task (i.e., attend to 3rd person *-s* as well as the indefinite article – the explicit focus of the instruction) and also because of the low saliency of 3rd person *-s*. It is also possible that, as the participants were of intermediate level, they had had prior exposure to the subject-stem structure (without the 3rd person *-s*), and the single lesson was not sufficient to have an impact on their use of the structure. Scores on the untimed grammaticality judgment test actually declined (by 17%), probably because the instruction directed at the indefinite article caused the learners to focus their attention on this structure and distracted them from attending consciously to 3rd person *-s* errors in the ungrammatical sentences of the test. In short, this study failed to demonstrate that any incidental acquisition of 3rd person *-s* had taken place.

Slimani's study indicated that incidental acquisition can take place in PPP. However, this is most likely to occur if the linguistic features are salient in the input and the learners are able to direct their attention to them. Frequency of input might be another important factor for incidental acquisition (e.g., Ellis, 2002). Clearly, more research is needed to investigate the conditions that make incidental acquisition possible in PPP lessons.

Two important issues emerge from this review of studies of incidental acquisition. The first issue is whether incidental learning takes place differently in TBLT and PPP. Incidental acquisition in TBLT involves learners acquiring a linguistic feature incidentally while they are attending to meaning, whereas incidental learning in PPP involves learners learning one linguistic feature incidentally while intentionally learning another. It would seem likely that the processes (cognitive and interpersonal) and the products (both contextual and decontextualized) of learning in these conditions are different. The second issue is whether the characteristics of the target feature influence the level of incidental learning. As Loewen et al. (2009) pointed out, the saliency or meaningfulness of the language feature might influence incidental learning. The study reported in the following chapters investigated both of these issues by examining the processes involved in the two types of instruction as well as their products, and by investigating two distinct grammatical structures that differed both in their saliency and meaningfulness.

Summary

I have looked at the difference between intentional and incidental learning and how intentional/incidental learning can take place in PPP and TBLT. I also discussed incidental acquisition in PPP and TBLT. Another question arises as to which type of learning is more effective, intentional learning versus incidental learning. In the current study, I thus operationalized this comparison with PPP (intentional learning) and TBLT (incidental learning) both focusing on the same language feature (vocabulary items). In the next section I will examine how incidental and intentional learning have been investigated in PPP and TBLT approaches.

How has incidental and intentional language acquisition been compared in previous studies?

The research that I will be reporting on later focuses on vocabulary learning in PPP and in TBLT, so I will restrict my review of comparative studies to those that have investigated the effects of these two different types of instruction on vocabulary acquisition. The question here is how effective are intentional and incidental learning?

In general, vocabulary acquisition researchers claim that intentional learning is more beneficial than incidental learning. Laufer (2005), for example, identified a number of limitations of incidental learning: if learners can understand the overall message then they may not pay attention to new words; they do not engage sufficiently with new words even if they succeed in guessing their meanings from context; and they may not meet new words a sufficient number of times to remember them. Elgort and Nation (2010) pointed out that intentional learning "can be used to quickly learn the 2,000 most frequent word families in English" (p. 101) and at more advanced stages can facilitate increased depth of knowledge of words that were first encountered incidentally. However, there are relatively few studies that have compared vocabulary learning in PPP-type instruction and TBLT. I will examine three such studies.

Laufer (2006) distinguished the two types of instruction. One – 'focus on form' (FonF) – "views the words attended to as tools for task completion, and the other – 'focus on forms' (FonFs) – treats the words attended to as the objects of study" (p. 150). Thus, taking use for task completion as criterial, her FonF condition involved incidental learning and the FonFs condition intentional learning. She conducted a study comparing the effect of comprehension-based FonF involving reading tasks and production-based FonFs involving written production exercises on the acquisition of new English vocabulary by Grade 11 students in Israel. The learners in the FonF condition were asked to read a text and answer comprehension questions using a bilingual dictionary if they needed. This condition catered to incidental language acquisition. In the FonFs condition the learners first received a list of target words with translations and explanations in English, and the teacher also explained each word orally. Then the learners worked on word production exercises. This catered to intentional language learning. Acquisition was measured by a discrete-item comprehension test involving L1 translation or L2 definitions of the target words. The results showed that the FonFs group outperformed the FonF group. Laufer argued that learners do not necessarily notice unfamiliar words in input and thus "the nature of lexical competence makes FonFs indispensable to vocabulary instruction." She also suggested that FonFs is of "major importance in any learning context that cannot recreate the input conditions of first-language acquisition" (p. 162).

In a follow-up study, Laufer and Rozovski-Roitblat (2011) again compared the effects of FonF and FonFs instruction on learner's acquisition of new words. The two types of instruction were operationalized in the same way as in Laufer (2006). However, this study examined long-term retention in unannounced tests and thus, according to the authors, investigated incidental acquisition in both instructional conditions. This study also investigated the effects of the frequency of exposure to the target words. The main finding was that the FonFs instruction supported by word focused exercises proved superior to FonF instruction when the words were met four times or more, but no difference was found when the exposure was limited to just two to three times.

Like many other studies, these findings suggest that intentional vocabulary learning is more effective than incidental vocabulary learning. This might be because intentional learning forces learners to "notice" the forms and meanings of words, but also because the tests used in most studies were essentially decontextualized form-focused types, which might not have reflected the learners' ability to use the words in communication. However, there are a number of studies that show that incidental instruction consisting of tasks can also provide opportunities for learners to 'notice' word forms and meanings (e.g., Gass & Torres, 2005). The key issue, then, might be the extent to which performing tasks leads to 'noticing' form meaning connections and also whether such noticing is needed to achieve the outcome of the task. It could also be argued that incidental acquisition is better suited to young beginner learners than intentional learning. Young learners are experienced in incidental acquisition from learning their L1.

De la Fuente (2006) compared the effects of PPP (catering to intentional learning) with those of production-based TBLT (catering to incidental learning) on university students in an elementary Spanish class. The PPP learners received 50 minutes of instruction consisting of the three phases of PPP: explanation of the new words (presentation), controlled oral and written production exercises (practice), and a role play performed in pairs (free production). The students in the two TBLT conditions worked on a restaurant task in pairs, where students needed to negotiate the meaning of the target words to complete the task. Acquisition was measured by means of a discrete-item oral production test. The two types of instruction proved equally effective in the immediate post-test. However, in the delayed post-test, the TBLT group outperformed the PPP group. Examining the interactions that occurred in each group, that is, the processes used by the students in the two approaches, de la Fuente found that the TBLT instruction provided more opportunities for the negotiation of meaning, production of the target words, and online retrieval of target words than did PPP. This study showed that incidental learning can lead to better vocabulary acquisition than intentional learning. However, as de la Fuente pointed out, a limitation of the study was that acquisition was only measured by means of a discrete-point test.

A key difference between Laufer's studies and de la Fuente's study lies in the opportunity the learners had to engage in interaction where they could 'negotiate' the target items in the TBLT context. De la Fuente's study suggests that when such an opportunity is available, incidental learning may be as or more effective than intentional learning.

Another issue is how learning is measured in these studies. The purpose of TBLT is to develop learners' ability to use the language in a communicative context. It is, thus, necessary to administer a test that requires the free use of the L2 as well as a discrete-point test that is biased in favour of PPP instruction. The present study included both discrete-point tests and tests requiring free use of the L2 to measure vocabulary learning, so that both contextual and decontextualized recall could be investigated. As I will report later, the results showed that input-based tasks provided opportunities for negotiation of meaning, which resulted in better vocabulary learning than intentional learning in the PPP context.

What theoretical perspectives support language acquisition through input?

As discussed earlier, TBLT in my study involved input-based tasks, which do not require learners to produce the L2. It is thus important to consider what theoretical perspectives support L2 learning through input. This section focuses on the issue of comprehensible input, that is, whether comprehending L2 input leads to acquisition.

Comprehensible input

The Input Hypothesis claims that what Krashen (1982, 1985, 1998) called 'acquisition' (as opposed to 'learning') occurs naturally and without consciousness when learners are exposed to comprehensible input. The Input Hypothesis, then, sees acquisition as entirely input-driven. Krashen argued that production plays no direct role in acquisition and that it serves only as a means of generating comprehensible input. In support of this position, Krashen (1998) cited empirical evidence that shows that (1) L2 acquisition occurs without learner output; (2) output, especially 'comprehensible output', is often scarce; (3) it is possible to attain high levels of linguistic competence without output; and (4) there is no direct evidence that output leads to language acquisition. This would strongly support the use of input tasks within a TBLT approach.

Ellis (2008) summarised studies that had investigated two key claims of the Input Hypothesis: (1) whether simplifying input (e.g., by lowering the speech rate and modifying input) aids comprehension and (2) whether comprehension results in acquisition (p. 247). The first issue was investigated by studies that operationalized 'simplified input' in various ways. Conrad (1989), for example, investigated the effects of simplifying input by lowering the speech rate. He compared the effects of different speech rates on three groups of participants: native speakers of English, English learners with high proficiency, and those with low proficiency. The results showed that reducing the speech rate helped the low-proficiency learners to recall the sentences they had heard. Griffiths (1990) compared the effects of different speech rates on the comprehension of a group of lower-intermediate adult English learners. Results showed that the moderately fast speech rate resulted in a significant reduction in comprehension, but that the slow rate did not lead to significantly lower comprehension scores than the average rate.

Other researchers investigated the effects of different ways of modifying input (e.g., by means of 'simplification' or 'elaboration'). Parker and Chaudron (1987) reviewed the effects of simplified and elaborated L2 modifications on comprehension in L2 studies and concluded that 'linguistic modifications' showed only mixed evidence of any effect on comprehension, whereas 'elaborative modifications' had a consistent effect. In a later study, however, Yano, Long, and Ross (1994) found that simplified input led to better comprehension than baseline input (i.e., input that had not been simplified) whereas elaborated input did not. Loschky (1994) and Ellis, Tanaka, and Yamazaki (1994) investigated the effect of oral input on comprehension. Their findings did not reveal any advantage for simplified input over baseline input. The conflicting results of these studies can be explained by the fact that they investigated different media (written vs. oral). Also, as Sharwood-Smith (1986) pointed, out comprehension does not just depend on the nature of the input (i.e., whether it is simplified) but on the interaction of factors such as the learner's real-world knowledge, their linguistic proficiency, and contextual support.

In Chapter 5, I will report how I, as a teacher, used simplified input as well as various kind of contextual support (e.g., gestures and visual materials) to ensure comprehension by the young, beginner learners.

Relation between comprehension and acquisition

Turning to the relationship between comprehension and acquisition, studies have also produced mixed results. Krashen and his co-researchers (e.g., Dupuy & Krashen, 1993; Mason & Krashen, 1997) investigated incidental L2 acquisition by asking L2 learners to view videos or engage in extensive reading. Mason and Krashen (1997) showed that a group of university students who experienced self-selected extensive reading plus summary writing outperformed those who just completed cloze exercises, even though acquisition was tested by means of a cloze test which favoured the latter group. Other studies have investigated simplified input and L2 acquisition. Leow (1993) examined the effects of simplified written input on the intake of linguistic items by learners of two different proficiency levels. Intake was measured by a multiple-choice recognition test. Results suggested that the simplification did not have a facilitating effect on learners' intake. Ellis (1995) investigated the effects of premodified oral input on vocabulary learning for low-proficiency learners of English. The task consisted of listening to directions about where to place specific kitchen objects in a picture of a kitchen. The results failed to show a consistent advantage for the simplified input group. Range (i.e., the number of oral texts in which each target word labelling the kitchen objects occurred) emerged as the aspect of the input most strongly related to acquisition of the target words. Overall the results of these and other studies indicate that acquisition is more likely if learners comprehend the input but that comprehension does not guarantee acquisition.

Ellis (2008) pointed out that the major problem with the Input Hypothesis is that comprehension can take place as a result of top-down processing, which removes the need for learners to process the input linguistically and make the necessary form-meaning mappings for those linguistic features they have not yet acquired. Færch and Kasper (1986) argued that acquisition can only take place when there is a gap between the input and the learners' interlanguage and when the learner perceives the gap as a gap in linguistic knowledge. In other words, as Schmidt (1990) so neatly put it, "it is unlikely that all input used in the comprehension of message meaning also functions as intake for the learning of form" (p. 139). So a question arises, which is important if we are to compare TBLT and PPP – How can we create the need for learners to process the input linguistically and make those important form-meaning mappings through interaction? The next section deals with this question.

In what ways does interaction in the classroom create opportunities for L2 learning?

As noted above, the key to successful incidental L2 learning seems to be whether learners pay attention to language while engaging in interaction. In this section I will consider how L2 interaction creates opportunities for form-meaning mapping. The discussion here is mainly informed by cognitive-interactionist theories that view the role of interaction as a source of input and an opportunity for output, which triggers the internal mental processing involved in 'acquisition', but also partly by sociocultural perspectives that see interaction as the actual location where 'learning' starts (see Newman & Holzman, 1997; Vygotsky, 1978).

I will start with introducing a key principle of cognitive-interactionist theories, 'focus on form' (Long, 1996), and consider how focus on form could take place in TBLT.

Focus on form

Long (1991, 1996) suggested that acquisition requires learners to attend to form, but that this has to take place while the learners' overall attention is on meaning. In other words, attention to form should be embedded in the communicative interactions that tasks give rise to. This has come to be referred to as 'focus on form', defined by Long (1991) as follows:

> Focus on form overtly draws students' attention to linguistic elements as they arise incidentally in lessons whose overriding focus is on meaning or communication.
> (pp. 45–46)

Focus on form emphasizes form-function mapping. That is, the learners' attention is drawn not just to a linguistic form but also to the semantic or pragmatic meaning realized by that form in the specific context in which it is used. Doughty (2001) suggested that attention to form facilitates acquisition in the "window of opportunity" (p. 257) that arises when learners are struggling to decode or encode a message that is communicatively important to them. Thus, focus on form requires two conditions – a primary focus on meaning and a short, temporary focus on form. PPP does not meet the first condition except possibly in the final production stage.

There are strong theoretical reasons for claiming that focus on form is not just facilitative of learning but may even be necessary. For example, Schmidt (2001) suggests the importance of 'noticing', the conscious registration of formal features in the input (e.g., there is an 's' at the end of a noun, which may signal 'more than one'). Schmidt (2001) pointed out that learners do not notice 'rules' but rather 'exemplars' of forms and the meanings they encode. That is, noticing does not involve awareness at the level of metalinguistic understanding, although it may subsequently lead to this deeper level of consciousness.

Researchers have investigated how focus on form takes place in classroom interaction. A seminal study by Ellis, Basturkmen, and Loewen (2001) examined the occasions and the various ways in which teachers drew learners' attention to form in what they called 'form-focused episodes' while tasks were being performed in a whole-class context in a private language school in New Zealand. The study also investigated the extent to which the learners successfully repaired their errors in these episodes. A follow-up study by Loewen (2005) investigated whether the form-focused episodes led to learning. He examined whether items that had been subject to focus on form in communicative lessons were acquired using tailor-made tests administered one or two days after the lessons and two weeks later. The results indicated that learners who successfully repaired their errors as a result of the focus on form during the lesson (i.e., suggesting that the focus on form had led to noticing) were more likely to demonstrate knowledge of the correct forms on the tests. The results indicate that incidental focus on form is beneficial, particularly if the targeted linguistic items were those that the learner had attempted to use.

In the following sections, I will consider three processes that might lead learners to attend to form in the classroom: when negotiation of meaning takes place, when learners are corrected during production, and when learners produce the L2. I will consider how these three processes create opportunities for learning in PPP and TBLT.

Negotiation of meaning in PPP and TBLT

Long (1996, but see also Long, 1983) suggested 'negotiation of meaning' is potentially facilitative of L2 learning. He proposed that acquisition takes place when (1) interactionally modified input (i.e., negotiation of meaning) assists learners to notice linguistic forms in the input, and (2) the forms that are noticed lie within the learners' 'processing capacity'. In other words, interactionally modified input was seen as promoting acquisition in two ways: (1) by providing the learner with 'positive evidence' (Long, 1996) and by prompting the learners to notice the gap between their own erroneous utterances and the target language input derived from negotiation; and

(2) by means of feedback signalling that learners had made an error (i.e., providing negative evidence) which then prompts them to modify their own output. In both cases, Long drew on Schmidt's ideas about the importance of 'noticing'. As Gass and Selinker (2001) noted, 'noticing' is "at the heart of the interaction hypothesis" (p. 298).

A number of studies have examined the effects of the negotiation of meaning on acquisition. As noted earlier, 'negotiation of meaning' takes place through the collaborative work that speakers undertake to achieve mutual understanding when there is some kind of communication problem (Ellis, 2009). One way of investigating the effectiveness of negotiation of meaning is by comparing an experimental group that experienced interactionally modified input with a comparison group that was exposed to baseline or premodified input. In Mackey (1999), for example, there were four experimental groups – (1) 'interactors' who received interactionally modified input through the negotiation of meaning, (2) 'interactor unreadies' who also similarly received interactionally modified input, (3) 'observers' who did not participate in the task interactions but were able to observe other learners' doing so, and (4) 'scripteds' who received premodified input but with no opportunity to interact. There was also a control group that received no treatment. In this study, Mackey also sought to control for the learners' stage of development on the grounds that negotiation would only be effective if learners were developmentally 'ready' to acquire the feature that was the topic of the negotiation. The results indicated that the 'interactors' advanced more than the non-interactors and that negotiation proved more effective than both premodified and baseline input. Clear evidence of the beneficial effect of negotiation on acquisition can also be found in two meta-analyses (Keck, Iberri-Shea, Tracy-Ventura, & Wa-Mbaleka, 2006; Mackey & Goo, 2007). Mackey and Goo (2007), for example, reviewed 28 interaction studies and concluded that "interaction plays a strong facilitative role in the learning of lexical and grammatical target items" (p. 405).

Negotiation, however, may only play a significant role in acquisition for intermediate level learners. Advanced learners may experience few comprehension problems and little difficulty in making themselves understood and so have little need to negotiate. As for beginner level learners, of the kind that figure in the study reported in this book, they lack the necessary L2 proficiency to take part in negotiation sequences although, as we will see, negotiation in the L1 is still possible.

Turning to the comparison of PPP and TBLT, negotiation of meaning is more likely to occur in TBLT where learners are attempting to achieve task outcomes using the L2. However, as pointed out, TBLT for complete beginners needs to be input-based. Since input-based tasks do not require production, the possibility of negotiation for meaning is reduced. Even so it can still arise when learners experience difficulty in comprehending the input. However, there are very few studies that have investigated the negotiation of meaning resulting from input-based tasks – particularly involving young learners.

One such study is Ellis and Heimbach (1997). They investigated vocabulary acquisition by young children aged five to six while performing an input-based task where the children listened first individually and then in small groups to teacher directions containing words unknown to them. They were encouraged to negotiate their understanding when they did not understand. The study examined the relationships between the learners' participation in the negotiation of meaning during the task, their comprehension, and their acquisition of new words embedded in the directions. The results showed that meaning negotiation aided comprehension but that there was no direct relationship between the amount that individual children negotiated and their acquisition of word meanings. The correlation between comprehension and acquisition was also weak. The study also showed that the children varied considerably in their ability or willingness to negotiate, leading Ellis and Heimbach to conclude that meaning negotiation may play a less prominent role in acquisition for children than it does for adults. Nonetheless, this study did demonstrate that simple listen-and-do tasks could induce some negotiation of meaning by children aged five to six, and as we will see, this is relevant for the present study.

In PPP, opportunity for the negotiation of meaning is most likely to arise in the final free production stage of a lesson as this requires learners to use the target items in the context of meaning-focused communication. The presentation and controlled practice stages of the lesson are unlikely to create the conditions for the negotiation of meaning because they are likely to discourage (or even prevent) learners asking for clarification. In the case of beginner learners, even the free production stage may not lead to negotiation and it is very possible that even in this stage the 'production' will take the form of the learners simply repeating sentences that were presented and practiced in the first two stages.

To summarize, negotiation of meaning can take place in the last stage of a PPP lesson and also in the performance of input-based tasks. However, the process of negotiation of meaning might be very different. In PPP, it is likely to occur when a student's utterance causes interactional breakdown and the teacher initiates the negotiation to resolve the problem. In input-based tasks, it will occur when learners are unable to comprehend a teacher's utterance and initiate negotiation to resolve the comprehension problem (as in Ellis & Heimbach, 1997). I will examine how negotiation of meaning took place in the PPP and the TBLT groups in my study by examining the interaction generated in the two kinds of instruction.

Error correction in PPP and TBLT

Corrective feedback

Another possible way to create opportunity for focus on form is thorough corrective feedback. In the L2 classroom, teachers often provide learners with feedback on their erroneous or inappropriate use of the L2 even though no breakdown in communication has occurred. Lyster (2001) called this 'negotiation of form' (i.e., the attention paid to form even when there is no communication problem) and argued that, like the negotiation of meaning, it can also facilitate acquisition. In fact negotiation of form is more common than the negotiation of meaning in many classrooms. A number of studies (e.g., Ellis, Loewen & Erlam, 2006; Lyster & Saito, 2010) have shown that the corrective feedback that teachers provide when negotiating for form during meaning-centred activities can facilitate acquisition in much the same way as the negotiation of meaning. However, whereas the negotiation of meaning can take place when learners are communicating between themselves, the negotiation of form usually requires the presence of a teacher.

There are now a large number of corrective feedback studies involving task-based instruction (see Ellis & Shintani, 2014 for a review). In general, however, these studies have been carried out with older learners – either secondary school students or adults. There is an absence of studies involving young children. One possibility is that young children will depend more on positive evidence (i.e., input in the context of meaning-focused communication) and thus will not benefit from correction to the same extent as older learners. In PPP lessons, however, corrective feedback is likely to be common even with young children. PPP requires the teacher to monitor the students' L2 production and provide feedback on their erroneous utterances and to prompt the use of the correct forms. In input-based tasks, on the other hand, corrective feedback is only possible if the learners voluntarily produce the L2. I will, thus, also examine how corrective feedback took place in the PPP and the TBLT lessons in the process analysis portion of my study.

Initiate-respond-feedback (IRF)

Corrective feedback in a traditional language lesson commonly takes place in a three-part interactional exchange – teacher's initiation–student's response–teacher's feedback (IRF). Such exchanges have been shown to be dominant in many classrooms. Berry (1981) explained why IRF is so prevalent. It arises because the teacher takes on the role of both 'initiator' and 'primary knower'. Only when the teacher either abandons the role of 'primary knower' or allocates the initiating role to the students do different discourse patterns occur. SLA researchers in the cognitive-interactionist tradition view IRF exchanges as limiting because they afford learners few opportunities for extended utterances, they restrict the range of language functions to be performed, and they remove the need for negotiating meaning, as communication breakdown is infrequent. As Van Lier (1996) put it "in the IRF exchange, the student's response is hemmed in, squeezed between a demand to display knowledge and a judgment on its competence" (p. 151). In other words, classrooms where the IRF dominates have been considered less than ideal for L2 acquisition.

The role that IRF plays in language learning, however, has been re-evaluated by some researchers. For example, Nassaji and Wells (2000) pointed out that richer contributions from students are likely if the initiation move involves the teacher questions that introduce issues for negotiation (e.g., "Do you agree with Nir?") rather than display questions that ask for information the teacher already knows (e.g., "Who was the king of France?"). Ohta (2001) found that the Japanese learners she investigated appropriated the language they were exposed to in IRF exchanges for use in subsequent group work. For example, she showed how IRF exchanges helped these learners to develop the interactional competence involved in producing appropriate listener responses (e.g., the use of *ne* as an aligning expression), which occur frequently in ordinary Japanese conversation. Antón (1999) also suggested that IRF plays an important part in prolepsis (i.e., an interaction where the teacher anticipates a difficulty that learners may be experiencing and attempts to deal with it). The teacher she investigated employed open-ended questions in IRF exchanges designed to help the learners to reflect on form and to lead them to verbalize a rule. Antón argued that this kind of proleptic teaching constitutes "effective assistance (i.e., a scaffold)" (p. 308).

I expect that IRF will occur frequently in the PPP but not in TBLT lessons in my study. The process analysis (Chapter 5) examines how IRF was manifested in the two types of instruction.

Role of output in PPP and TBLT

Another opportunity for noticing arises when learners produce output. Swain (1985) noted that whereas comprehension does not necessarily require bottom-up processing, as learners can rely on top-down processing by using the context and their encyclopaedic knowledge to infer meaning, output does require bottom-up processing as learners need to select the words and structures to express what they want to say, and thus are more likely to pay attention to form. In particular, 'pushed output', where learners have to struggle to make their meaning clear, is likely to do so. Swain (1995) discussed three ways in which output could contribute to grammatical competence. First, it serves a consciousness-raising function by triggering 'noticing'. That is, producing language helps learners to notice their problems. Second, producing language enables learners to test out hypotheses about the L2. One way in which this occurs is through the modified output that learners produce following negative feedback. Third, output allows learners to reflect consciously about L2 forms. This can occur in the context of performing a communicative task that stimulates negotiation of form (what Swain called 'languaging'). Output also serves another role – as De Bot (1996) pointed out, it can help learners to achieve greater fluency by increasing control over those forms they have already partially acquired. This would be the case for PPP in which learners are engaged in producing the L2 in a gradual shift from controlled exercises to more fee production activities. In later chapters I will show that the production practice in PPP lessons led to accurate production of the target vocabulary items by the beginner learners.

In the interaction approach, which informed Swain's initial ideas about the importance of output, it would seem that output is of value for helping learners to acquire fuller control over those L2 forms that they have already partially acquired but are not able to use accurately. From this perspective, pushed output might not play a role in the acquisition of new linguistic forms and thus is of less relevance for the complete beginners who engaged in tasks in the study reported in this book. Many of the studies that have investigated the role of output (Izumi, Bigelow, Fujiwara, & Fearnow, 1999; Lyster & Ranta, 1997; Nobuyoshi & Ellis, 1993; Pica, Holliday, Lewis, & Morganthaler, 1989; Shehadeh, 2001) looked at adult intermediate or advanced learners. Only a few studies have investigated the task-based output of young, low-proficiency learners in a foreign language context. Van den Branden (1997) investigated 11–12 year old children performing two two-way communicative tasks. He reported that children who had been pushed to modify their output in the first task produced significantly more output, more essential information, and a greater range of vocabulary in the later task than did children who had not been pushed. De la Fuente (2002) examined 10-year-old students with two years of learning English in the classroom. Their negotiated interaction included pushed output that helped them acquire new words and this combination worked better in this respect than either premodified input or negotiated interaction without pushed output. However, the question remains as to whether complete beginner learners produce output when performing input-based tasks. In fact, the study reported in the following chapters showed that the children in input-based lessons did engage in L2 production. I will examine in Chapters 5 and 6 what roles such output played in the performance of the task and in L2 acquisition.

One study is of special interest to the present investigation. Pinter (2006) compared adults' and children's performance of a required information exchange task by examining the strategies they used. The children in this study were relative beginners. She observed various differences in the way the child and adult learners handled the demands of the task. She concluded that children were quite limited in their ability to complete the task due to their failure to make use of strategies such as top-down search, narrowing the focus, referring to potential problems, and acknowledging outcomes. She also found that the children made little use of opportunities for production (e.g., co-constructing utterances with the help of peers, requesting clarification, elaborating on previous turns or prompting). Pinter's study suggests that two-way information gap tasks may be too demanding for young learners with very limited L2 proficiency. I employed listen-and-do tasks, which are one-way information gap tasks, in the current study. As we will see in Chapters 5 and 6, the children in the TBLT lessons enthusiastically produced output during such tasks although not initially in the target language (English).

What does previous research tell us about task repetition?

A limitation of Ellis and Heimbach's (1997) study was that the children only performed each task once. Children may benefit from repeating the same task and are more likely to engage in the negotiation of meaning when their confidence in performing the task increases but they still experience difficulty in comprehending the input. My own experience as a teacher tells me that young learners need to repeat activities to learn. Thus, in the study reported in the following chapters the children performed the same tasks a number of times.

Samuda and Bygate (2008) suggest that repeating tasks allows learners to try out new aspects of language. Drawing on Levelt's speech production model, Bygate (1996, 2001) suggested that repeating tasks makes it easy for learners to conceptualize their ideas and formulate them as messages because they are familiar with task procedures and the language forms that need to be used. Bygate (1996, 2001) reported that repeating the same task resulted in more fluent, accurate, and complex sentences in oral production tasks. This is in line with Skehan (1998, 2012) who argued that learners have difficulty in attending simultaneously to both meaning and form and, as a result, prioritize one or the other. Thus, tasks that are excessively demanding and push learners to achieve the outcome may not work for learning because they fail to involve any focus on form. He also pointed out that "for any task-based approach to work, conditions have to be created so that form is not forgotten" (Skehan, 2012, p. 398). His solution to this problem was to give learners the opportunity to plan the task. Task repetition also can be considered as involving planning.

There are a number of studies showing that task repetition is beneficial for young learners. Swain and Lapkin (2008), for example, asked French immersion children to complete a series of activities in pairs in five sessions: (1) role-play, (2) transcribing their own role play, (3) comparing their transcription to a reformulated version, (4) reflecting on their role play in a stimulated recall, and (5) re-doing their role play. They reported that the children remained engaged in the activity over the five sessions and that the repetition helped them to notice differences between their own language use and that of others. Van den Branden (1997) investigated the performance of 10 and 11-year-old Belgian children learning Dutch while they were performing a picture-description task in pairs. One of the two groups was requested to repeat the task with another partner. The learners in this group used a greater range of vocabulary in the second round, recycling the new words that arose in their interlocutor's utterances in the first performance. Pinter (2005) examined 10-year-old Hungarian

EFL learners with 2-years' experience of formal instruction of English in a 'Spot-the-Difference Task' performed in pairs. The same task was repeated three times with three- or four-day intervals. Pinter reported that the students became more talkative and used their L1 less. Also, they used more systematic search strategies and their grammatical accuracy improved. Pinter concluded that the repetition boosted the learners' confidence in L2 production.

These studies all investigated production-based tasks. Repeating input-based tasks is also likely to help learners to attend to different aspects of language in input, which might increase opportunities for incidental learning. Also, if repeating production-based tasks encourages young learners' production, as Van den Branden and Pinter showed, it is possible that young learners performing input-based tasks might also try out some of the language they have heard as they become familiar with the task. Later I will show that as the children became familiar with the tasks, they engaged more actively in negotiating for meaning when they did not understand. To begin with they did so in their L1 (Japanese) but as Van den Branden (1997) found in his study, over time they also negotiated using their newly acquired L2.

What do we currently know about how young, beginner L2 learners acquire vocabulary and grammar?

Learning L2 vocabulary

One of the aims of the study is to investigate vocabulary learning in the context of task-based and PPP instruction. As the learners were complete beginners at the start of the study, it was natural to focus on vocabulary rather than grammar as there is ample evidence to show that the early stages of L2 acquisition are lexical in nature. In this section, then, I address the theoretical perspective that informed my investigation of vocabulary learning by children.

Jiang's theory of lexical representation

Jiang (2000) argued that representation of lexical information in a second language is fundamentally different from that of the first language. In the first language, lemmas (i.e., the semantic and syntactic information about words) and lexemes (i.e., morphological information) are highly integrated within a person's memory for a given word, and therefore stimulating the meaning of a word automatically activates its form. Thus, in the process of establishing a semantic system in L1 acquisition, a child learns new semantic and formal specifications simultaneously. However, in L2 acquisition, due to the entrenched L1 semantic system, learners inevitably acquire words in relation to their L1 equivalents. In other words, whereas L1 words are learned as both semantic (i.e., lemmas) and formal entities (i.e., lexemes), learning L2 words (initially at least) only involves developing new lexemes because meaning is already available through the L1 lemmas.

Jiang suggests there are three stages of L2 lexical development. In the first stage of learning an L2 word, learners acquire the new lexeme. Semantic and grammatical information is available through the link with the L1 lexeme. By repeatedly making the link between the L1 form and the L2 form/meaning learners move into the second stage, namely the L1 lemma mediation stage, where the L2 lemma is developed by copying the information from the L1 lemma. In the last stage, the L2 integration stage, the learners establish the L2 lemma independently of the L1 lemma. This creates a strong representation of the L2 word and allows for efficient processing. Jiang points out the need for learners to comprehend and produce new words in context in order to encourage the deep processing that will enable the final L2 lemma stage to be reached.

The form of TBLT instruction employed in my study involved listen-and-do tasks where learners were required to comprehend the teacher's oral commands in the L2 and demonstrate their understanding of it without any requirement that they produce in the L2. The PPP in this study, on the other hand, required learners to produce the target L2 features particularly the practice and production stages. Thus, the comparison of TBLT and PPP in my study also involved the comparison of comprehension-based and production-based instruction. This raises an important question: Does a comprehension-based approach only result in receptive lexical knowledge or does it also contribute to productive knowledge? Jiang's theory suggests that receptive and productive knowledge of L2 words are available at each stage and also can be strengthened through both comprehension and production of the words. This theory, then, predicts that comprehension-based instruction can contribute to productive knowledge of L2 words as well as receptive knowledge. The study I will be reporting showed that the input-based tasks did lead to productive knowledge of the vocabulary items (see Chapter 6).

The Involvement Load Hypothesis

I will also draw on Laufer and Hulstijn's (2001) Involvement Load Hypothesis to examine the differential effect of the two kinds of instruction on word learning. This hypothesis proposes that the effectiveness of instruction depends on 'need' (i.e., whether the instructional activity creates a need to learn the word), 'search' (whether the activity involves learners in searching for the meaning of a word), and 'evaluation' (whether the activity requires learners to assess the appropriateness of a word for a particular context). Laufer and Hulstijn examined a range of studies to determine the relative effectiveness of different learning methods on vocabulary learning. They concluded that activities that involved more need, search, and evaluation were more effective. For example, Hulstijn, Hollander, and Greidanus 1996) showed that learning was greater if learners had to look words up in a dictionary (involving 'search') than if the meanings of the words were provided in a gloss (no 'search').

Of particular importance to my study is 'engagement'. One possibility is that receptive activities may not engage learners sufficiently to ensure productive knowledge of L2 words and that the development of productive knowledge requires engagement in production activities. However Laufer and Hulstijn's (2001) theory predicts that the effectiveness of vocabulary instruction depends less on the medium of the instruction than on the extent to which the activities involve 'need', 'search', and 'evaluation'. The theory claims that activities that involve all three will be more effective than those that involve just one or two. The key question, then, becomes the extent to which the comprehension-based and production-based instructional activities used in my study involved need, search, and evaluation.

Learning L2 Grammar

As we have already seen, PPP and TBLT draw on very different theories of how L2 grammar is acquired. Here I summarise the different theoretical positions that underlie these two approaches to teaching.

PPP draws on skill-learning theory, in particular Anderson's (1983) Adaptive Control of Thought (ACT) Model. Learning commences with (1) a declarative stage, followed by (2) a procedural stage, and finally (3) an automatic stage. As noted in Chapter 2, these three stages correspond neatly to the three stages of a PPP lesson. In the presentation stage learners are provided with declarative information about the target feature. In the practice stage they develop 'procedures' and finally in the production stage they develop the automatic processing needed to make use of the target feature in communication. DeKeyser (2007) argued that the automatisation of procedural knowledge will depend on the extent to which the cognitive operations involved in production of the target feature match those involved in a natural communicative context. For this reason the final stage of the PPP sequence – the free production stage – is essential.

TBLT draws on a variety of theories to explain the learning of L2 grammar, but common to all of them is (1) that the acquisition of new grammatical features takes place incidentally, and that it is facilitated by (2) drawing learners' attention to linguistic features (e.g., various pro-active and reactive strategies designed to attract the learners' attention to form while their primary focus is on achieving some communicative purpose). Like PPP, then, TBLT aims to help learners acquire the grammatical knowledge needed to engage in free communication. However, unlike PPP, TBLT is premised on the view that there is no need for the explicit presentation of the target feature to develop declarative knowledge or the need for controlled practice. Rather, it assumes that acquisition largely occurs incidentally in and through attempts to communicate.

As Ellis (2003) pointed out, tasks can be either focused or unfocused depending on whether or not there is a specific pre-determined linguistic focus. In my study I will make use of focused tasks as a type of 'proactive form-focused instruction' that involves "preplanned instruction designed to enable students to notice and to use target language features that might otherwise not be used or even noticed in classroom discourse" (Lyster, 2007, p. 44). Such instruction provides repeated opportunities for noticing, awareness, and practice (Ranta & Lyster, 2007) of specific grammatical features, processes that are unlikely to occur when unfocused tasks are used.

What steps can be taken to improve the validity of a comparative method study?

Issues in research methodologies comparing TBLT and PPP

I have looked at theoretical issues to be considered in the comparison TBLT and PPP, but I also need to consider the methodological background of my research. In this section, I will focus on two research methods that I employed, that is, method comparison to examine the learning products of the two types of instruction, and conversation analysis to examine the classroom processes that resulted from implementing the two teaching procedures.

Comparative method studies

The study I am reporting in the following chapters compared two teaching methods – TBLT and PPP in language classrooms. This type of approach is called a comparative method study (Ellis, 2012). Although this approach addresses issues that are of interest to teachers (i.e., what teaching method is more effective than the other), it is challenging in a number of ways.

Comparative method studies attempt to compare two or more types of language instruction to decide which is more effective in promoting L2 learning. Ellis (2012) classifies such studies into (1) 'global studies', which examine methods/approaches for teaching a second language (L2) over a long period of time and assess learning outcomes in terms of general language proficiency or achievement; and (2) 'local studies', which investigate the impact of a particular procedure of methods/approaches over a relatively short period of time and assess learning outcomes in terms of the acquisition of specific linguistic features. Although global method studies were popular in the 1960s and 70s (e.g., Asher, 1972; Levin, 1972; Smith, 1970), they generally failed to produce conclusive evidence of the superiority of one method over another. As a result such studies fell out of favour. However, Ellis (2012) argued that 'local studies' are more insightful and avoid the methodological problems of the global studies.

The main problem with comparative method studies, particularly of the 'global' type, was their failure to establish that the different instructional goals and techniques of the methods being investigated were implemented successfully in the classroom – in other words, there was no attempt to investigate whether the approaches being compared were implemented as intended. The idea of a "method" is a pedagogical construct – it constitutes a work plan for action. That is, it is defined externally in terms of approach, method, and technique (Anthony, 1963). However, it cannot be assumed that there is a close match between a work plan and the activity that arises when the work plan is implemented in the classroom. Kumaravadivelu (2001) rightly argued that teachers will necessarily re-interpret any externally defined specification of teaching when making online decisions that are part and parcel of actual teaching. This is likely to especially the case if the period of instruction is lengthy – the more all-encompassing the programme of instruction is, the more difficult it will be to distinguish the different approaches. This is why Seedhouse (2005) emphasised the importance of examining tasks – one type of workplan – in terms of how they are implemented in the classroom.

Ellis (2012) identified six design problems with previous global method studies: (1) the groups of learners being compared were not equivalent; (2) the teachers who taught the groups were not equivalent; (3) there was no observation of the actual teaching; (4) no account was taken of individual learner differences; (5) many of the studies lacked control groups; and (6) many of the studies failed to guard against test bias. Ellis concluded that comparative method studies "are of value, but only if they avoid the methodological pitfalls of the earlier method studies" (p. 19).

Conversation analysis

In order to investigate the process of the two types of instruction, I elected to use conversation analysis. Conversation analysis is a method for analysing the moment-by-moment processes of oral interaction. It is based on the assumption that contexts are not fixed in advance of an encounter, but rather are continually created through the active talk of the participants (Duranti & Goodwin, 1992). In this approach, interaction is studied by transcribing what people say and do, and then analysing how the interaction is collaboratively constructed (Hutchby & Wooffitt, 1988). Conversation analysis allows the researcher to focus on how each turn in a conversation is connected to what came immediately before, and how each turn sets up possibilities for subsequent turns. Investigating the characteristics of turn taking might show differences in the conversational patterns of the different classroom contexts arising out of PPP and TBLT.

Conversation analysis has been increasingly used in second language acquisition (SLA) research and has been shown to be a strong tool for investigate classroom interaction in detail (Markee, 2005). One of the most complete applications of CA to the study of classroom instruction can be found in Seedhouse (2004), which examined how conversational features are reflexively related to the pedagogical focus. He analysed the types of interactions that took place in four different L2 classroom contexts: form-and-accuracy, meaning-and-fluency, task-oriented, and procedural contexts. His analysis focused on two aspects of conversation: the organization of 'turn-taking' and 'repair'.

The study of turn-taking involves examining how the turns that speakers take in a conversation reflect what is said and how it is said, and how this affects the length of a turn (Hutchby & Wooffitt, 1988). Turn-taking occurs either when the current speaker selects the next speaker or when the next speaker self-selects (Sacks, Schegloff, & Jefferson, 1995). The examination of turn-taking is a central feature of CA. The analysis of turn-taking shows us who controls the conversation and to what extent the conversation is similar or dissimilar to one in a naturalistic context. This is important because we need to know whether the task-based instruction actually involved different interactional patterns from PPP.

'Repair' refers to a set of practices for dealing with problems relating to hearing, speaking, and understanding talk (Schegloff, Jefferson, & Sacks, 1977). Repair entails both 'repair initiation' and 'repair solution'. Repair can be self-initiated (initiated by the speaker who was the source of the problem) or other-initiated (initiated by the recipient of the problematic turn). Repair can also be completed by either side (self-repair or other-repair). In other words, the organization of repair can take a number of forms: (a) self-initiated self-repair, (b) self-initiated other-repair, (c) other-initiated self-repair, and (d) other-initiated other-repair (Schegloff, Jefferson, & Sacks, 1977). This classification is useful for examining corrective feedback and negotiation of meaning that takes place in the L2 classroom. I will examine in Chapter 5 how these different types of repair occurred in the PPP and the TBLT lessons in my study.

Markee (2008) employed a different approach to investigate the process features of an L2 classroom. Specifically, he adopted a 'learning-behaviour tracking' (LBT) methodology that involved (1) learning object tracking and (2) learning process tracking. The former involved identifying when a specific learning object (e.g., a word or a grammatical feature) occurred in the interactions involving the same learner(s) over a period of time. The latter involved showing "how and when participants orient to, and potentially incorporate, particular learning objects that occur in different speech events in their interactional repertoires" (p. 409). An example of this can be found in Shintani and Ellis (2014). This study documented how the children repeating the same input-based tasks moved from (1) comprehending two adjectives, *big* and *small*, to (2) repeating the words after the teacher, and then finally to (3) producing them themselves. Markee argued that this approach is important because it examines a particular object that the participants themselves choose to focus on in their talk rather than an object that the researcher has selected as a target item for learning. In his study, the word 'prerequisites' happened to occur in the interactions that took place between a teacher and a group of Chinese professors in a language skills development course, and Markee tracked the use of the word through the lesson. He was able to show how one learner gradually increased control over the use of this word in the interactions in which it occurred. Markee's LBT methodology can help to show how learning behaviours change over time and thus how learning-as-a-process takes place. However, Markee cautioned that often "it is impossible to demonstrate successful language learning behaviour because there is no evidence of independent productive use of a new learning object" (p. 409).

In the study reported in this book, I will make use of both Seedhouse's and Markee's approaches. Specifically, I will examine the characteristics of the turn-taking and repair that occurred in the two different L2 classroom contexts (i.e., PPP and TBLT) to investigate whether the two approaches resulted in different kinds of interaction. But as well as making use of Markee's learning-behaviour tracking methodology to investigate how learners 'pick up' linguistic items from the interactions they participate in, I will also use the evidence of learning obtained from tests to examine whether "independent productive use" was achieved as well.

However, the current study differs from typical conversation analysis-for-second language acquisition (CA-for-SLA) (e.g., Markee, 2005) which uses CA to investigate key constructs in SLA (e.g., recasts, as in Hauser, 2005) or interaction in the task-based classroom (as in Seedhouse, 2004). Instead, I have elected to use CA as a means of supplementing experimental research to provide an 'internal' perspective on the different types of instruction. Although Seedhouse (2004) used CA to examine classroom conversation, his purpose was to identify the different interactional patterns in different classroom contexts. No study, to my knowledge, has used CA to identify the differences in the specific process features of different teaching methods.

Conclusion

This chapter has raised a number of issues in research on PPP and TBLT. First, there is very little research on TBLT with young, beginner learners. This is important because young learners are more likely to benefit from incidental learning, where they pick up the language in natural interactions, than from intentional learning. In order to examine whether TBLT can be a better alternative to PPP for young learners, it is necessary to conduct experimental research comparing the two types of instruction in a classroom context. The research reported in the following chapters is such a study.

Second, very few studies have specifically investigated incidental grammar acquisition in the L2 classroom, and no study has examined whether incidental acquisition takes place in PPP and TBLT when the lesson targets another language feature. In order to fully examine the differences between TBLT and PPP, it is necessary to investigate two sets of comparisons: (1) intentional learning in PPP versus incidental learning in TBLT, to compare the approaches in terms of their supposed respective strengths; and (2) incidental learning in PPP versus incidental learning in TBLT, comparing the two approaches in terms of the same learning process. In the former case, TBLT needs to employ focused tasks that target the same L2 features as the PPP lesson. With this in mind, the current research employed new vocabulary items for the target. For the latter comparison, I needed to measure incidental learning of the same L2 features but which were specifically *not* the target of the lessons (i.e., not vocabulary). Hence two grammatical features – plural *-s* and copula *be* – were investigated in the current study to see whether there was any incidental acquisition that took place in the two teaching contexts.

As I have argued, in order to implement TBLT for young, beginner learners, input-based tasks are needed. On the other hand, PPP requires learners to *produce* the L2. The comparison in this research, therefore, also involves two sets of variables – production-based versus comprehension-based instruction, and PPP versus TBLT. In this sense, the current study can be called a 'method comparison study' (Ellis, 2012). As Ellis (2012) pointed out, traditional method comparison studies have a number of problems that can lead to their findings being inconclusive. To avoid these, the project carried out detailed analyses of the process-features before looking at the outcomes of the two types of instruction. Care was also taken in designing the experimental part of the study, and these methods are described in detail in the next chapter.

CHAPTER 4

Introducing the comparative method study of PPP and TBLT

In this chapter, I present the design and procedures used in the study in detail. As outlined in the previous chapter, the investigation compared two types of instruction – presentation-practice-production (PPP) and task-based language teaching (TBLT) for young beginner learners. As shown in Chapter 1, PPP is a widely used traditional teaching approach (Byrnes, 1986; Ur, 1996) in which a specific language feature is presented to the student in the beginning of lesson, followed by controlled practice exercises, and then moving toward free production activities. In contrast, TBLT centres lessons on 'tasks'. A task should be designed so that when doing it, learners are mainly concerned with comprehending or conveying messages, there is some kind of 'gap' (e.g., information), and there is a defined outcome other than the use of language. In a task, learners should use their own resources (linguistic and non-linguistic) in order to complete the activity. In input-based tasks, which were used in this study, learners should comprehend language input to do something by using their own language knowledge and any other source of information (e.g., contextual knowledge and non-verbal information).

As explained in the previous chapter, the current study is a type of comparative method study. I argued that there is a need for 'local' rather than 'global' method comparisons, and that it is necessary to investigate not only the learning outcomes, but also the process features of instruction. The current study was designed as a 'local' comparison by identifying specific target features as the focus of instruction, and then teaching them over a relatively short period of time (i.e., five weeks) which, although short, was still instructionally relevant. Both the process (i.e., how the learners worked) and product (i.e., what they learned) of the lessons were examined. The process aspects of the instruction were investigated using conversation analysis (CA), while the product of learning was investigated by employing a between-subjects design to compare the two groups of students, using a pre-test, immediate post-test and delayed post-test design.

The four research questions outlined below reflect this approach. First, I wanted to establish whether there were any differences between the two types of instruction in terms of the process features that they used (Research Question 1). Second, I wanted to see whether there were any differences in the learning outcomes (Research Questions 2 and 3). More specifically, the study investigated the effect of instruction on both vocabulary learning (Research Question 2) and incidental grammar learning (Research Question 3). The four research questions were the following:

1. In what ways did the classroom process features differ between presentation-practice-production (PPP) and task-based language teaching (TBLT)?
2. Which instructional approach (PPP or TBLT) resulted in greater vocabulary acquisition?
3. Which instructional approach (PPP or TBLT) was more effective in facilitating the incidental acquisition of grammatical features?
4. What relationship does the data suggest between process and product of PPP and TBLT?

Research Question 2 involves a comparison between intentional and incidental learning (see Chapter 3). In the TBLT group, the learners were not made aware that the purpose of their lessons was to learn vocabulary, whereas the PPP learners were told this explicitly and were directly taught the target words. However, neither group of learners was told that the purpose of the lessons was also to learn grammar (i.e., the learners in the PPP lessons were only told that the aim was to learn was vocabulary). For this reason, Research Question 3 addresses incidental grammar learning in both groups. Research Question 4 attempts to make a link between the findings of process and product analyses.

Participants

To recruit participants for the study, an advertisement was published in a local free paper in Toyota City. It addressed the following points:

> We recruit six-year-old children who are willing to participate in an educational research project. The children can receive nine free English lessons.
>
> The conditions for the participants are: (1) the child has not received any English lessons anywhere; (2) the child should be a new primary student; (3) the child can attend twice a week, for three months.

The advertisement was framed in this way because the criteria for recruitment were that the children should be all six years old with no prior experience of learning English.

A total of 45 Japanese children were recruited through the advertisement. The parents of the children were informed that the children would be participating in the study and their consent was obtained. The 45 children were randomly divided into three groups of 15: the presentation-practice-production (PPP) group, the task-based language teaching (TBLT) group, and the control group. Each group was further divided into two classes of between six to nine students each to enable effective examination of the process features of the lessons. Addressing the ethical issue of the possible unequal opportunities for the children to receive potentially effective instruction, each group received a shorter version of the treatments they had not received once the data collection for this study was completed (e.g., the control group received one PPP and one TBLT lesson).

All groups met twice a week during the project and did not receive any English instruction other than that provided in this study. The number of students in each group and class is shown in Table 4.1.

Table 4.1. Number of students in each group or class

Groups (student number)	Class (student number)
PPP group (n = 15)	PPP-A (n = 7) PPP-B (n = 8)
TBLT group (n = 15)	TBLT-A (n = 6) TBLT-B (n = 9)
Control group (n = 15)	Control-A (n = 8) Control-B (n = 7)

Each of the classes was held in a small classroom in the private school. Students sat around the large table and the teacher stood on one side of the table. A video-camera was placed the other side of the teacher and an audio-recorder was placed in the middle of the table. A typical classroom layout is presented in Figure 4.1.

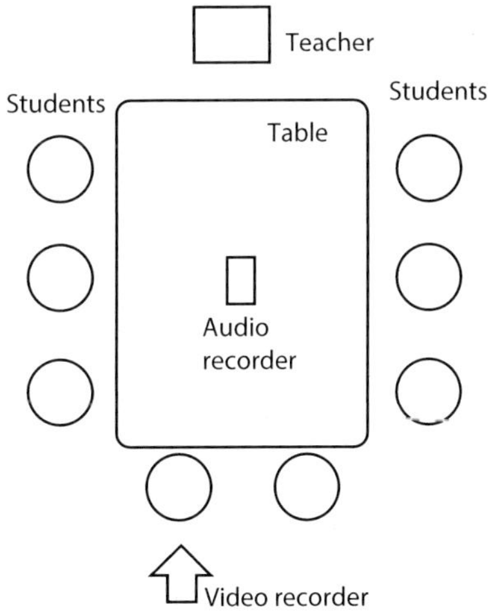

Figure 4.1. Classroom layout

Instructional treatments

Instructional materials and procedures for the PPP group

Prior to each PPP lesson, the goal of the activities (to learn new vocabulary) was made clear to the students. Each lesson then consisted of five activities representing the three phases of PPP (presentation- practice-production). The first activity, which served as the 'presentation' phase, involved the children repeating individual words. The second and third activities, which served as the 'practice' phase, involved the students' saying the word shown on flash cards – both chorally and individually. The fourth and the fifth activities served as the 'production' (i.e., free production) phase. Both of these activities involved the children naming the objects shown on the flash-cards chorally as part of a game. All five activities were carried out in each lesson and were repeated six times with different sets of items.

In PPP, the syllabus is linear (see Chapter 3). Accordingly, the three sets of words (Sets A, B, and C in Table 4.2) were introduced in different lessons for the PPP group. Each set consisted of eight nouns and four adjectives. Set A was introduced in Lessons 1 and 2, Set B in Lessons 3 and 4, and Set C in Lessons 5 and 6. Each set was taught once again in Lessons 7, 8, and 9, which served as review lessons. In order to balance the time difference between exposure to the target items and the post-tests, the PPP group reviewed the previous set of target items in each lesson. Both nouns and adjectives were introduced in accordance with PPP methodology; that is, the form and meaning of the words were introduced explicitly before production practice.

Table 4.2. Distribution of target items in three sets for the PPP class

	Nouns	Adjectives
Item A	*camel, ostrich, crocodile, hippopotamus, squirrel, seal, polar bear, peacock, crocodiles, peacocks*	*brown, gray, heavy, light*
Item B	*pan, ladle, chopsticks, cutting board, plate, soap, battery, toothbrush, batteries, toothbrushes*	*black, blue, big, small*
Item C	*green pepper, eggplant, chestnut, radish, leek, pear, mandarin, persimmon, pears, mandarins*	*purple, white, long, short*

For the PPP group, the target adjectives were introduced in the same way as the target nouns. Each adjective was depicted in a picture card. The colour adjectives were represented by coloured cards and the dimension adjectives were represented by pictures showing two objects that differed in size or shape (e.g., a picture of two balloons with an arrow pointing to the bigger balloon to represent '*big*').

I, as a teacher, used English during the activities, but Japanese was also used to explain the procedures for each activity whenever necessary. I made every effort to provide corrective feedback using recasts, since previous research (e.g., Lyster and Ranta, 1997) has shown this to be teachers' favoured strategy for correcting errors. Corrective feedback was provided both when the learners chose a wrong word (e.g., 'banana' instead of 'pear') and also when they chose the wrong grammatical form (e.g., 'pear' instead of 'pears'), on the grounds that this constitutes standard practice in PPP. As the learners had difficulty following the task procedures in the first few lessons, some of the activities were shortened in order to finish the lesson within the 30-minute time limit. The five activities are described below.

Activity 1: Listen and Repeat

Fourteen flash-cards representing eight target nouns plus two plural nouns, and four adjectives were presented one by one to the learners. I presented each flash-card in turn to the class, naming the item represented on the card. The children were asked to repeat the word after the teacher chorally. Each flash-card was presented twice. The activity was then repeated one more time.

Activity 2: Guess the hidden items

I asked all the students to name each flash-card in English while displaying and placing it face up in a holder. After 13 cards were placed in the holder, I placed the last card face down in the holder and asked the children to try to name the hidden item. I provided feedback to indicate whether a student was correct or incorrect and recast any wrong answers. This activity was repeated four times.

Activity 3: Throwing dice

All the flash cards were placed in the holder face down. Each card was numbered. One of the children threw a dice. I then picked up the card corresponding to the number shown on the dice and asked a child to name the item. If the answer was wrong, the teacher provided a recast and turned the card face down again. If the answer was correct, the card was left face up. This was repeated until each child had had two turns.

Activity 4: Production Bingo game

The students were instructed to choose nine cards from a set of 14 small flash cards. Each student had an individual set of cards, which were laid in a 3 × 3 formation in front of them. I also had a set of cards. I asked one of the children to pick up one card from her set and to show it to the other children. Then, all the children named the word on the card chorally and turned over the same card in their own set. This continued for six cards. I checked each learner's Bingo score (the number of turned-over cards). Two or three rounds were played depending on the available class time.

Activity 5: Kim's game

This activity required the students to produce all the vocabulary items. The four sets of flash-cards (a total of 56 cards) were spread randomly on the table face down. The children took turns flipping over one of the cards, and then all repeated the word shown on the card aloud. When a student turned a card over that was the same as one of the cards already face up, he/she was allowed to keep the pair of cards. If the children could not name the card, or provided a wrong answer, I responded with a recast. After all the cards had been turned over, the number of pairs collected by each child was counted and the winner announced.

Instructional materials and procedures for the TBLT group

Three tasks were designed in accordance with Ellis's (2003) definition of tasks; that is, they included a gap, they required learners to focus primarily on meaning and to make use of their own linguistic resources, and they had a clearly defined outcome (see Chapter 1). They constituted what Ellis calls input-tasks; that is, they were focused tasks that were designed in such a way that the outcome could only be achieved if the learners were successful in comprehending the input. Each task involved the learners listening to the teacher's commands and responding to them. All three tasks, thus, designed to involve teacher-learner interaction and there were no collaborative tasks between learners in pairs or groups. The three tasks were performed in each lesson, and were repeated in each of the nine lessons.

TBLT instruction typically involves exposure to a range of different language features (Ellis, Basturkmen, & Loewen, 2002). In order to achieve this, the TBLT lesson was designed in such a way that all the target words appeared in every lesson. However, the nouns and adjectives appeared in different ways. Students had to identify picture cards that corresponded to the nouns according to the teacher's directions. Each direction involved one or two nouns, and all 24 nouns appeared in every lesson. On the other hand, the adjectives arose only spontaneously in the process of performing the tasks. Both dimension adjectives and colour adjectives were introduced by me (the teacher) when I wanted to describe the target nouns to help the children understand the directions. In other words, the adjectives appeared whenever there was a need to elaborate the input. The students did not see any pictorial cards designed to show the meanings of the adjectives in any of the lessons.

There was no 'pre-task' phase where the target words were taught to the children. In this respect, the study differed from previous task-based studies (e.g., de la Fuente, 2002). In other words, the TBLT learners were required to perform the listen-and-do tasks without any prior knowledge of the target words. However, to assist them in comprehending the words, I, as a teacher, provided both verbal and non-verbal (e.g., gesture) support. Examples of this will be provided in the next chapter.

At the beginning of each lesson, the goal and task procedures were explained to the students. The students' primary attention was directed at the meaning of the teacher's commands by making sure that they were focused on the task goal. At no point were the children told the linguistic goal (i.e., learning vocabulary or grammar). While the teacher made every effort to use English during the performance of the tasks, it was necessary to switch to Japanese at times to ensure understanding of the task. The three tasks are described below.

Task 1: Help the zoo and the supermarket

Task 1 was a one-way information gap task where the teacher had the information and the students did not. The students had to make use of their own resources (including their L1 and L2 knowledge) to perform the task. The outcome of the task involved placing cards in the correct position.

The students listened to the teacher's commands and tried to find the cards corresponding to the target item(s). A total of 30 small flash cards for the 30 target items (including the six plural items), one three-sided board with 30 pockets to hold flash cards on the pictures of the "zoo" and the "supermarket", and one small empty box for incorrectly chosen cards were prepared. The children were informed that the purpose of this task was to help the zoo or the supermarket by finding the right cards and placing them in a pocket in the holder. They listened to a command, found the matching card, and then, when told to do so by the teacher, displayed the card they had chosen. The teacher then indicated whether they had chosen correctly. Those children who had chosen correctly placed the card in the pocket on the board while those who had answered incorrectly returned the card they had chosen to the table and put the correct card in their "incorrect" box. Care was taken to prevent the children from simply imitating the other children in two ways: (1) the three-sided board was designed to keep each student's responses hidden from other students; and (2) they were told to hide the card they had chosen in their hand until the teacher asked them to show it. After finishing the commands for all 30 items, each student counted the number of cards in his or her incorrect box. The student with the fewest cards was the winner.

Figure 4.2 shows one of the classrooms during this task.

Figure 4.2. A classroom during Task 1 in TBLT group

Task 2: Help the animals

Task 2 was also a one-way information gap task. The children were told that the purpose was "to help the animals" by finding the object(s) (represented on the cards) that the different animals needed. The goal of the task was to collect as many cards as possible.

The same 30 flash cards used in Task 1 were also employed here. Each student had a set of cards. The teacher explained in Japanese that the goal of the task was to help the animals by finding the pairs of cards which corresponded to the teacher's statements. For example, if the teacher said "The polar bear needs the batteries", they had to find the card showing a single "polar bear" and the card showing two "batteries". The students held up the pair of cards they had selected so that the teacher could indicate whether they had chosen correctly. They were allowed to change their selections until they identified the correct cards. Altogether each student collected ten pairs of cards.

Task 3: Listening Bingo game

This task was a form of Picture Bingo – a game which students are very familiar with. The learners began by choosing nine out of the ten cards they were given and laid them out in a 3 × 3 formation in front of them. In every lesson, a different set of ten cards from those used in tasks 1 and 2 was chosen. Each set included some cards representing plural objects. The teacher then called out a word naming one of the pictures. If a student had a card showing the picture of this word, he or she turned it face down. After presenting six words (some of which were singular and some plural), each child's Bingo score (i.e., the number of turned-over cards) was checked by the teacher. Between one and three rounds were played depending on the available class time.

Instructional materials for the control group

The control group was included to provide a basis for comparison in which students should not have acquired much or any of the targeted forms but simply changed or developed in all other ways similar to how the treatment groups had. Each lesson in the control group consisted of three activities: (1) practicing English songs, (2) practicing verb phrases using Total Physical Response (Asher, 1977), and (3) tracing and copying the alphabet on worksheets. The songs were *London Bridge*, *Mulberry Bush*, and *Twinkle Twinkle Little Star*. These introduced the verb phrases *get up, wash your face, get dressed, eat breakfast, go to school, go home, do your homework, eat dinner, watch TV, take a bath, go to bed, play soccer, play tag, sing a song, play tennis*, and *draw a picture*. Care was taken to avoid using the target words in the classroom, but the students were exposed to some plural *-s* items and, inevitably to copula *be* in the teacher's utterances and in the songs.

Research design

In order to undertake a careful comparison between PPP and TBLT of both process and product, the study employed a quasi-experimental design (Dörnyei, 2007; Mackey & Gass, 2005). As described earlier, the PPP group engaged in a set of activities that matched PPP methodology, while the TBLT group experienced task-based learning consisting of input-based tasks. In carrying out this kind of comparison, it is very important to be precise about the activities chosen, and about how they are carried out, and ensure that the activities do genuinely represent the teaching approaches that we want to investigate (see Chapter 1). These are described in detail below. In order to check whether the outcome of the PPP and TBLT sessions was different from what would have happened without either kind of session, the control group participated in a variety of activities that did not expose them to any of the target words. As controlling time-on-task is important when comparing different types of instruction (de la Fuente, 2002, Ellis & He, 1999, Ellis, Tanaka, & Yamazaki, 1994; Loschky, 1994), the lesson time for each group was set to approximately 30 minutes. All the lessons for the three groups were taught by the same teacher (i.e., the researcher).

Six tests were designed to measure language ability. In order to provide a balanced picture of the children's learning, we used production tests as well as comprehension tests. Since prior experience of comprehension activities can influence performance on production tests, the three production tests were administered prior to the three comprehension tests. This testing regime was repeated three times as pre-test, post-test 1, and post-test 2. The pre-test was used to check learners' starting points and was conducted two weeks prior to the first lesson. Post-test 1 was conducted one week after the treatment round in order to find out the immediate impact of the lessons, and post-test 2 was conducted four weeks after post-test 1, in order to find out how much what the students knew in post-test 1 they still retained. The test data was analysed quantitatively by employing statistical procedures. All the treatment classrooms were video- and audio-recorded and transcriptions were prepared in order to investigate the process features of the instruction. An overview of the research design is shown in Table 4.3.

Recording and transcribing of lessons

In each lesson, students sat around a square table with nine seats. One video-camera was positioned at one side of the classroom, focused on the students. The audio-recorder was placed in the middle of the table (see Figure 4.1, p. 61). A broad transcription of all the lessons was first made by the researcher. Every effort was made to identify individual student utterances by referring to the video-recordings. In order to investigate the process features in detail, selected sequences were further transcribed using CA conventions (see Chapter 5).

Table 4.3. Overview of the research design

	PPP groups	TBLT groups	Control groups
Week 1		Pre-test (4 tests)	
Week 2		Pre-test (4 tests)	
Week 3	PPP lesson 1, 2	TBLT lesson 1, 2	Unrelated lessons
Week 4	PPP lesson 3, 4	TBLT lesson 3, 4	Unrelated lessons
Week 5	PPP lesson 5, 6	TBLT lesson 5, 6	Unrelated lessons
Week 6	PPP lesson 7, 8	TBLT lesson 7, 8	Unrelated lessons
Week 7	PPP lesson 9	TBLT lesson 9	Unrelated lessons
Week 8		Post-test (4 tests)	
Week 9		Post-test (4 tests)	
Week 13		Delayed post-tests (4 tests)	
Week 14		Delayed post-tests (4 tests)	

Target features

The study investigated the acquisition of a number of selected vocabulary items and two grammatical features: plural *-s* and copula *be*.

Target vocabulary items

The target vocabulary items included two different word categories: nouns and adjectives. Nouns are considered easier for young learners to learn since they are more likely to evoke images and are thus more easily acquired than verbs (N. Ellis, 1994; N. Ellis & Beaton, 1993). In contrast, adjectives are considered to be more difficult for children to learn than nouns. Summarising studies of first language (L1) vocabulary acquisition, Gasser and Smith (1998) proposed three reasons for why learning adjectives is more difficult than learning nouns: (1) common nouns label objects that are similar across many inter-related and correlated features (e.g., a 'car' indicates a vehicle with four wheels) whereas dimensional adjectives label objects that are alike on only one abstract property (e.g., a white car, white bread, a white paper); (2) common nouns all classify objects at one level (e.g., classifying 'a car' and 'a bicycle' requires simple decision making) whereas adjectives are typically mutually exclusive within a dimension (e.g., a big dog versus a small dog) but overlap across dimensions (e.g., a big dog will be smaller than a small house); (3) adjectives associate with a wide range of nouns, whereas nouns tend to associate with a relatively fixed set of adjectives (e.g., 'white' man, fridge, egg).

Twenty-four nouns and 12 adjectives were selected as the target items. Three criteria guided the selection of the target words: (1) the L1 equivalents of the words would be known by the Japanese children; (2) the words were not in the *List of English Loanwords in Japanese* (Daulton, 1999), avoiding the possibility that children could identify the words' meanings by using their L1 knowledge; and (3) the adjectives served as common descriptors of the target nouns. First, three semantic categories that the Japanese children would be familiar with were chosen: animals, home appliances, and fruit and vegetables. Eight nouns for each category were selected which satisfied criteria 1 and 2. Then, 12 adjectives (six colour adjectives and six dimension adjectives) were selected. However, as a result of satisfying criteria 3, most of the adjectives did appear in Daulton's list (the exceptions being 'purple', 'small', and 'short'). I decided to prioritize the criterion (3) over (2) because the adjectives needed to be used to describe the nouns in the tasks.

In order to expose the children to the plural form of the nouns, two items from each set were introduced in both singular and plural form. Thus, there were a total of ten words for each set (i.e., eight in singular form and two in the plural form).

The 24 nouns and 12 adjectives and the two items from each set that were introduced in both singular and plural form are shown in Table 4.4.

Table 4.4. Target vocabulary items

Categories	Nouns		Adjectives
	Singular form	Plural form	
Animals (12)	*camel, ostrich, crocodile, hippopotamus, squirrel, seal, polar bear, peacock,*	*crocodiles, squirrels*	*brown, gray, heavy, light*
Home appliances (12)	*pan, ladle, chopsticks, cutting board, plate, soap, battery, toothbrush,*	*toothbrushes, batteries*	*black, blue, big, small*
Fruit & vegetables (12)	*green pepper, eggplant, chestnut, radish, leek, pear, mandarin, persimmon*	*pears, mandarins*	*purple, white, long, short*

Note that although the target words were carefully chosen to ensure that the referents would be familiar to Japanese children of this age, we could not avoid the possibility that some of them did not know the equivalent L1 word. Thus, despite our intentions, the instruction might still have involved some concept learning as well as learning of new L2 words.

Target grammatical features

The study investigated the incidental acquisition of two grammatical features: plural *-s* and copula *be*. Plural *-s* was chosen because it constitutes a difficult learning feature for

Japanese speakers, but is meaning bearing. Copula *be* was chosen because it is highly frequent in input but conveys no meaning, that is, it is relatively redundant.

According to Processability Theory, (Pienemann, 1998; Pienemann & Håkansson, 1999) plural *-s* requires the processing resources associated with the category procedure (i.e., lexical items are categorized, and include grammatical information such as number and gender to nouns, and tense to verbs). This constitutes the first processing operation acquired after the word/lemma stage. In contrast, copula *be* is a variational feature, acquirable at any stage of development depending on the learner's orientation (i.e., norm-oriented learners are more likely to acquire it earlier than functionally-oriented learners) (Meisel, Clahsen, & Pienemann, 1981).

Table 4.5 lists the factors that Ellis (2006) proposed to account for the learning difficulty of different grammatical structures as implicit knowledge. This comparison indicates that overall the copula is likely to pose greater learning difficulty than plural *-s*. It has lower functional value and is less regular (i.e., it occurs in many different forms). However, copula *be* occurs more frequently in the input than plural *-s*.

Table 4.5. Comparative difficulty in plural *-s* and copula *be*

Factors	Plural *-s*	Copula *be*
Frequency	Less frequent	More frequent
Saliency	Not very salient (a bound morpheme)	Not very salient in the contracted form
Functional value	High	Low
Regularity	Regular	Less regular (various forms; full and contracted forms)
Processability	Easy	Easy (as a 'variational' feature it is not subject to developmental constraints)

Testing materials

The importance of using multiple types of assessment is now universally recognized (Beretta & Davies, 1985; R. Ellis, 2004, 2005; Laufer, 1998; Schmitt, 1994; Takimoto, 2009). Accordingly, the study included eight tests: four vocabulary tests, two plural *-s* tests, and two tests for the copula *be*.

Vocabulary tests

Multiple-choice comprehension test

In this test, learners were asked to listen to an audio-recorded word and choose the appropriate picture from six pictures. The test contained 36 questions for each of the 36 target words. The test was administered to the children in groups. For the dimension adjectives, pictures showing the size of different objects were used. For example, for the adjective 'heavy' the learners had to select a picture showing an elephant from a set of six pictures the other five of which represented light objects (e.g., an ant). The target nouns were not used for testing the adjectives to avoid confusing the children. Five seconds were given for each question. One point was assigned for each correctly chosen item, and the highest possible score was 36. Care was taken to ensure the children could not see other learners' test papers during the test. Figure 4.3 shows a part of this test.

Figure 4.3. Multiple-choice comprehension test

Discrete-item production test

The discrete-item production test was administered to the children individually by the researcher. In this test, the researcher asked the child to name 36 target vocabulary items displayed on flashcards. The six colour adjective cards created for the PPP lessons were used in this test. For the dimension adjectives, different items from the ones used in the PPP lesson were prepared to avoid any bias in favour of the PPP group. The adjectives were tested after the noun items. One point was awarded for each correctly produced item, irrespective of whether they made any morphological or pronunciation errors (e.g., *too-brush* for 'toothbrush' or *cuttin boar* for 'cutting board') as long as it was clear the child knew the word. However, an answer was considered incorrect if they only produced part of the target word (e.g., *bear* for 'polar bear' or *chops* for 'chopsticks').

Category task

In this test, which was performed individually, the learners were asked to listen to sentences containing target nouns and decide which specific situation each corresponded to. For example, learners heard the sentence "A polar bear is walking slowly on the rock", and were asked to point to one of four pictures representing different situations (e.g., "fruit and vegetable shop", "home appliance shop", "land area of the zoo", and "sea area of the zoo"). In order to test the adjectives, each of the four pictures included an image of a child holding or wearing one of four items (e.g., a balloon, a bag, a hat, and a butterfly net) which had different colours or sizes. The learners listened to sentences such as "The boy has a blue balloon" and identified the picture with a blue balloon. Definitions of the nouns used for the adjective questions were provided in both English and Japanese prior to the test. Thirty-six sentences – one sentence for each target word – were prepared and presented in a random order. The children were awarded one point if they chose the correct category (i.e., identified the correct picture) for a sentence. The maximum score possible was 36.

Same-or-Different task

The children also took this test individually with the researcher. They were given a sheet with 12 pictures showing singular objects, and 12 showing plural objects. Five out of the 12 plural objects represented items introduced during the treatment (i.e., 'crocodiles', 'batteries', 'mandarins', 'toothbrushes', and 'squirrels'), while the other seven represented 'new' items (i.e., 'camels', 'peacocks', 'green peppers', 'pans, 'seals', 'chestnuts', and 'radishes'; see Figure 4.4). The researcher had a 'teacher sheet' consisting of 12 pictures. The children were instructed to speak in English to find out which pictures on their sheet were the same as those on the researcher's sheet. The researcher asked the children to name the object shown in a picture and told the children the name of the object in her picture. If the student's and researcher's pictures were the same they marked the picture with a check. If they were not the same they put a cross. The children were awarded one point for each item they produced correctly. The criterion for correct production used for the discrete-item vocabulary production test was also employed for this test. The maximum score possible in the Same-or-Different Task was 36.

Plural tests

Plural -s comprehension test

This test was completed by the children in groups. Two of the words appearing in the treatment and three new words were used. Each word was tested in both its singular and plural form. The students were given a test sheet consisting of ten pairs of pictures. Each set had two pictures (one representing the item in singular form and one in plural form; see Figure 4.5). They then listened to an audio-recorded word and were asked to indicate which picture corresponded to the word they had heard. They had five seconds to respond to each item.

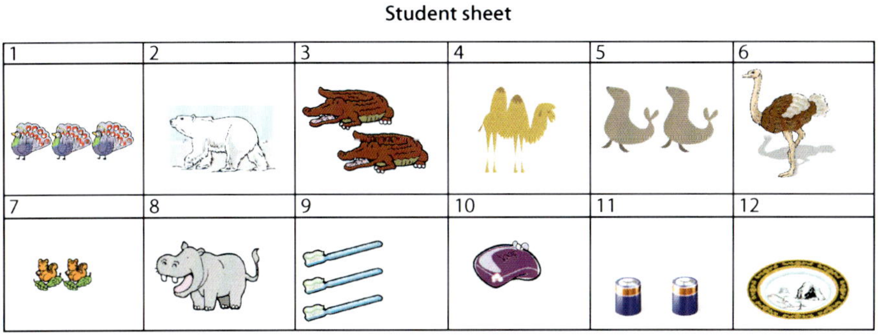

Figure 4.4. Same-or-Different task

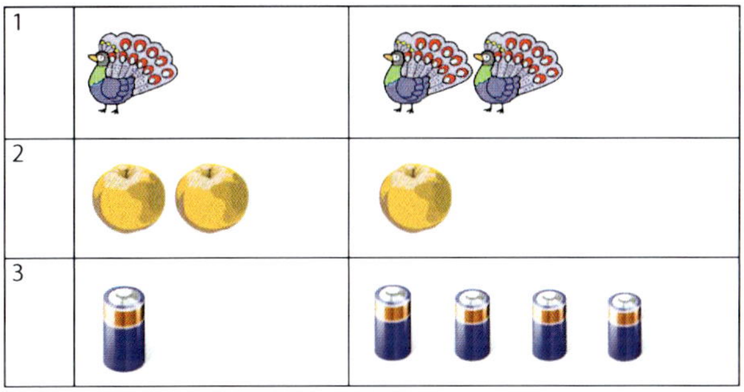

Figure 4.5. Plural -s comprehension test

Wug test

This test was adapted from Berko (1958). The test was administered to the children individually by the researcher and consisted of ten items: five which had been introduced in the treatment and five nonsense words (see Figure 4.6). The researcher first provided the singular form orally while pointing to the single item picture (e.g., "This is a wug"), and then pointed to the plural item picture and elicited a plural noun orally from the learner by saying "There are two of them. There are two ____". The instructions were provided in English first, but Japanese was used if a student did not understand them. Ample time was given for the learners to answer. If a learner was unable to provide an answer or only said the singular form of a word for three consecutive items, the test was stopped.

Copula tests

Task-based copula 'be' production test: Tell-and-Do task

The aim of this test was to measure children's structural knowledge of the copula *be* by having them produce the structure during a one-way information-gap task.

Figure 4.6. The Wug test sheet

Two different sheets for the children and the researcher were prepared. The children's sheet had ten pictures (five depicting singular items and five plural items) with various colours. The researcher's sheet had the same ten pictures as the children's sheet but with no colours. The children were asked to tell the researcher to colour her pictures in the same manner as their own sheet. The ten items consisted of five target items and five items from the *List of English Loanwords in Japanese* (Daulton, 1999). The colours used in the test were selected from Daulton's list, but excluded the target adjectives.

This test was scored for 'production' and 'accuracy'. The children obtained one point each time they produced an utterance with *be* regardless of subject-verb agreement. They obtained an additional point if there was correct subject-verb agreement. The maximum score possible was 10 for 'production' and a further 10 for 'accuracy'.

Discrete-item copula be production test: Sentence production test

This test measured children's ability to produce the correct form of *be* in sentences consisting of subject + *be* + complement. A test sheet with pictures of 12 nouns (six in singular form and six in plural form) with various colours was prepared. The 12 nouns consisted of six target items and six items from the *List of English Loanwords in Japanese* (Daulton, 1999). The first two pictures (one depicting a singular noun and the other a plural noun) were used by the researcher to provide examples of what the children needed to say. Additionally, flash cards were used to present all the vocabulary items required for this test. Next, the researcher gave the test sheet (Figure 4.7) to the child and used the first two pictures on the sheet to show them how to make sentences consisting of subject + *be* + noun, for example, "The mandarin is orange" and "The green peppers are green". The child was then asked to make sentences for the rest of the six pictures. This test was scored in the same way as the Tell-and-Do task.

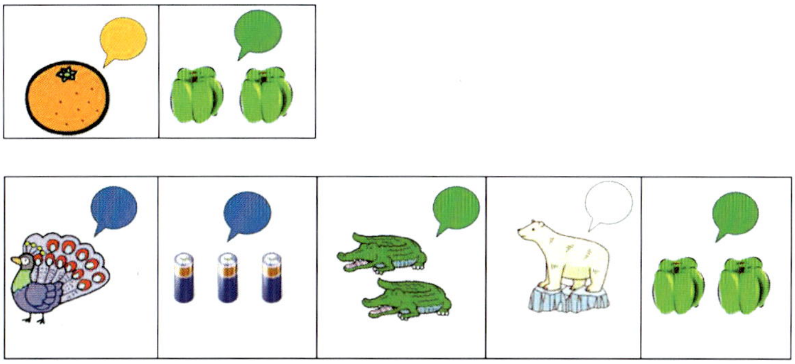

Figure 4.7. Discrete-item copula be production test: Sentence production test

Testing order

The order of the tests is shown in Table 4.6. In order to avoid inter-test effects, production tests were all administered prior to comprehension tests.

Table 4.6. Testing order

	Test	Objective	Type of test	Modality
1	Same-or-Different task	Vocabulary Plural -*s*	Task-based	Production
2	Discrete-item vocabulary production test	Vocabulary	Discrete-item	Production
3	Wug test	Plural -*s*	Discrete-item	Production
4	Tell-and-Do task	Copula *be*	Task-based	Production
5	Sentence production test	Copula *be*	Discrete-item	Production
6	Category task	Vocabulary	Task-based	Reception
7	Multiple-choice word test	Vocabulary	Discrete-item	Reception
8	Multiple-choice plural -*s* test	Plural -*s*	Discrete-item	Reception

Reliability of the testing instruments

The internal reliability of all the tests was estimated using the combined post-test 1 scores for the PPP and the TBLT groups (n = 30). The decision to use the post-test 1 scores was made because most of the children scored zero on the pre-test; thus, it was not possible to conduct a reliability analysis for this test. The reliability estimate (Cronbach alpha) was relatively high for all the vocabulary tests: α = .834 for the discrete-item comprehension test, α = .793 for the Category Task, α = .815 for the discrete-item production test, α = .782 for the Same-or-Different Task. The plural *-s* comprehension test showed a lower reliability estimate, α = .667, but the alpha level for the two plural *-s* production tests was α = 1.000. The estimation was low for the comprehension test presumably because the students tended to choose an item randomly when they were unable to differentiate the singular and plural forms. The two tests for the copula *be* also showed high reliability estimates: α = .988 for both tests. All eight tests were thus considered to be relatively reliable.

Data analysis

In order to answer Research Question 1, the process features of the two types of instruction were first examined. Class A from the PPP group and the TBLT group were chosen for this analysis (see Table 4.1). The transcribed data for the two classes were analysed in terms of the organization of turn-taking and repair, and learning behaviour, over time using conversation analysis. A detailed account of the procedures followed as well as the results of the analysis will be provided in the next chapter.

To address Research Questions 2 and 3, the quantity and the quality of the input (i.e., target words/grammatical features heard by the students) and output (i.e., target words/grammatical features produced by the students) that occurred in the two groups were examined first. Then all test scores were analysed in terms of descriptive statistics, and then through within- and between-group comparison tests using SPSS version 19. A series of repeated measures ANOVAs with pair-wise comparisons using Bonferroni adjustments were employed to check for significant differences between the groups and over time. For the data that did not meet the assumption of normality, non-parametric tests (i.e., the Wilcoxon Signed Ranks Test and Mann-Whitney U test) were used.

The Same-or-Different Task served as the production test for both vocabulary and plural *-s*. The test scores were counted in two ways: (1) the number of target words each child produced for vocabulary; and (2) accuracy scores for the plural *-s* morpheme based on whether a child supplied this morpheme in obligatory context. They were scored by the researcher. To ensure intra-rater reliability the researcher scored the tests at two different times, with 100% agreement.

For plural *-s* and copula *be*, neither of the analyses based on mean scores nor rank-order was appropriate as most of the students failed to show any improvement in either structure. The scores were, thus, used to determine whether each learner had or had not acquired plural *-s* based on an 80% criterion level (Jia, 2003) based on the individual scores. The number of children who had 'acquired' or 'not acquired' the two structures was counted and the difference between the two experimental groups was compared using a Chi-square test.

Alpha was set at .05. Effect sizes for the comparative effects of two variables were estimated using the correlation coefficient effect size *r*. For the chi-square tests, Cohen's *w* was used. Effect size values were interpreted as small = .1, medium = .3 or large = .5 according to Cohen's (1988) recommendations.

Conclusion

The next chapters will present the results. The comparison will start with a focus on processing differences; that is by examining the nature of the interactions that occurred in the two types of instruction. It will then turn to focus on the product of the interventions, by examining the learning outcomes as measured by the battery of tests of both receptive and productive knowledge.

The study differs from much of the previous task-based research in a number of ways. Firstly, it explores the viability of using a task-based approach with complete beginners. Whereas most other task-based studies have investigated speaking tasks, this study looks at input-based tasks. Additionally, unlike most other studies which were cross-sectional in design, this study is semi-longitudinal in nature, lasting five weeks. Another way in which this study differs from most previous studies is that it investigated both the instructional processes in the interactions that arose as the tasks were performed and learning outcomes. Finally, by asking the children to complete the same tasks nine times, the study investigates task repetition in much greater depth than other studies. My aim was to develop teaching and testing materials and procedures not just for my study but for use in other contexts involving young children so that potentially the study could be replicated.

CHAPTER 5

Comparing the process features of the two types of instruction

This chapter examines in depth the process of the instruction taking place in the presentation-practice-production (PPP) and the task-based language teaching (TBLT) interventions that were delivered in the current study. The goal of this chapter is to establish the extent to which the processes of the two types of instruction were similar or different, offering an internal (i.e., what actually happened) as opposed to an external (i.e., what was planned) perspective on the instruction.

The chapter will seek to answer Research Question 1 addressed in Chapter 4:

> In what ways did the classroom process features differ between presentation-practice-production (PPP) and task-based language teaching (TBLT)?

I will address this question by conducting a micro-analysis of the conversation that took place in the two instructional contexts. Seedhouse (2004) argued that the way in which interaction in a language lesson or class is organized varies according to the context. In this respect, he distinguished between: (1) 'form and accuracy oriented contexts', (2) 'meaning and fluency oriented contexts', (3) 'task-oriented contexts', and (4) 'procedural contexts' (i.e., where the teacher explains how to carry out an activity; see Chapter 3). Seedhouse reported that in 'form and accuracy oriented contexts', the focus is on producing the accurate target L2 forms while in 'meaning and fluency oriented contexts' it is on establishing mutual understanding. Conversation in 'task-oriented contexts' focuses on the completion of the task. Seedhouse argued that in 'task-oriented contexts,' learners' tends to "narrowly focus on getting the task finished" (p. 131) rather than on either form (as in form and accuracy oriented contexts) or on meaning (as in meaning and fluency oriented contexts). He further argued that 'task-oriented contexts' tend to be characterized by minimal and highly indexicalised language as illustrated by this extract:

L1: what?
L2: stop.
L3: dot?
L4: dot?
L5: point?
L6: dot?
LL: point point, yeah.

L1: point?
L5: small point.
L3: dot. (Lynch, 1989 cited by Seedhouse, 2004, p. 126)

It could be argued, however, that if the learners are beginners and have no experience of using the L2 for communication – as was the case with the learners in my study – such language use could be considered evidence of the early development of communicative competence. In this chapter, I will examine whether the actual conversations that took place in the PPP and TBLT lessons correspond to the types of language use described by Seedhouse (2004) and, in this way examine to what extent and in what ways the classroom processes that arose in the two types of instruction differed.

The analysis focuses on two conversational features that have been frequently analysed in CA-for-SLA (see Chapter 3) research: 'turn-taking' (i.e., how each of the interlocutors contributes to the conversation) and 'repair' (i.e., how conversational problems are dealt with). Researchers argue that various classroom factors such as the orientation of lessons or learner differences influence the characteristics of these processes (e.g., Seedhouse, 2004; Ohta, 2001; see also Chapter 3).

Due to time constraints I selected two classes (i.e., the TBLT-A class, which consisted of six students, and the PPP-A class, which consisted of seven) for this analysis (see Chapter 4). The video-recorded data and the transcribed audio-recoded data of the 18 lessons (nine lessons for each class) were used for the analyses. The spoken data were transcribed following CA conventions (Jefferson, 2004; see Appendix A). Supplementary video-recorded data were used to identify the speakers' nonverbal actions. Some of the data were quantified by counting the occurrences of specific types of conversation patterns in three of the nine lessons (Lessons 1, 5, and 9). These lessons were chosen because they occurred at the beginning, in the middle, and at the end of the instructional treatment and thus helpful to capture the general overview of and to document changes across the nine lessons.

Turn-taking

Turn-taking refers to "an organization of practices designed to allow routine achievement of what appears to be overwhelmingly the most common default 'numerical' value of speakership of talk-in-interaction: one party talking at a time" (Schegloff, 2000, p. 1). The central turn structure identified by conversation analysts is the 'adjacency pair'. An adjacency pair refers to two turns that are functionally related to each other in such a way that a first turn requires a second turn, such as a question-answer pair (Sacks & Schegloff, 1979; Sacks, Schegloff, & Jefferson, 1974). However, the turn structure that has been traditionally identified in classroom interaction is a three-part structure: teacher's initiation, student's response, and the teacher's feedback (IRF) exchange (Sinclair & Coulthard, 1975). Seedhouse (2004) showed that in a form and accuracy oriented context, adjacency pairings consist of a teacher prompt (e.g., "What is the past form of go?"), followed by a student response (e.g., "Went."), which in turn was followed by an optional evaluation turn (e.g., "Good."). In this examination of the turn structure, the term adjacency pair will be used to refer to interactions that involve pairs of turns, while IRF will be used to refer to the three-part structure.

A question turn can be initiated by referential questions (i.e., questions where the answers are not known by the person asking them) or display questions (i.e., questions where the answers are already known to the person asking them). While referential questions are common in a naturalistic context (outside of the classroom), in second language classrooms teachers tend to use display questions (Brock, 1986; Long & Sato, 1983). It is possible, then, that display questions will predominate in the PPP activities but referential questions will be more common in the TBLT activities. Thus I will examine the types of questions that occurred in the PPP and TBLT to see if this is the case.

Studies have also suggested that turn-taking in L2 classrooms is characterized by a strict allocation of turns by the teacher (Markee, 2000; McHoul, 1978). Seedhouse (2004) reported this occurs particularly in a 'form and accuracy oriented context'. Conversations in a large L2 classroom often involve a turn in chorus with the whole class repeating after the teacher's model. This might not happen in TBLT lessons as there is no 'presentation' phase in the lesson. Thus I decided to examine who is controlling the conversation, and also whether turns in chorus occurred in the two types of classroom activity.

Seedhouse (2004) also reported that in a 'form and accuracy oriented context' students do not develop a new topic in the conversation. However, Seedhouse also reported that in a 'meaning and fluency oriented context' the teacher only controls turns at the beginning and the end of the lesson and the students often develop a new topic when they are controlling the conversation. I examined this aspect as well.

Finally I examined the length and frequency of turns in the two types of instruction. Studies have shown that in language classrooms teacher turns are longer than those of students (e.g., Markee, 2000). I would expect this to be the case for both the PPP and TBLT classes because of the students' limited productive skills, but some differences between the two types of instruction might be expected in line with Seedhouse's claims about the type of language use associated with different classroom contexts.

In the next sections, therefore, I will examine the following six aspects of turn-taking:

1. occurrence of IRF exchanges;
2. question types;
3. control of turn-taking;
4. occurrence of turn in chorus;
5. topic development;
6. length and frequency of turns.

I will start with examining the PPP lessons.

Characteristics of turn-taking in the PPP lessons

Occurrence of IRF exchanges

In the PPP group, IRF exchanges were frequently observed throughout the five activities. Conversation often involved short sequences typically consisting of a single IRF exchange. The IRF exchanges in this group were mostly focused on the accurate production of the vocabulary items targeted in the lessons. This was the case not only in the first phases of PPP (i.e., presentation and practice) but also in the production phase. Two examples from Activity 1 and Activity 5 are shown below. Activity 1 was designed as the presentation phase of the presentation-practice-production (PPP) approach. This activity required the students to repeat a target word after the teacher, which was also displayed on a flashcard. This led to the kind of exchange shown in Excerpt 5.1.

Excerpt 5.1
1. T: ((shows a card to the class)) crocodile
2. Ss: croco[di:]
3. T: [cro]codile
4. Ss: crocodi:
5. T: okay

(Activity 1 in Lesson 4, PPP)

In turn 1, the teacher presents the target word form, and in so doing asks the class to say the word. This led to choral repetition by the students. The teacher's second turn serves as a positive evaluation of the learners' production as well as a request for further repetition by the class. The students respond by again producing the word chorally, and the sequence concludes with the teacher's evaluation in turn 5. In other words, the first phase of PPP consisted of a typical IRF exchange – teacher's initiation (turns 1 and 3), students' response (turns 2 and 4), and the teacher's feedback (turn 5).

Activity 5 required the students to flip one card and to match it with another card face-up on the table. Students were required to name the item on the card as they turned it over. Although this activity was designed as the last phase of PPP approach (i.e., free production), the actual conversation tended to follow the typical IRF pattern, as shown in Excerpt 5.2.

Excerpt 5.2
1. T: okay, your turn (3.0)
2. S1: ((turns over one card on the table))
3. T: ((looks at the card)) what colour is this? ((looks at L1)) what colour is this?
4. ((takes the card from S1's hand and shows it to S1)).
5. S1: ((looks away))
6. T: black.
7. S1: bla[ck.]
8. T: [okay] ((puts the card on the table and looks at the next student)) your turn.
(Activity 5 in Lesson 4, PPP)

The teacher asked S1 a question in turn 3 (i.e., initiation), and treated S1's next turn (turn 5) as a display of ignorance (i.e., response). In turn 6, the teacher said the word for the student, which led to the learner's repetition of the word in turn 7, followed by the teacher's evaluation in turn 8 (i.e., feedback). The turn-taking structure was similar to Excerpt 5.1 – the sequence was centred around an IRF exchange which was targeted on the accurate production of the target word, 'black'. In other words, although the activity constituted the last phase of PPP (aimed at encouraging free production), the actual exchange was very similar to the first two phases of PPP (presentation and controlled practice).

Question type

Question turns in the PPP lessons were predominantly initiated by the teacher and mainly consisted of display questions. Table 5.1 shows the frequency of two types of questions classified along two dimensions: (1) teacher-initiated versus student-initiated and (2) display versus referential questions. The table shows that teacher-initiated display questions were dominant. There were relatively few referential questions. A student-initiated question occurred only once in Lesson 5, and involved a referential question.

Table 5.1. Types of question turns in Lessons 1, 5, and 9 in the PPP class

Type of questions		Lesson 1	Lesson 5	Lesson 9
Teacher-initiated	Display questions	448	425	411
	Referential questions	31	25	18
Student-initiated	Display questions	0	0	0
	Referential questions	0	1	0

An example of a teacher-initiated display question can be seen in Excerpt 5.2. Referential questions occurred predominantly in Activities 4 and 5 when the teacher checked how well the students were performing the activities, as illustrated in Excerpt 5.3. Such sequences, however, still involved an IRF exchange.

Excerpt 5.3
1. T: how many pairs have you got?
2. S: one, two, three, four, (.) [five, six]
3. T: [five, six] six pairs (.) great.
(Activity 5 in Lesson 7, PPP)

There were also a few cases where a learner initiated a question to ask about the meaning of a target word (or receive confirmation about it). This was almost always expressed in Japanese (the L1), as shown in Excerpt 5.4.

Excerpt 5.4
1. S: crocodile tte wani? ((tr: does 'crocodile' mean crocodile?))
2. T: yes. yes.
(Lesson 1 in Activity 4, PPP)

The above analysis shows that the question turns in the PPP lessons were almost exclusively initiated by the teacher, in accordance with the pedagogical purpose of the activity – eliciting the students' accurate production of the target language feature (i.e., vocabulary items).

Control of turn-taking

In the PPP lessons, turn-taking was strictly controlled by the teacher. The above extracts show that the teacher decided who said what and when. In Excerpt 5.1, the teacher's turns 1 and 3 were requests which set up the students' choral responses. These turns created the interactional context for the teacher's evaluation that closed the exchange. In Excerpt 5.2, the teacher used the first turn to ask S1 to perform the activity. In the following turns (turns 3, 4, and 6), the teacher asked S1 to produce the target word. Then, the teacher nominated another student to respond in turn 8. There were no turns taken by the other students during the exchange. In Excerpt 5.3, the teacher used the first turn (turn 1) to allocate the following turn to one of the students. In Excerpt 5.4, there was no teacher allocation of turns, but this type of exchange occurred very rarely in this group, as shown in Table 5.1.

This suggests that the interactions in the PPP classes were similar to those which are typical in a 'form and accuracy oriented context' according to Seedhouse (2004). As a result, the opportunity for students to take control of the conversation was limited. In other word, the interactions were very different from those found in a naturalistic context.

Turns in chorus

As Table 5.2 shows, learners' choral production occurred frequently in the PPP lesson, both when requested by the teacher and in response to the teacher's feedback. This type of choral turn is typical of many classrooms (Markee, 2000; Van Lier, 1988) and is especially common in classrooms with very young learners for whom choral responses might be more acceptable compared with older learners. The numbers decreased over time as the learners became more able to produce the target words.

Table 5.2. Frequency of student turns in chorus in Lessons 1, 5, and 9 in the PPP group

	Lesson 1	Lesson 5	Lesson 9
Requested repetition	91	84	68
Response to feedback turn	45	24	9

An example of 'requested repetition' can be seen in Excerpt 5.1, where the learners were asked to repeat after the teacher. Learner turns in chorus also occurred immediately after the teacher's feedback turn in IRF exchanges, as shown in Excerpt 5.5. In turn 1, when the teacher found that the students could not produce the target word following her request, she said the word herself (turn 3), which led to the students' choral repetition in the next turn.

Excerpt 5.5
1. T: ((shows a card to the class)) what is it?
2. Ss: ((silence)) (2.0)
3. T: squirrel.
4. Ss: squirre:l

(Activity 2 in Lesson 4, PPP)

Following Seedhouse, the frequent occurrence of students' turns in chorus indicates that the PPP lessons were typical for L2 classrooms where the focus is on the accurate production of the target language.

Topic

There was no opportunity for the learners to initiate or develop a topic. As shown in the above excerpts (Excerpts 5.1, 5.2 and 5.5), the interactions were focused on the learners' accurate production of the target vocabulary items except for a few occasions where students asked a question about language (Excerpt 5.3) and the teacher checked the students' performance of the activities (Excerpt 5.4). The students' output was strongly guided by the teacher's requirement to display linguistic knowledge, as shown in the above excerpts. Seedhouse (2004) argues that topic does not apply to interactions in form and accuracy oriented contexts (p. 104). The focus of the PPP lesson – the accurate production of the target language feature – may actually prevent the learners from developing new topics in the conversation.

The students' limited L2 knowledge may be another reason for the lack of topic development. However, as I will show in the later section, the TBLT lessons did provide opportunities for students to develop and introduce topics on their own initiative.

Length and frequency of turns

In the PPP lessons, student turns in the L2 were predominantly one-word utterances with the exception of one utterance involving counting cards (see Excerpt 5.3). The teacher's turns, on the other hand, mostly consisted of multi-word utterances. Table 5.3 shows the frequency and the average length of turns in each activity in the PPP lessons in the three lessons. Non-verbal turns and L1 turns were excluded from this analysis.

Table 5.3. The frequency and the length of turns in the ppp lesson (Lessons 1, 5, and 9)

	Activity	Lesson 1		Lesson 5		Lesson 9	
		Teacher	Student	Teacher	Student	Teacher	Student
Number of turns	Activity 1	50	38	45	42	48	48
	Activity 2	118	60	102	76	98	72
	Activity 3	58	35	61	32	48	39
	Activity 4	88	15	70	22	68	32
	Activity 5	201	68	188	95	191	85
	Total	515	216	466	267	453	276
Mean length of turn*	Activity 1	2.6	1.0	2.4	1.0	2.5	1.0
	Activity 2	5.5	1.0	5.6	1.0	4.0	1.0
	Activity 3	3.9	1.0	4.5	1.0	3.5	1.0
	Activity 4	5.0	1.0	6.1	1.3	6.8	1.2
	Activity 5	5.4	1.1	6.7	1.5	7.2	1.4
	Whole lesson	4.5	1.0	5.1	1.2	4.8	1.1

* The length of turn was calculated by counting the number of L2 words in one turn (not including L1 turns or non-verbal turns)

The table shows that both the teacher and the students produced a substantial number of turns during the lesson. The teacher produced more turns than the students, reflecting the fact that most exchanges were of the IRF type, where the teacher typically took the first and the third turns while the students took the second turn only. The mean number of words per turn shows that the teacher talked more than the students. The mean length of students' turns was greater in Activities 4 and 5 than other activities in Lessons 1 and 5 because there were frequent occasions where the learners were counting the number of cards they had collected (e.g., "one, two, three, four. four bingos").

The table shows that the PPP lessons involved a typical L2 classroom pattern – the teacher dominates the conversation – which was evident throughout the three phases of the lesson.

Summary

Table 5.4 summarizes the characteristics of turn-taking in the PPP. Overall, the interactions taking place in the PPP lessons showed strong similarities with of the typical features of 'form and accuracy oriented contexts' as identified by Seedhouse.

Table 5.4. Characteristics of turn-taking in the PPP lessons

Aspects of turn-taking	Characteristics of turn-taking
IRF exchanges	Short sequences typically involving a single IRF exchange
Question type	Predominantly initiated by the teacher with display questions
Control of turn-taking	Tight control of turn-taking (i.e., teacher decides who says what and when.)
Turns in chorus	Learner turns were frequently produced in chorus.
Topic	Topics were not developed. The interactions were focused on the learners' accurate production of the target vocabulary items.
Length and frequency of turns	Teacher turns were longer than student turns.

Now I will move on to the TBLT lesson and examine how turn-taking in this group differed from the PPP lessons.

Characteristics of turn-taking in the TBLT lessons

Occurrence of IRF exchanges

In the TBLT lessons, adjacency pairs often consisted of a student question and a teacher answer. Feedback turns rarely occurred. Several question-answer exchanges occurred simultaneously and involved more than two speakers. Excerpt 5.6 shows a sequence from Lesson 4 with these characteristics.

Excerpt 5.6

1. T: okay (1.0) u::::m. okay (.) let's go to the zoo (.) please take the (1.0) squirrel (.) [squirrel]
2. S1: [squirrel]
3. S5: [squirrel]
4. T: Yeah (.) [squirrel]

5. S1: [whito?]
6. S2: supermarketto?
7. S1: whito?
8. T: (.) no no no [no].
9. S3: [zoo] (.) zoo [zoo].
10. T: [zoo] yeah (.) to the zoo (.) squirrel to the zoo.
11. S1: whito? (.) [whito?]
12. S2: [white?]
13. T: [no] no no no (.) not [white].
14. S4: [blue?]
15. T: not blue ((looks at the card in her hand and smiles)) (2.0) brown.
16. S2: brown?
17. T: and very ((shows 'small' with her hand)) small. (1.0) [small and]
18. S2: ((looks at the teacher with frowning face)) [brown tte nani?] ((trs: *what's brown?*))
19. S4: brown tte nani? ((trs: *what's brown?*))
20. S3: ((picks up one card from his set and looks at the teacher)) [one?]
21. T: [brown?] ((walks to the wall to point something brown)).
22. S3: ((shows his pointing finger to the teacher)) one? (1.0) [one?]
23. S2: [brown?]
24. T: ((shows her pointing finger)) one (.) yeah (.) very small ((gesture)). very small ((gesture)) and brown (.) brown ((goes to the wall and points to brown)) and small (.) okay, three (.) two (.) [one (.) Go]
24. S5: [one (.) Go:]
25. Ss: ((hold up their selected cards))
29. T: ((shows the correct card)) this is the (.) squirrel (.) squirrel, squirrel. Okay.

(Task 1 in Lesson 4, TBLT)

In the first part of the sequence, two exchanges occurred. One of them was initiated by S1's question (turn 5), which was repeated in turn 7 and turn 11 as his question was not answered. In turn 12, another student (S2) asked the same question in a louder voice, which was answered by the teacher in the next turn. The other exchange was initiated by S2's question '*supermarketto*?' in turn 6, which was answered by the teacher in turn 8. S5 provided additional information ('*zoo*'), and the teacher elaborated in turn 9. Both exchanges were initiated by students, were responded by the teacher, and involved more than one student.

The above analysis suggests that the interactions exchanges that took place in the TBLT lesson were very different from the PPP interaction in two ways; the conversation in the TBLT lessons led to longer sequences than those in the PPP lessons, and it consisted of multiple exchanges that involved overlapping. This indicates that the conversation in this group was more naturalistic than the PPP.

Question types

The question turns in the TBLT lessons were first analysed using the same dimensions as the PPP group (i.e., teacher-initiated versus student-initiated and display versus referential questions). As Table 5.5 shows, the question turns in the TBLT lesson were exclusively referential questions, and were initiated by students more often than by the teacher. This pattern contrasts markedly with the question turns in the PPP class (see Table 5.1).

Table 5.5. Types of question turns in Lessons 1, 5, and 9 in the TBLT groups

Type of questions		Lesson 1	Lesson 5	Lesson 9
Teacher-initiated	Display questions	0	0	0
	Referential questions	2	8	12
Student-initiated	Display questions	0	0	0
	Referential questions	0	70	84

The above sequence also shows that the learners' questions had various functions: they were used to help other students to provide an answer (turn 12), to repeat a question turn when it was not answered (turns 7 and 11), to answer a question posed by another student (turn 9), and to request information from the teacher (turns 5, 6, 14, 18 and 20). This shows that in the TBLT lessons, the students voluntarily produced one-word utterances directed at achieving the outcome of the task, for example by obtaining information from and helping other students. This suggests the TBLT lessons created a context where students use the L2 as a communicative tool.

The TBLT lessons also involved some teacher-initiated questions (see Table 5.5). Such exchanges typically occurred when the teacher asked the students to describe how they were performing the task, as in Excerpt 5.7.

Excerpt 5.7
1. T: how many bingos have you got?
2. S1: (1.0) one, two
3. T: oh, only two? okay.

(Task 3 in Lesson 7, TBLT)

The fact that display questions did not occur here suggests that the question turns observed in the TBLT lesson were aimed at conveying messages rather than testing the students. The questions were mostly initiated by the students. This shows that the actual conversation in the TBLT lessons reflects the purpose of this teaching approach – providing learners with opportunities to use the L2 as a tool to achieve a goal rather than just practising linguistic forms.

Control of turn-taking

Teacher allocation of turns was relatively rare in the TBLT lessons. In Excerpt 5.6, for example, although the sequence was initiated by the teacher's instruction (turn 1), the subsequent student turns were not allocated by the teacher. Table 5.5 clearly shows that all the initiation turns were produced by the students. The teacher's utterances were produced in response to the students' questions. Finally, in turn 24, the teacher took control of the interaction with her instruction, "okay, three, two, one, go", which requested the students to show the cards they had selected. This shows that the teacher started and ended the sequence, but within the sequence the learners mostly controlled the turns. Seedhouse (2004) observes that in meaning and fluency oriented classroom contexts, turn-taking is managed by students but eventually controlled by the teacher. The above sequence follows a similar pattern.

Topic

Seedhouse (2004) claims that in a 'task-based context', learners tend to focus only on the successful completion of the task rather than on meaning such as on the topic at hand or on expressing personal meaning (see p. 80). However, in some of the conversations the learners did engage in the development of the topic, as Excerpt 5.8 shows.

Excerpt 5.8
1. T: please take the crocodile to the supermarket.
2. S1: ((taking the 'crocodile' card from his table)) (2.0) *supermarketto*?
3. T: oh, sorry, zoo, zoo. not supermarket.
4. S2: crocodile, supermarket ((gestures))
5. T: yeah, it's scary isn't it, if a crocodile is in the supermarket.
6. S1, S2: ((laugh))

(Task 1 in Lesson 9, TBLT)

S1's first turn indicates that he successfully identified the meaning of the word 'crocodile'. He then produced "*supermarket*" with a rising intonation with the intention of pointing out the teacher's error. In turn 4, S2, who was sitting next to S1, playfully articulated the idea of a crocodile appearing in the supermarket, which the teacher then took up and extended, causing the students to laugh. This indicates that there were occasions when the learners engaged in the development of the topic that the task had created. In this respect, some of the interactions s corresponded to Seedhouse's (2004) 'meaning and fluency oriented context'.

Length and frequency of turn

As in the PPP, the teacher's turns in the TBLT lessons were generally longer than those of the students (Table 5.6).

Table 5.6. The frequency and the length of turns in the TBLT lessons (Lessons 1, 5, and 9)

	Task	Lesson 1		Lesson 5		Lesson 9	
		Teacher	Student	Teacher	Student	Teacher	Student
Number of turns	Task 1	71	62	57	117	64	108
	Task 2	116	22	91	12	85	8
	Task 3	42	8	32	11	28	6
Mean length of turn*	Task 1	6.5	1.1	8.2	1.1	9.2	1.3
	Task 2	10.1	1.0	15.5	1.2	14.0	1.1
	Task 3	14.8	1.0	18.0	1.1	13.2	1.1

* The length of turn was calculated by the number of L2 words in one turn (not included L1 turn or non-verbal turn)

However, the length and number of turns varied depending on the task. In Task 1, the students' turns were more frequent than the teacher's turns, as there were many occasions when more than one student contributed to an exchange. The teacher's turns in Task 1 were shorter than those in the other tasks because the teacher frequently gave short one-word answers in response to the students' question turns. In Tasks 2 and 3, on the other hand, the teacher's turns were more frequent and longer than the students' turns, as a result of which there was less opportunity for student production. This was because Tasks 2 and 3 allowed the students to change their cards until they had found the correct card. For example, as Excerpt 5.9 shows, in Task 2 the learners showed the card they had chosen to the teacher and waited for the teacher's feedback rather than negotiating the meaning of the word in question. This inevitably led to the students' L2 turns becoming less numerous and the teacher's turns longer and more frequent than in Task 1.

Excerpt 5.9
1. T: peacock and the chestnut. peacock and a chestnut.
2. S2: chestnut?
3. T: yes, do you know? peacock. peacock. blue bird. blue bird. and the chestnut is very small.
4. S1: ((shows the teacher the cards in his hand))
5. T: ((points to S1's card)) that's a crocodile. peacock and a battery.
6. S2: ((shows the teacher the cards in his hand))
7. T: ((points S2's card)) no. no, that's an ostrich, and a, a, an eggplant. peacock is a blue bird. blue bird
8. S2: ((shows the teacher another card))
9. T: ((looks at the card)) yes. blue bird. peacock, blue bird, and a chestnut, a chestnut.
10. S3: ((shows the teacher the cards in his hand))

11. T: ((looked at S3's cards)) no no no. ((points to one of the cards)) it's okay. this is okay. no no no. okay. the peacock and, yes, peacock is okay, peacock is a blue bird right? chestnut is brown, small
12. S4: ((shows the teacher another card))
13. T: ((looks at S4's cards)) yes that's right. small, brown, vegetable. small brown vegetable.
14. S1: ((shows the teacher another card))
15. T: ((points to S1's cards)) yes that's right. small brown vegetable.
16. S5: ((shows the teacher the cards in his hand))
17. T: ((points to S5's cards)) yes that's right. ((points to S2's cards)) no no no no. peacock is a blue bird.
18. S2: ((changes his card))
19. T: yes (.) and the chestnut is ((point to a card on S2's table)) this one (.) yes that's right. put it into the box.

(Task 2 in Lesson 5, TBLT)

Seedhouse (2004) uses an example of a learner-learner interaction resulting from an information gap activity to claim that there is a tendency towards minimalisation and indexicality in learner language in a 'task-based context', since the learners are focused on accomplishing the task. The learner production in Task 2 supports Seedhouse's contention; the learners' turns are manifestly constrained by the task design. However, as shown in Table 5.4, the learners' turns in Task 1 served various purposes, such as providing information to other students, helping other students to obtain information, and requesting information from the teacher in order to complete the tasks, which involved using the target vocabulary items. Considering the fact that these learners had no English learning experience prior to this project, Task 1 seems to have created a situation where they were pushed to use their L2 in a communicative way. This task motivated the learners to achieve the task outcome. If the language produced by the learners was 'minimal', this was not because of the task but because these beginner learners' linguistic resources were limited (see Ellis, 2003, for a similar argument).

Finally, although the learners' production in Tasks 2 and 3 can be described as 'minimal', Excerpt 5.8 shows that the exchanges afforded the learners rich contextualized input. The teacher's turns in this extract helped the learners to complete the task by scaffolding the learners' comprehension of the target items, thus enabling them to identify the correct cards.

Summary

The preceding analyses reveal that the organization of turns in the TBLT lessons was markedly different from the PPP lessons as summarised in Table 5.7. Turn-taking in Task 1 can be characterized as typical of a 'meaning and fluency oriented context'; the turn-taking sequences were varied and there were many occasions where the students controlled the turn-taking. There was little evidence to show the kind of restriction that Seedhouse argues is typical of a 'task-oriented context'. However, as previously discussed, turn-taking in Tasks 2 and 3 did manifest such restrictions.

Table 5.7. Characteristics of turn-taking in the TBLT lessons

Aspects of turn-taking	Characteristics of turn-taking
IRF exchanges	Longer sequences involving several exchanges that involved overlapping.
Question type	Mostly initiated by the students with referential questions. Questions had various functions.
Control of turn-taking	Turn-taking often managed by students, but the beginning and the end of the sequence were controlled by the teacher.
Turns in chorus	The learners turns never occurred in chorus.
Topic	Conversation was focused on the successful completion of the task. There were some occasions when the learners' initiated development of the topic that the task created.
Length and frequency of turns	Teacher turns were longer than student turns. The learners' turns were constrained by the task design and their limited L2 proficiency.

The analysis shows that the characteristics of the turn-taking in the PPP group correspond to Seedhouse's 'form and accuracy oriented context', whereas in the TBLT lessons turn-taking displayed a mixture of the characteristics found in the 'meaning and fluency oriented' and 'task-oriented' contexts.

This analysis of the interactions in the two groups supports Seedhouse's (2004) claim that there is a reflexive relationship between the pedagogical focus and the organization of turn taking (p. 101). However, it has also been shown that it is possible for the turn-taking in a 'task-oriented context' to take on characteristics of the 'meaning and fluency oriented context' if the task is carefully designed.

Conversations in the PPP group typically involved short sequences consisting of single IRF exchanges, frequent occurrence of teacher-initiated display questions, the teacher's tight control of turn-taking, and numerous turns in chorus. Topics were not developed because the interactions were focused on the learners' accurate production of the target vocabulary items. Turn-taking in the TBLT group, on the other hand, displayed features Seedhouse associated with 'meaning and fluency oriented contexts' and 'task-based contexts'. There were longer sequences with several exchanges that involved overlapping, frequent occurrences of student-initiated referential questions, more student control of turn-taking, and no occurrence of turns in chorus. The types of learner turns were more varied than in the PPP group, and there were some occasions when the learners initiated development of the topics that the task created. Some of the limitations of a 'task-based context' that Seedhouse pointed out (e.g., occurrence of minimalisation and indexicalisation in student's turn) appeared in Tasks 2 and 3, but not in Task 1, indicating that careful design and implementation of tasks can engage learners in authentic conversations.

Repair

Repair is defined as the "treatment of trouble occurring in interactive language use" (Van Lier, 1988, p. 183). TBLT frequently leads to 'trouble'. As discussed in Chapter 1, tasks should have some kind of gap (e.g., information gap), which aims at creating problems that can be solved by using the L2. The process of solving such problems can lead to a focus on form (see Chapter 3), which has been argued to be facilitative of learning. In PPP repair typically occurs in a different way. As PPP requires learners to produce the accurate form of the target feature, learners' erroneous production constitutes the 'trouble' which the teacher solves by providing feedback. The characteristics of repair, thus, seem very different in these two contexts. I will examine repair in the PPP and the TBLT classes in terms of the focus of repair (medium- or message-oriented) and the agent of repair (self- or other-initiated/completed).

Van Lier (1988) distinguishes 'medium-oriented repair' (i.e., repair that focuses on the form and function of L2) and 'message-oriented repair' (i.e., repair that focuses on the transmission of thoughts, information and feelings).[1] The term 'message' involves both meaning and form. In other words, message-oriented repair focuses on problems that originate in meaning but also involves the link between meaning and form. On the other hand, medium-oriented repair only focuses on problems relating to language form. Seedhouse (1999) argues that "within each context a particular pedagogical focus combines with a particular organization of repair which is appropriate to that focus" (p. 60). Hence, in a PPP lesson where the pedagogical focus is on linguistic accuracy, repair is likely to be medium-oriented. On the other hand, in a TBLT lesson, which aims to direct the learners' attention to both meaning and form, it is possible that both message-oriented and medium-oriented repair occur.

Another way to analyse the characteristics of repair is in terms of the four basic types of repair proposed by Schegloff, Jefferson, and Sacks (1977): (1) self-initiated self-repair, (2) self-initiated other-repair, (3) other-initiated self-repair, and (4) other-initiated other-repair. In naturalistic settings, self-initiated self-repair occurs

1. Van Lier (1988) also talks about 'activity-oriented repair' (i.e. repair that focuses on the organization and structure of class environment), but I found only one instance in the data where a student clarified the procedure of a task using the L1. Therefore, I did not include this type.

when a speaker rephrases his or her utterance because it was problematic in some way. However, studies have shown that repair in L2 classrooms is often different from that found in naturalistic conversation. Van Lier (1988) showed that self-initiated other-repair occurs frequently in L2 classrooms, and noted that it is a "special feature of L2 classrooms" (p. 201). Seedhouse (2004) reported that in 'form and accuracy oriented contexts', repair is typically initiated and completed by the teacher, while in 'task-oriented contexts' it is often initiated by the students and completed by either themselves (or other students) or the teacher. Researchers (e.g., Swain & Lapkin, 1995) argue that self-initiated repair promotes learning by inducing noticing and attention. On the other hand, the Vygotskyan sociocultural perspective claims that learners first rely on the assistance of experts to correct an error ('other-regulation'), but eventually achieve independence and self-regulate, correcting their own erroneous forms with little or no intervention (DiCamilla & Antón, 2004). Thus, I will examine the above four types of repair (self-initiated self-repair, self-initiated other-repair, other-initiated self-repair, and other-initiated other-repair) in the PPP and TBLT lessons.

Instances of repair were identified by using the three phases of repair organization proposed by Schegloff, Jefferson, and Sacks (1977): the trouble source or the repairable (R), the initiation of repair (IR), and the actual accomplishment of repair (AR). The following analysis focuses on repairs resulting from trouble sources originating in the learners' production or comprehension (repairs relating to trouble sources in the teacher's language were not considered).

Characteristics of repair in the PPP lessons

Repairs in the PPP lesson were all centred around the purpose of the lesson – the students' successful production of the target words). The vast majority of repairs in the PPP lessons were medium-focused. They were predominantly other-initiated other-repairs. This supports Seedhouse's (2004) claim that the repair that occurs in form and accuracy oriented contexts tends to be 'didactic repair'. Table 5.8 shows the type of repair in one of the PPP lessons which was typical of other PPP lessons.

Now I will discuss the extent to which each of the repair types occurred (or did not occur) in the PPP lessons.

Self-initiated self-repair

None of the repairs observed in the PPP lessons fell into this category. Two factors might explain this: the participants' proficiency level and the teacher's control of turn-taking. The participants were all aged six and had no experience of learning English prior to the project. Studies have shown that both age and proficiency affect the amount and nature of self-repair (Camps, 2003; Kormos, 1999; Verhoeven, 1989). The absence of this type of repair might also be due to the nature of the conversation in the PPP.

Table 5.8. Repair in PPP lessons 1, 5, and 9

Orientation of repair	Type of repair	Frequency			Functions
		L1	L5	L9	
Medium-oriented	Self-initiated self-repair	0	0	0	
	Self-initiated other-repair	0	1	1	when a learner asked the teacher linguistic questions
	Other-initiated self-repair	0	7	15	when the students were unable to produce the target word, and the teacher provided the first phonological part of the form to prompt learner's production (covert scaffolding)
	Other-initiated other-repair	85	65	21	when the teacher provided the correct form following a student's turn (overt scaffolding)
	Total	85	73	37	

In the PPP lessons, as discussed, the teacher tended to control the turn-taking. This prevented the learners from initiating and completing repair themselves, as shown in Excerpt 5.10.

Excerpt 5.10
1. T: ((points one of the two boys in a card)) this boy is?
2. S1: smo[::]
3. T: [short]
4. Ss: sho::
5. T: short (.)short (.)short (.) Okay?
(Activity 2 in Lesson 4, PPP)

In turn 3, the teacher immediately reformulated S1's erroneous utterance in turn 2. In turn 4 the whole class repeated the teacher's recast, but not to the satisfaction of the teacher. This led her to provide another recast and then close the sequence by saying "okay?" This excerpt illustrates a general tendency – whenever learners produced an erroneous utterance it was followed by the teacher's immediate correction, thus depriving the students of an opportunity to self-correct their error.

Self-initiated other-repair

In the PPP group, self-initiated other-repair occurred on a few occasions when the learners asked linguistic and vocabulary-related questions. In this type of repair, question turns were exclusively produced by the students in their L1, as Excerpt 5.11 shows.

Excerpt 5.11
1. T: this pencil is? (3.0) short.
2. Ss: shor:

3. T: short, short.
4. S1: *shor tte chiisai tteiu koto*? ((tr: does '*shor*' mean small?))
5. T: *uun, mijikai, mijikai* (.) *kore, nagai disyo. nagai, mijikai*. ((tr: no, it means short. this is long, right? long, short))

(Activity 2 in Lesson 3, PPP)

In turn 1, the teacher asked the question while showing a picture of a long and short pencil with an arrow pointing to the short pencil. The teacher then produced the word 'short' as the students were not able to come up with the word themselves. As S1 was not sure of the meaning of the word 'short' (R, i.e., the repairable), she sought confirmation of her hunch about its meaning using her L1 (IR, i.e., the initiation of repair) in turn 4. This led to the teacher providing a translation in Japanese (AR, the repair). This repair was directed at establishing a connection between the form and meaning of the word. Therefore, it was classified as a medium-oriented repair.

This type of repair only occurred a few times during the PPP lessons. This may be because the method of instruction did not require the learners to work out the meanings of the target words for themselves, as the target items were presented alongside pictorial images in all five activities. In the first activity, the meanings of the target words were illustrated with pictures while the teacher provided the phonological forms. In the following four activities, the students were asked to produce the phonological form while observing the images on the cards. Thus, there was no need for the children to inquire about the meaning of the target word except on a few occasions where they failed to understand the pictorial image, as in Excerpt 5.11.

Other-initiated self-repair

This type of repair occurred frequently in the PPP group when the teacher noticed that the students were unable to produce a target word. The teacher would then prompt its production by providing the first syllable of the word's form, as shown in Excerpt 5.12.

Excerpt 5.12

1. T: what's this?
2. S: ((gaze the teacher))
3. T: *pi:*
4. S: peacock
5. T: that's right. peacock.

(Activity 5 in Lesson 5, PPP)

In turn 2, the student indicated that he was unable to produce the target word (R). This led the teacher to provide the first syllable of the target word in turn 3 (IR). The student then produced the full form of the word 'peacock' in turn 4 (AR). As the teacher's repair focused on the phonological form of the word, it was classified as medium-oriented repair.

Other-initiated other-repair

Other-initiated other-repair was the most common type of repair in the PPP lessons. As shown in Excerpt 5.13, this type of repair often occurred when the teacher provided the target word when a student failed to produce it.

Excerpt 5.13
1. T: ok, your turn.
2. S: ((turns over one card on the table))
3. T: what is it?
4. S: ((gaze the teacher)) (2.0)
5. T: eggplant
6. S: eggplant
7. T: ((looks away) okay, your turn.

(Activity 5 in Lesson 2, PPP)

The teacher interpreted turn 4 as a signal that the students were not able to produce the required L2 form (R) and responded by producing it herself in turn 5 (IR and AR). The teacher's turn in line 5 seems to function as a repair and at the same time as a request to the learners to reproduce the word. This is evident in the student's repetition of the target in turn 6 and the following evaluation by the teacher in turn 7. This type of learner repetition after the teacher had supplied the target word occurred frequently in the PPP lessons. As the teacher focused on the form of the learner's language, this repair was classified as medium-oriented repair. This also suggests that although Activity 5 was designed to be the 'free-production' phase of PPP, which might be expected to elicit message-oriented repairs, the actual repairs that occurred were still medium-oriented.

Excerpts 5.12 and 5.13 illustrate how the teacher scaffolded (see Chapter 3) the learners' production of the target items in the PPP classroom. In Excerpt 5.13, the teacher provided overt scaffolding (presenting the full form of the target word) to enable the student's production of the target. In Excerpt 5.12, the scaffolding was more covert, but nevertheless successfully prompted the student's production of the full form of the word. In the PPP lessons, it seems that other-initiated repairs tended to be 'other-repairs' when the scaffolding was overt, and became 'self-repairs' when the scaffolding was covert.

Summary

Two main characteristics of repair in the PPP activities were identified. Firstly, the repairs were predominantly medium-oriented; very few message-oriented repairs were identified. This indicates that the focus of the conversation was entirely on the accurate production of the language. There seemed to be very limited opportunities for the students to deal with message-oriented problems. Secondly, the majority of repairs were other-initiated other-repair; there was an absence of self-initiated repair. This corresponds to the analysis of turn-taking above, documenting the strict teacher control of the conversation throughout the five lessons. Again, this indicates that the

PPP activities corresponded to Seedhouse' (2004) 'form and accuracy oriented contexts', where repair is typically initiated and completed by the teacher.

Characteristics of repair in the TBLT lessons

The TBLT lesson consisted of listening tasks inviting the learners to try and understand the message. This resulted in numerous comprehension problems, which were then repaired. Thus repair in the TBLT lessons mostly involved problems related to comprehending a message (Schegloff, 1991).

As Table 5.9 shows, Repairs in TBLT lessons were almost entirely message-oriented. This was because most of the repairs focused on the meaning of the teachers' instructions rather than on the learners' language, reflecting the design of the instruction (i.e., tasks that required the learners to comprehend the teacher's input).

Table 5.9. Repair in Lessons 1, 5, and 9

Orientation of repair	**Type of repair**	**Frequency**			**Functions**
		L1	L5	L9	
Medium-oriented	Self-initiated, self-repair	0	0	0	
	Self-initiated, other-repair	0	2	1	when a learner asked linguistic questions (either in their L1 or in L2), and the teacher provided a direct answer
	Other-initiated, self-repair	7	3	2	1. when the teacher encouraged students to use the L2 rather than the L1 2. when a student's utterance caused miscommunication that was then repaired by the student
	Other-initiated, other-repair	0	0	0	
	Total	7	5	3	
Message-oriented	Self-initiated, self-repair	8	5	4	when a student asked the teacher's help but the teacher provided only implicit information to foster the learner's self-repair
	Self-initiated, other-repair	5	44	80	when a learner asked information to accomplish the task or to confirm if their choice was correct, and the teacher provided a direct answer
	Other-initiated, self-repair	31	22	0	when the teacher identified the student's miscomprehension and provided indirect information to prompt the student's repair
	Other-initiated, other-repair	4	5	4	when the teacher corrected the students' card choice
	Total	48	76	88	

I will now examine each type of repair in detail.

Self-initiated self-repair

There were no occasions where the students demonstrated self-initiated self-repairs that focused on their own language (i.e., medium-oriented repairs). This might be because of the participants' age and limited proficiency, as discussed previously. However, self-initiated self-repair did occur when students negotiated for meaning as a result of a comprehension problem and the teacher responded indirectly. In the CA literature, when the teacher's indirect answer prompts the student's correct answer, it is classified as 'self-repair' (Seedhouse, 2004; Van Lier, 1988). In Excerpt 5.14, for example, the learner (S1) asked for the teacher's help in identifying the correct card and the teacher provided an indirect answer.

Excerpt 5.14
1. T: crocodiles (.) crocodiles
2. S1: one?
3. T: crocodiles (1.0) okay
4. S1: one?
5. T: okay, listen listen listen(.) stop stop (.) listen lisetn listen. ((shows a card)) This is a crocodile, and ((shows another card)) crocodiles. one crocodile and three crocodiles. okay, now, please take the crocodiles to the zoo. okay? (1.0) three (.) two (.) one (.) go.
6. S1: ((change his singular card to the plural card)
7. Ss: ((show their selected cards))
8. T: crocodiles. only S1. Okay.

(Task 1, Lesson 5, TBLT)

In this excerpt, S1 was unable to identify whether the target item was plural or singular (R, i.e., the repairable), so he asked the teacher "one?" in order to identify the correct card (IR, i.e., the initiation of repair). However, instead of giving a direct answer, the teacher responded indirectly, encouraging the student to work out the answer for himself. She demonstrated the difference between the plural and singular phonological forms (turn 5), which prompted the student to change his card in line 6 (AR, i.e., the accomplishment of repair). In this excerpt, the learner is clearly initiating repair in order to complete the task.

This repair sequence shows how opportunities to focus on form can arise in input-based tasks. The student's attention was on the meaning (i.e., to find the card), but also on form (i.e., 'crocodile' and 'crocodiles'). The teachers' response to one student's problems seems to have supported other students' successful performance of the task. Thus, it is possible that this repair sequence helped the negotiating student (S1), as well other overhearers of the sequence to notice the form at stake. This repair sequence also indicates how the teacher provided scaffolding for the TBLT group. Instead of providing a direct answer to the student's question, she presented information to the whole class, which enabled learner self-repair and directed attention to the message.

Self-initiated other-repair

Medium-oriented, self-initiated other-repair was observed only twice in the TBLT group. It occurred when a student asked a question about a linguistic problem in their L1 as in Excerpt 5.15.

Excerpt 5.15
1. S: *ne: ne:* (.) *kore,* mandarin? *orange janaino*? ((tr : well, is this 'mandarin'? isn't it 'orange'?))
2. T: ah (.) *orange wa marukute ookino* ((gesture)) *mandarin wa mikan. chiisai yatsu ne.* ((tr: 'orange' is the round and big one. 'mandarine' is mandarin, the smaller one)).
3. S: *fu:n.* ((tr: I see))

(Task 1, Lesson 3, TBLT)

Here, the student asked about the meaning of the word 'mandarin' because he mixed it up with the synonym 'orange' in turn 1 (IR). This was answered by the teacher in Japanese (AR).

A similar type of repair occurred in the PPP activity (Excerpt 5.11): A student asked a question in their L1 to unravel the meaning of a vocabulary item and the teacher responded in the L1. This suggests that both in the PPP activities and the input-based tasks, students tried to establish L2 form-meaning connections by using the information given, but that when the information was not sufficient, students tended to use their L1 to ask help from the teacher. In both cases (Excerpts 5.11 and 5.15) the teacher provided the answer immdiately in the L1, which solved the problem. This suggests that when repair was initiated by a student and was medium-oriented, it was likely to be initiated and completed in the L1. This seems appropriate for young, beginner learners. As pointed out earlier, this type of repair was rare perhaps because the pictures often sufficed for the students' to establish the form-meaning mapping.

Message-oriented repair, on the other hand, was the most frequent type in TBLT activities. This type of repair was typically observed in Task 1, when the students asked for information to enable them to accomplish the task and the teacher responded directly. The trouble source (R) was generally the learners' non-comprehension or mis-comprehension of the teacher's instructions. Excerpt 5.6 (p. 88) includes several repair trajectories initiated by the students and completed by the teacher. The first repair, for example, starts with S1 asking the colour of the target word in turn 5 ("*whito?*": IR), which was repeated in turn 11 ("*whito? whito?*") as the answer was not provided. S2 asked the same question in turn 12 ("white?") and the teacher finally provided the answer in turn 13 ("no no no no. not white": RA). Another example, in turn 15, revolved around an unknown word (i.e., 'brown'). S2 asked its meaning in her L1 in turn 18 ("*brwon tte nani*? ((=what's brown?))": IR), which was repeated by another student in the next turn. The teacher responded to both verbally ("brown?") and by pointing to a brown object in the classroom (AR).

These repairs were aimed at obtaining the information needed to complete the task. Therefore, they can be considered to be message-oriented repairs. However, some of them seemed to have more specific sub-goals, such as the repair in (4), where the learner focused on understanding the meaning of the unknown word in the teacher's utterance.

Excerpt 5.6 also shows that the learners' questions addressed various aspects of the target word, such as its descriptive features (e.g., *whito*), its category (e.g., supermarket) or its number (e.g., one). In other words, the learners were using the L2 resources at their disposal in various ways in order to achieve the task goal.

This analysis shows that the message-oriented self-initiated self-repair in the TBLT group provided the learners with opportunities to focus on form, as I argued in Chapter 3. I have shown that negotiation of meaning in input-based tasks is likely to be learner-initiated because it is the learner who needs to solve the communicative breakdowns (i.e., comprehension problems). I also argued that even in an input-based task, it is possible that learners voluntarily use the L2 to negotiate meaning. The above analysis showed that the input-based tasks, Task 1 in particular, were successful in providing the students with such opportunties. However, as I will show in the following sections, the repair in Task 2 and Task 3 had different characteristics.

Other-initiated self-repair

Other-initiated other-repair in this group was mostly message-oriented. This type of repair occurred frequently in Task 2 and Task 3. The repair involved the teacher addressing the students' comprehension problems and providing implicit information to support self-repair. Excerpt 5.16 shows an example of this type of repair.

Excerpt 5.16
1. T: ((looks at S's cards)) no, that's a persimmon (.) radish is the long one (.) white and green.
2. S: ((picks up the correct card))
3. T: that's right.

(Task 3 in Lesson 5, TBLT)

In this extract, the teacher identified the student's incorrect choice (R) and provided a description of the target word (IR) which enabled the student to choose the correct card (AR). The teacher focused on solving the student's comprehension problem to help the student complete the tasks; thus, it was classified as a message-oriented repair.

This type of repair did not occur frequently in Task 1, as the teacher did not have to evaluate any choices made by the students. However, it occurred on a few occasions when the teacher provided an elaborative explanation to address a student's failure to comprehend, as shown in Excerpt 5.17.

Excerpt 5.17
1. T: Okay, the next. Please take the toothbrush to the supermarket.
2. S: <u>Two</u> *dakara kore*. (It's 'two' so it's this one).
3. T: Please take the, please take the toothbrush. I didn't say two. I didn't say two. ((shows one finger)) one toothbrush (.) ((shows two fingers)) two toothbrushes (.) okay?
4. S: ((puts back the card in his hand and take the card with one 'toothbrush' on it))
(Task 1 in Lesson 8, TBLT)

In this example, turn 2 indicated that the student believed 'toothbrush' was referring to 'two', and selected the plural card instead of the singular card (R). The teacher then demonstrated the difference between the plural and singular forms of 'toothbrush' (IR), which led the student to choose the correct card in turn 4 (AR). Although the repair involved linguistic form (i.e., the distinction between the plural and singular forms), the problem originated in the learner's difficulty to comprehend the teacher's utterance. Therefore, this repair was classified as message-oriented.

There was one occasion where a student's utterance caused miscommunication, but the student eventually repaired his own utterance, as shown in Excerpt 5.18.

Excerpt 5.18
1. T: chestnut is small
2. S: *bato*?
3. T: what?
4. S: *bato*?
5. T: black? (.) sorry? (1.0) it's very small.
6. S: big? big?
7. T: not big, not big, not big. small. very small ((gesture))
(Task 1 in Lesson 7, TBLT)

In this excerpt, the student's turn 2 was incomprehensible to the teacher (R). The teacher requested clarification in turn 3 (IR) but could not solve the problem ('black? sorry'), so she provided the correct word in turn 5 (AR). The student then corrected his utterance in turn 6. The repair was initiated by the teacher but completed by the student. It was thus classified as message-oriented, other-initiated, self-repair.

On a few occasions, other-initiated self-repairs were produced by students when one student repaired another student's failure to comprehend, as shown in Excerpt 5.19.

Excerpt 5.19
1. T: okay the next. please take the toothbrushes. please take the toothbrushes to the supermarket. toothbrushes.
2. S1: *nanko*? *nanko*? ((tr: how many? how many?))
3. T: listen listen. please take the toothbrushes.
4. S2: ((hold the card with one toothbrush on it)) *ikko dayo* ((tr: It's one))
→ 5. S3: ((talk to S2)) *sanko dayo* ((tr: it's three))

6. S2: *ikko dayo* ((tr: it's one))
→ 7. S3: /z/ *dayo* ((tr: it's /z/))
8. S2: ((changes his card to the card with three toothbrushes))
(Task 1 in Lesson 9, TBLT)

S3 identified a problem in S2's turn in line 4 (R) and attempted to correct it in turn 5 (IR). As the next turn showed that repair was not completed, S3 provided further information to persuade S2 to correct the error (turn 7), which led S2 to correct his choice in turn 8 (AR). This repair involved S3 directing S2's attention to form (i.e., "it's /z/"), but the problem originated in the S2's miscomprehension of the teacher's instruction. Thus, the repair can be classified as a message-oriented, other-initiated, self-repair.

These examples show that Tasks 2 and 3 did not provide an opportunity for the students to negotiate meaning before their choice of card was evaluated, which resulted in the teacher initiating the repair.

Contrary to message-oriented repair, medium-oriented repair of this kind occurred only rarely. An example of this type is shown in Excerpt 5.20. The repair in this sequence occurred when the teacher encouraged students to use English rather than relying on Japanese.

Excerpt 5.20
1. T: okay the next. please take the camel.
2. S1: camel
3. T: camel to the zoo. the camel is also.
4. S2: black?
5. T: not black. not black. very big.
6. S3: *omoi?* (heavy?)
7. T: yeah I think so. heavy and…
8. S4: pata pata suru (does it flap?)
9. T: *Pata pata suru?* that's Japanese. that's Japanese.
10. S3: heavy?
11. T: uh?
12. S3: heavy?
13. T: I think so, heavy. and big.
14. S2: blue?
15. T: no no no.
→16. S4: *chairo?* (brown?)
→17. T: *chairo* is Japanese. do you remember?
→18. S2: brown?
→19. T: brown yes. brown. brown, big, heavy. are you ready? camel. camel. three, two, one, go.
20: all students: (showing their cards)
21. T: okay.
(Task 1 in Lesson 4, TBLT)

The teacher treated S4's use of the L1 in turn 16 as a problem (R) and encouraged her to use the L2 in turn 17 (IR), leading to an attempt to supply the L2 word in turn 18 (AR).

Other-initiated other-repair

There were no medium-oriented repairs of this type in the TBLT lessons. This might be because the teacher tended to ignore learners' linguistic errors, as Excerpt 5.21 shows.

Excerpt 5.21
1. T: okay the next. please take the hippopotamus to the zoo. hippopotamus.
2. S: *hippopopomus*
3. T: yes, to the zoo.

(Task 1 in Lesson 8, TBLT)

Although the student failed to produce the word correctly (turn 2), the teacher accepted the student's utterance and continued her instruction in turn 3, presumably because the student's error did not affect the performance of the task. Studies have shown that teacher's feedback on learners' grammatical errors occurs frequently in the language classroom compared to conversations between native speakers and non-native speakers in a naturalistic context (Chaudron, 1988; Chun, Day, Chenoweth, & Luppescu, 1982). Seedhouse (2004), however, pointed out that incorrect linguistic forms are frequently ignored in 'meaning and fluency oriented contexts' in the classroom unless they lead to breakdowns in communication. The above extract indicates that this happened in the TBLT lessons.

However, message-oriented repairs frequently occurred when the teacher corrected a learner's card selection in Task 2 or Task 3, as these tasks allowed the students to change their selection of cards at any time while performing the task.

Excerpt 5.22
1. T: no no that's a persimmon, mandarin is this one ((shows a picture card with a picture of 'mandarin))
2. S: ((looks at the picture and turns over the correct card))

(Task 1 in Lesson 2, TBLT)

In this excerpt, the teacher identified the student's incorrect choice (R) and showed the correct card (IR and AR). Here, the teacher was again focused on helping the learner to complete the task successfully; therefore, this repair was classified as a message-oriented repair.

Summary

Overall, repairs in the TBLT lessons were mostly message-oriented, focusing on the task outcome, that is, identifying the card that the teacher asked the student to find. The above analyses have shown that both the students and the teacher in the TBLT group were engaged in solving the 'problems' that the tasks created. When repair was initiated by the students, it was mainly realized by means of a one-word utterance or in their L1. One might argue that the repair in the TBLT lessons differed from that in naturalistic conversation. Seedhouse (2004) argued that in 'task-oriented contexts' repair tends to be decontextualized and involve only limited production. However, the above excerpts also show that the young, beginner learners voluntarily initiated repair by using their very limited L2 knowledge. When their L2 knowledge was not sufficient to repair the trouble, they resorted to their L1 and other non-linguistic resources such as gestures. I would argue that the behavior involved in such repair is similar to that found in a naturalistic context. The tasks in the TBLT lessons were successful in creating such opportunities.

It needs to be noted, however, that student-initiated repair did not occur in all the tasks which were performed in the TBLT lessons. As Table 5.10 shows, self-initiated self-repair mostly occurred in Task 1 while other-initiated self-repair generally occurred in Tasks 2 and 3.

Table 5.10. Type of repair in each task in Lessons 1, 5, and 9

Task	Type of repair	L1	L5	L9
Task 1	Self-initiated, self-repair	8	5	4
	Self-initiated, other-repair	0	41	73
	Other-initiated, self-repair	5	4	0
	Other-initiated, other-repair	0	0	0
Task 2/Task 3	Self-initiated, self-repair	0	0	0
	Self-initiated, other-repair	5	5	8
	Other-initiated, self-repair	33	21	2
	Other-initiated, other-repair	4	5	4
Total		55	81	91

The table shows that repair in the TBLT activities occurred in two ways: repair was either initiated by the students and completed by the teacher; or repair was initiated by the teacher and completed by the students. The former occurred because the learners needed to ask the teacher questions in order to accomplish the task and the teacher provided answers (as in Task 1). The latter occurred because the teacher identified the students' comprehension problems and provided implicit information to help the students fix them by themselves (as in Tasks 2 and 3). This indicates that the design and implementation of tasks may influence the type of repair that occurs. It also suggests that, in either case, the repair in this group involved the collaborative work of both the teacher and the students. In addition, this indicates that although the tasks used in this study were of the simple one-way information type, they created opportunities for the teacher and the students to repair conversation problems collaboratively using the L2, the L1, and non-linguistic resources.

Differences between the two groups

The types of repair in the PPP and the TBLT are summarised in Table 5.11 (below). There were a similar number of repairs in the two groups, but the characteristics of the repairs differed markedly. First, repairs that occurred in the PPP were almost entirely medium-oriented while those in the TBLT repair tended to be message-oriented. The 'trouble' to be repaired in the PPP predominantly focused on the accurate production of the target vocabulary items, which corresponds to Seedhouse' (2004) 'form and accuracy oriented context'. On the other hand, the 'trouble' in the TBLT was caused by the comprehension problems that the tasks created. The type of repair in the TBLT was similar to that found in the 'task-based context' as suggested by Seedhouse. I have argued that such repair is useful for young, beginner learners.

Table 5.11. Number of types of repair in Lessons 1, 5, and 9 in the two groups

Focus of repair	Type of repair	PPP lesson			TBLT lesson		
		L1	L5	L9	L1	L5	L9
Medium-oriented	Self-initiated, self-repair	0	0	0	0	0	0
	Self-initiated, other-repair	0	1	1	0	2	1
	Other-initiated, self-repair	0	7	15	7	3	2
	Other-initiated, other-repair	85	65	21	0	0	0
Message-oriented	Self-initiated, self-repair	0	0	0	8	5	4
	Self-initiated, other-repair	0	0	0	5	44	80
	Other-initiated, self-repair	0	0	0	31	22	0
	Other-initiated, other-repair	0	0	0	4	5	4
Total		85	73	37	55	81	89

Second, a single type of repair was dominant in the PPP lessons (message-oriented, other-initiated, other-repair). This again corresponds to Seedhouse's (2004) 'form and accuracy oriented context', where it is "the teacher who evaluates the accuracy of the learner's forms and who therefore predominantly initiates the repair" (p. 147). Repair occurred when the teacher provided the correct form of a target vocabulary item when students could not produce it or produced an erroneous form. The teacher often used 'recasts' (Excerpts 5.13), which have been found to be the most common type of corrective feedback in L2 classrooms (Lyster & Ranta, 1997). This indicates that the repair in the PPP was typical of the L2 classroom. Repair in the TBLT, however, was often initiated and/or completed by the students. If self-initiated repair promotes learning (e.g., Swain & Lapkin, 1995), then the analyses indicate that the TBLT lessons provided opportunities for noticing and attention to form to a greater extent than the PPP lessons did. It should be also noted that repair in the TBLT lessons was more varied than in the PPP. The fact that in the TBLT group repair was either initiated by the students and completed by the teacher or initiated by the teacher and completed by the students indicates that repair in this group involved collaborative work by the teacher and the students. If language learning occurs through 'collaborative dialogue' (Swain, Kinnear, & Steinman, 2011), the input-based tasks seem to have created such opportunities to a greater extent than the PPP did.

Finally, the analyses showed that while in the PPP learners received substantial corrective feedback (i.e., mainly medium-oriented other-initiated other-repair), the TBLT learners did not. In fact, corrective feedback did not occur in Lessons 1, 5, and 9 in the TBLT class.

Repair in the TBLT group mostly led to successful comprehension of the teacher's instructions. However, the question can be raised to what extent comprehension leads to acquisition (see Chapter 3). While corrective feedback has shown to be beneficial for L2 learning, studies have shown mixed results for the effects of comprehensible input on learning. I will examine this in more detail in Chapter 6.

Conclusion

The purpose of this part of the study was to establish to what extent the actual classroom activities in the two types of instruction were truly different. I adopted an internal perspective by using CA to analyse various aspects of the interaction that took place in both conditions. The analysis revealed a clear difference between the classroom interactions resulting from the two types of instruction. The essential external difference between TBLT (in this study) and PPP is that the former aims to teach through input and the latter though output. In fact, when the TBLT intervention was implemented, learners frequently engaged in the production output, albeit on a voluntary rather than required basis. However, the nature of learner output in the two instructional conditions was clearly different. Overall, the differences in the process features can be summarized as follows: whereas the interactions that occurred in the PPP classroom were essentially 'pedagogic', those in the TBLT group classroom were primarily 'conversational'.

Overall, the interactions in the PPP group corresponded to the kinds of classroom conversations reported in previous studies, whereas the TBLT lessons resulted in more naturalistic and meaning-focused interactions. This supports Seedhouse's claim that classroom conversation varies according to context. The analyses have also shown that the design and implementation of tasks in the TBLT group influenced the occurrence and types of conversation, indicating that tasks can create contexts that involve meaning-focused, authentic conversation when they are designed and implemented carefully.

An additional point of interest is that this investigation is unusual in using CA to explore teacher-class interactions with young beginner learners. The analyses reveal the ways in which the nature of the classroom conversations reflected the limited proficiency and low age of the participants – as is shown for example in the student's one-word turns. Students' choral turns in the PPP lesson are another typical characteristic of classroom interaction with young children. However, the analyses also showed that young children with no experience of L2 learning were able to initiate conversation using their limited L2 and to conduct 'self-initiated' repair when an input-based task required them to do so. As Ellis (2003) notes, simple listening tasks can be devised such that they can be performed even with zero competence in the L2.

CHAPTER 6

Learning vocabulary through PPP and TBLT

In this chapter, I report on the relative effectiveness of presentation-practice-production (PPP) and task-based language teaching (TBLT) in promoting L2 vocabulary acquisition. I present the results and discussion of the second general research question stated in Chapter 4:

> Which instructional approach (PPP or TBLT) results in more vocabulary being acquired?

As explained in Chapter 4, the 45 six-year-old learners were randomly divided into three groups (TBLT, PPP and control) and received nine lessons over five weeks. A total of 24 nouns and 12 adjectives were taught in both treatment groups. Vocabulary learning was measured by four tests (i.e., the Category Task, the discrete-item word listening test, the Same-or-Different Task, and the discrete-item word production test) which were conducted as a pre-test, post-test 1, and post-test 2.

It should be recalled that whereas the PPP lessons were designed to introduce both nouns and adjectives, the tasks in the TBLT lessons were designed to introduce only nouns; adjectives arose only incidentally in the process of performing the different tasks. Given this difference in the way the lessons were planned, the decision was made to examine the effects of the two types of instruction separately for nouns and adjectives.

The test scores for nouns showed that both the PPP and the TBLT groups learned the target nouns as a result of the instruction they received and were able to maintain their knowledge over time. In other words, both types of instruction were effective in enabling the learners to acquire both receptive and productive knowledge of the nouns. Overall, the two groups did not differ in the acquisition of the target nouns. There was no significant difference in the Same-or-Different Task, the discrete-item production test or the multiple-choice listening test. However, in the Category Task, the TBLT group achieved significantly higher scores than the PPP group.

As the study was based on cognitive-interactionist theories, which see input, output, and interaction as the main sources of second language learning (see Chapter 3), it is important to examine whether the opportunities for input and output of the target vocabulary items were similar or different in the two groups. To this end, I also examined the quantity and the quality of the input (i.e., the target words the students were exposed to) and output (i.e., the target words produced by the students) that occurred in the two groups.

In the following sections, I will first present test results followed by the process analysis where I consider the frequency and the types of input and output that occurred in the classroom to better understand the factors that may have contributed the test results.

Test results for nouns

Table 6.1 shows the descriptive statistics of the test scores for the nouns. The maximum score for each test was 24. Both the PPP group and the TBLT group increased their scores from the pre-test to post-test 1 on all tests and the gains were maintained at post-test 2 while little change was evident in the control group.

The detailed statistical test results are reported in Appendix B. In the following summary of the findings, the effect sizes (*r* for the test scores, *w* for the categorical scores) were interpreted as small = .1, medium = .3 or large = .5, as suggested by Cohen (1988).

Table 6.1. Descriptive statistics for the target nouns

Test	Group	Pre-test		Post-test 1		Post-test 2	
		Mean	SD	Mean	SD	Mean	SD
Same-or-Different Task	PPP (n = 15)	.20	.56	7.87	4.05	7.20	3.97
	TBLT (n = 15)	.20	.56	5.07	2.52	6.33	2.74
	Control (n = 15)	.13	.35	.20	.56	.20	.56
Discrete-item production test	PPP (n = 15)	.20	.56	8.40	3.74	8.93	4.20
	TBLT (n = 15)	.20	.56	6.53	2.64	7.93	2.02
	Control (n = 15)	.20	.56	.27	.59	.40	.74
Category Task test	PPP (n = 15)	1.47	1.25	10.53	3.27	10.60	3.36
	TBLT (n = 15)	.80	.94	13.13	3.09	13.53	3.27
	Control (n = 15)	1.67	1.05	1.60	1.35	2.67	1.67
Multiple-choice listening test	PPP (n = 15)	4.40	2.56	16.60	4.39	16.33	4.05
	TBLT (n = 15)	5.20	3.41	15.33	4.12	15.13	4.19
	Control (n = 15)	4.00	2.00	3.73	1.91	3.73	1.91

Table 6.2 summarises the changes over time for each group. The PPP group improved in all tests from pre-test to post-test 1 and from pre-test to post-test 2 with large effect sizes. However, the PPP group failed to show improvement from post-test 1 to post-test 2 on any of the tests. The TBLT group also significantly improved from the pre-test to

post-test 1 in all the tests again with large effect sizes. Improvement was also evident from post-test 1 to post-test 2 in the two production tests (i.e., the Same-or-Different Task test and the discrete-item production test) with small effect sizes.

Table 6.2. Effect sizes for the changes over time in noun scores

Tests	PPP group			TBLT group			Control group		
	Pre-post1	Pre-post2	Post1-post2	Pre-post1	Pre-post2	Post1-post2	Pre-post1	Pre-post2	Post1-post2
S-or-D Task	.80*	.78*	.08	.80*	.84*	.23*	.07	.07	0
Dis-production	.84*	.83*	.07	.86*	.93*	.29*	.06	.15	.10
Category Task	.88*	.88*	.01	.94*	.94*	.06	.03	.34	.33
M-C listening	.86*	.87*	.03	.80*	.79*	.02	.07	.07	0

S-or-D Task = Same-or-Different Task; Dis-Production = Discrete-item production test; M-C listening = Multiple-choice listening test; Pre-post1= improvement from pre-test to post-test 1; Pre-post2 = improvement from pre-test to post-test 2; Post1-post2 = improvement from post-test 1 to post-test 2; * = the difference was significant at $p = .05$ level

I will now examine whether there were any differences between the groups on the tests scores for the nouns. The results of the between-group differences are summarized in Table 6.3. In the pre-test, there were no significant differences between the three groups on any of the tests. On post-tests 1 and 2, both the PPP and the TBLT groups outperformed the control group with large effect sizes. There were no significant differences between the PPP and the TBLT groups in three of the post-tests (the Same-or-Different Task, the discrete-item production test and the Multiple-choice listening test). In these tests, the PPP group scored higher than the TBLT group but the effect sizes for this comparison were either negligible or small, and the difference was not

Table 6.3. Comparative effect sizes of the three groups for the acquisition of nouns

	Pre-test	Post-test 1			Post-test 2		
	PPP-TBLT-Cntl.	PPP-Cntl.	TBLT-Cntl.	TBLT-PPP	TBLT-Cntl.	TBLT-Cntl.	TBLT-PPP
S-or-D Task	0	.80*	.80*	.39	.84*	.84*	.13
Dis-production	0	.84*	.85*	.28	.92*	.92*	.15
Category Task	.29	.87*	.92*	.38*	.90*	.90*	.41*
M-C listening	.13	.89*	.87*	.17	.87*	.87*	.14

Cntl. = Control group; S-or-D Task = Same-or-Different Task; Dis-Production = Discrete-item production test; M-C listening = Multiple-choice listening test; Pre-post1= improvement from pre-test to post-test 1; Pre-post2 = improvement from pre-test to post-test 2; Post1-post2 = improvement from post-test 1 to post-test 2; * = the difference was significant at $p = .05$ level (the TBLT group significantly outperformed the PPP group) statistically significant. However, the TBLT group outperformed the PPP group in the Category Task on both post-test 1 and 2.

Test results for adjectives

Table 6.4 shows the descriptive statistics for the target adjectives. The maximum score possible for all tests was 12. Both the PPP group and the TBLT group increased their scores for all tests from the pre-test to post-test 1 while the control group did not show much change. The TBLT group consistently scored higher than the PPP group in post-tests 1 and 2, but there was no notable improvement in either group from post-test 1 to post-test 2. The control group did not show any statistically significant improvement over time. The detailed statistical test results are reported in Appendix B.

Table 6.4. Descriptive statistics for the target adjectives

Test	Group	Pre-test		Post-test 1		Post-test 2	
		Mean	SD	Mean	SD	Mean	SD
Same-or-Different Task	PPP (n = 15)	.67	1.45	1.67	1.80	1.67	1.76
	TBLT (n = 15)	.60	1.30	4.47	2.77	4.87	3.14
	Control (n = 15)	.60	1.24	.73	1.58	.67	1.40
Discrete-item production test	PPP (n = 15)	1.47	1.06	3.27	2.43	3.00	2.17
	TBLT (n = 15)	1.73	1.53	5.53	2.95	6.53	2.75
	Control (n = 15)	1.40	.91	1.13	.99	1.07	.96
Category Task	PPP (n = 15)	1.40	1.96	5.53	2.77	5.67	2.85
	TBLT (n = 15)	1.73	1.94	8.07	3.17	8.60	3.02
	Control (n = 15)	1.00	1.31	1.60	1.50	1.60	1.59
Multiple-choice listening test	PPP (n = 15)	2.53	2.20	7.27	2.66	7.20	2.48
	TBLT (n = 15)	3.40	2.35	10.13	1.19	10.60	.99
	Control (n = 15)	2.67	1.95	2.53	2.00	3.13	1.55

Table 6.5 provides a summary of the changes over time for each group. As can be seen, the PPP group improved significantly from the pre-test to both post-test 1 and post-test 2 on all the tests except the Same-or-Different Task, where the gains from the pre-test to post-test 2 were non-significant. The TBLT group showed significant gains from the pre-test to both post-test 1 and post-test 2 on all tests, including the Same-or-Different Task. The effect sizes for the TBLT group were larger than the PPP in all comparisons. Both experimental groups did not show any significant decrease

from post-test 1 to post-test 2, indicating that the effects were durable. The control group did not show any significant gains.

Table 6.5. Changes over time in adjective scores

Tests	PPP group			TBLT group			Control group		
	Pre-post1	Pre-post2	Post1-post2	Pre-post1	Pre-post2	Post1-post2	Pre-post1	Pre-post2	Post1-post2
S-or-D Task	.29*	.30	.00	.67*	.67*	.07	.04	.02	.02
Dis-production	.43*	.41*	.06	.63*	.74*	.17	.14	.17	.03
Category Task	.65*	.66*	.02	.77*	.81*	.09	.21	.20	.00
M-C listening	.70*	.71*	.01	.88*	.89*	.21	.04	.14	.18

S-or-D Task = Same-or-Different Task; Dis-Production = Discrete-item production test; M-C listening = Multiple-choice listening test; Pre-post1= improvement from pre-test to post-test 1; Pre-post2 = improvement from pre-test to post-test 2; Post1-post2 = improvement from post-test 1 to post-test 2; * = the difference was significant at $p = .05$ level

Table 6.6 shows that there were no significant differences between the groups on any of the pre-tests. On post-tests 1 and 2, the PPP group outperformed the control group on three of the tests with small to medium effect sizes, but failed to outperform the control group in the Same-or-Different Task on post-test 2. The TBLT group outperformed the control group on all the post-tests with medium to large effect sizes.

Table 6.6. Summary of the between-group effect sizes (r) for the acquisition of adjectives

	Pre-test		Post-test 1		Post-test 2	
	PPP-Cntl.	TBLT-Cntl.	PPP-Cntl.	TBLT-Cntl.	PPP-Cntl.	TBLT-Cntl.
S-or-D Task	.03	.00	.33*	.63*	.30	.65*
Dis-production	.04	.13	.50*	.71*	.50*	.80*
Category Task	.12	.22	.66*	.80*	.66*	.82*
M-C listening	–.03	.17	.71*	.92*	.73*	.96*

Cntl. = Control group; S-or-D Task = Same-or-Different Task; Dis-production = Discrete-item production test; M-C listening = Multiple-choice listening test; Pre-post1= improvement from pre-test to post-test 1; Pre-post2 = improvement from pre-test to post-test 2; Post1-post2 = improvement from post-test 1 to post-test 2; * = the difference was significant at $p = .05$ level (the TBLT group significantly outperformed the PPP group)

To summarise the test results, overall, TBLT proved to be more effective than PPP. As Table 6.11 shows, the TBLT group performed as well as the PPP group on the noun tests (both comprehension and production) in spite of the limited opportunity to produce the target items. On the Category Task for nouns, the TBLT group outperformed the PPP group. It should be noted, that, while the PPP group outscored the TBLT on the two production tests (see Table 6.7), the differences between the two groups were small and not significant. However, for the acquisition of adjectives, the quality of the interactions in the two types of instruction appears to have been a key factor, with TBLT proving to be superior in gains on all measures.

Table 6.7. Comparative results and effect sizes (*r*) of the acquisition of nouns and adjectives

	Nouns		Adjectives	
	Post-test 1 (*r*)	Post-test 2 (*r*)	Post-test 1 (*r*)	Post-test 2 (*r*)
S-or-D Task	PPP = TBLT (.38)	PPP = TBLT (.13)	TBLT > PPP (.51)	TBLT > PPP (.53)
Dis-production	PPP = TBLT (.28)	PPP = TBLT (.15)	TBLT > PPP (.39)	TBLT > PPP (.58)
Category Task	TBLT > PPP (.38)	TBLT > PPP (.41)	TBLT > PPP (.39)	TBLT > PPP (.45)
M-C listening	PPP = TBLT (.17)	PPP = TBLT (.14)	TBLT > PPP (.57)	TBLT > PPP (.67)

( ): Effect size *r*; "PPP = TBLT": There was no significant difference between the two groups; "TBLT > PPP": The TBLT group significantly outscored the PPP group

Input and output in the classroom

I will first report the quantity of the input and output by counting the frequency of the target words produced by the teacher (i.e., input for the students) and by the students (i.e. output) throughout the nine lessons. Then I will examine the quality of the input to the learners (i.e., the teacher's language) and the learners' output (i.e., their production) separately.

Frequency of target words in the teacher's and the students' production

The frequency of the target word tokens in the teacher's and the students' production during the nine lessons is shown in Table 6.8. A student token was counted only once when the students produced a word chorally.

Chi-square tests indicated that the frequency of the target words as produced by both the teacher and the students differed significantly in the PPP and TBLT lessons. However, considering that the students were exposed to the target language produced by other students as well as the teacher, the input that the students received is better reflected in the total number of student and teacher tokens. Calculated in this way, there was no difference in the total input that the two groups experienced (see Appendix B for statistical values). In other words, both groups were exposed to a similar amount of input, but the opportunity to produce output was much greater in the PPP group than in the TBLT group.

Table 6.8. Frequency of target words in the teacher's and the students' production

	Teacher's production			Students' production		
	PPP	TBLT	Difference (*w*)	PPP	TBLT	Difference (*w*)
Nouns	3,264	5,888	sig. (−.46)	2,766	52	sig. (.96)
Adjectives	1,362	2,219	sig. (−.15)	1,080	301	sig. (.56)

sig. = the difference was statistically significant at $p = .01$ level.; ( ) = effect size *w* between the PPP and the TBLT groups

Types of teacher production

I noticed that the teacher's L2 utterances in the PPP lessons often consisted of one target word, while the teacher's commands or elaboration in the TBLT lessons meant that the target vocabulary items were 'embedded' in sentences. In order to achieve the task outcome, the TBLT students needed to process the full utterance and infer the meaning of the target item using the contextual information provided. I suggest that this required the learners to 'search' (Laufer & Hulstijn, 2001) for the key word and comprehend it in a way that was more similar to how the words might occur in a naturalistic context (Lightbown, 2008).

An example of an 'embedded' production is shown in Excerpt 6.1. 'Embedded' words often occurred in the teacher's instructions, and also in the additional information the teacher gave to help the learners select the appropriate cards representing the nouns. In these cases, the target items were embedded in complete utterances.

Excerpt 6.1
1. T: Please take the <u>peacock</u>, <u>peacock</u> to the zoo.
2. S: Peacock.
3. T: Yeah. The <u>peacock</u> has a beautiful feather. It's a <u>blue</u> bird. <u>Blue</u>.
4. S: Blue.
5. T: Yeah. The <u>peacock</u> is <u>blue</u>. Okay? Ready?

(TBLT; Lesson 3)

On the other hand, the teacher produced an 'isolated' word when providing feedback on the learners' erroneous production, as shown in Excerpt 6.2,

Excerpt 6.2
1. T: (pointing to the shorter pencil in the picture card), this pencil is...?
2. S: small.
3. T: <u>short</u>.
4. S: short.

(PPP: Lesson 3)

Table 6.9 shows the frequency of these two types of teacher production. When the teacher used a word in a longer utterance, it was coded as 'embedded'. If the teacher's turn consisted solely of the target word, it was coded as 'isolated'. As the table shows, the TBLT group was exposed to embedded nouns and adjectives much more frequently than the PPP group.

Table 6.9. 'Embedded' and 'isolated' word production by the teacher

	Nouns			Adjectives		
	PPP	TBLT	Difference (*w*)	PPP	TBLT	Difference (*w*)
Embedded	152	3,991	sig. (−.93)	52	2,057	sig. (−.95)
Isolated	3,112	1,897	sig. (.24)	1,310	162	sig. (.78)

sig.: the difference was statistically significant at $p = .01$ level.; ( ): effect size *w* between the PPP and the TBLT groups

Chi-Square tests showed that there were significant differences between the two groups in the number of 'embedded' and 'isolated' tokens for both nouns and adjectives. The TBLT learners experienced the target words (both noun and adjectives) in an embedded form whereas the PPP learners encountered them as isolated words.

Cross-tabulation tests showed that in the PPP lessons, the frequency of the teacher's embedded and isolated nouns and adjectives was very similar. However, there were significant differences in the way the teacher used nouns and adjectives in the TBLT lessons. In the teacher's embedded utterances, the adjectives were produced more frequently than the nouns, while in the isolated utterances the opposite was the case. In other words, in the TBLT lessons adjectives were more likely to be embedded than nouns whereas in the PPP group both nouns and adjectives were produced in a similar way.

Types of learner production

The learner production was first categorised according to whether it was 'optional' or 'required'. The conversation analysis in Chapter 5 showed that the students in the TBLT often initiated repair in order to obtain information to achieve the task outcome. I noticed that many such utterances consisted of adjectives (e.g., 'white?' in Excerpt 5.6 in Chapter 5), some of which were targeted in this study (see Chapter 4). In the PPP condition, on the other hand, the conversation often consisted of IRF (initiation–response–feedback) exchanges where the students were asked to produce the L2. Thus, in general, most of the L2 production by the PPP students was 'required' by the teacher. Assuming that self-initiated production is beneficial for learning (e.g., Swain & Lapkin, 1995), I wanted to see whether the students' production of the target nouns and adjectives differed in the two groups in terms of whether it was optional or required. In the analysis, production was deemed to be 'optional' if the teacher made no attempt to elicit a target word from the students, and it was considered 'requested' whenever the teacher explicitly elicited a target word. For example, in Excerpt 6.1 (from the PPP group), the student's production of "small" (turn 2) was requested by the teacher while "short" (turn 4) was optional.

I then examined whether the 'optional' tokens were 'self-initiated' or 'borrowed'. All the above examples of 'optional' learner production consisted of repetitions of a part of the teacher's utterances. However, I also noticed that in the TBLT lessons, students sometimes produced a word which was not a repetition of the teacher's utterance, i.e., they produced the target words spontaneously. Excerpt 6.3 shows an example. In turns 2, 4, and 6, the students initiated the production of adjectives which were not in the teacher's utterance in turn 1.

Excerpt 6.3
1. T: please take the ostrich to the zoo.
2. S1: green?
3. T: not green.
4. S1: blue?
5. T: no.
6. S1: gold?
7. T: gold? no. the ostrich is big.
(TBLT: Lesson 5)

As shown in Chapter 5, repetition occurred frequently in both the PPP and the TBLT lessons in this study. Repetition itself is considered to be beneficial for language learning. However, the independent production of an L2 word shows the learner had control over the use of the word in the interactions, which can be considered an indication of learning having taken place (Markee, 2008; Shintani & Ellis, 2014; also see Chapter 3). In the analysis, a target word was considered to be 'self-initiated' if the learner was the first person in a sequence to use it. It was considered to be 'borrowed' if the target word had occurred in an utterance earlier in a sequence and the learner was just repeating or imitating it.

Table 6.10 shows the frequency of the 'requested/optional' and 'self-initiated/borrowed' adjective and noun tokens produced by the two groups in the nine lessons.

Table 6.10. Number of requested/optional and self-initiated/borrowed tokens by the students

		Nouns			Adjectives		
		PPP	TBLT	Difference (*w*)	PPP	TBLT	Difference (*w*)
Requested		2,601	0	–	1,028	0	–
Optional	Self-initiated	6	2	n.s. (.16)	3	263	sig. (.98)
	Borrowed	159	50	sig. (.46)	49	38	n.s. (.13)

sig.: the difference was statistically significant at p = .01 level.; n.s.: the difference was statistically non-significant; ( ): effect size *w*

There were no 'requested' tokens in the TBLT group. There was a significant difference in the frequency of the 'self-initiated' tokens for adjectives but not for nouns. In the case of the 'borrowed' tokens, the reverse was true – there was a significant difference in the frequency of nouns but not adjectives. Cross-tabulation analyses showed a significant difference between the nouns and adjectives in terms of the number of 'self-initiated' and 'borrowed' tokens in the TBLT group. The difference was non-significant in the PPP group.

Table 6.11 summarises the above analyses. The PPP and TBLT instruction resulted in markedly different discourse processes in ways to be expected from the external descriptions of these two types of instruction.

Table 6.11. Differences in the types of input/output in the PPP and TBLT Groups

Types of input/output		PPP	TBLT
Input	Frequency of exposure to target items	Frequent exposure to the target items	Frequent exposure to target items
	Isolated vs. embedded	Target items generally occurred in isolation.	Target items often embedded in utterances. The adjectives were more often embedded than the nouns.
Output	Frequency of production of target items	Frequent opportunities to produce the target words	Fewer opportunities to produce the target words
	Requested vs. optional	The production of the target words was mostly requested in IRF exchanges.	The production of the target words only occurred optionally.
	Initiated vs. borrowed	Learners produced the nouns and adjectives by borrowing them from the teacher's utterances.	The production of nouns mostly occurred by borrowing from the teacher's utterances. However, the production of adjectives was often initiated by the students in order to negotiate the meaning of the nouns.

It is clear that that the two types of instruction led to marked differences in the input the learners experienced and in their opportunity to produce the target items. In the PPP lessons, the learners were frequently exposed to the target words but almost always in an isolated manner. They produced the target words only when requested to do so by the teacher and only rarely initiated production themselves. As seen in Chapter 5, the teacher's requests typically triggered the three-part exchange (i.e., initiation-response-feedback, or IRF; Sinclair & Coulthard, 1975) so typical of PPP instruction, as shown in Excerpt 6.1. As other studies (Brock, 1986; Long & Sato, 1983) have shown, these IRF exchanges involve display questions (i.e., questions where the speaker already knows the answers) rather than referential questions (i.e., questions where the speaker is seeking new information). Furthermore, when the PPP learners produced the target words, they frequently 'borrowed' them from the teacher's corrective feedback moves. These process features suggest that the PPP learners were treating the target words as objects that had to be 'performed' and remembered.

The TBLT group was also frequently exposed to the target words as might be expected in an approach using input-based tasks. However, the nature of this exposure was very different from that of the PPP group. The target words were frequently embedded in the teacher's complete sentences. Thus, the TBLT instruction exposed the learners to the target words in a contextualized and more naturalistic way. When the learners produced the target words, they did so because they had opted themselves to produce them, rather than being required to do so, again reflecting the nature of the input-based instruction. Interestingly, the adjectives were embedded more frequently than the nouns. This was because the learners engaged in self-initiated repair by initiating the use of the adjectives in order to comprehend the teacher's commands (see Excerpt 6.3). In other words, the TBLT instruction created a situation where the learners needed to use their own linguistic resources and where the target words were tools to help them complete the tasks.

Discussion

Based on the analyses above, I will now consider the test results by answering three questions: (1) Why did both TBLT and the PPP show similar results for nouns?; (2) Why did the TBLT group perform better than the PPP group on the Category Task for nouns?; (3) Why did the TBLT group perform better than the PPP group for adjectives on all four tests?

Why did both TBLT and the PPP show similar results for nouns?

The process features of the two types of instruction were very similar in the case of the nouns (see Table 6.11). This may explain the similar levels of acquisition in the PPP and TBLT conditions. Both groups experienced extensive exposure to the target nouns. In both groups, the nouns were introduced one at a time in a pre-planned manner. The learners in both groups tended to borrow the nouns from the teacher's utterances rather than initiate their production themselves. Although there were some differences in the process features (e.g., in the PPP group the learners were exposed primarily to isolated use of the nouns whereas in the TBLT group they were exposed to embedded use), these do not seem to have made a difference. What seems to have been important is whether the meanings of the nouns were made transparent. The PPP instruction mostly involved requesting the learners to produce the target nouns one by one (e.g., teacher: "Okay next, what's this?"). Thus, as shown in Excerpt 6.1, each conversational sequence focused on one vocabulary item. Similarly, in the TBLT group, each conversational sequence was centred around a teacher's instruction, which also targeted one noun at a time.

Why did the TBLT group perform better than the PPP group in the category task for nouns?

The only significant group difference was in the Category Task, where the TBLT learners outscored the PPP learners. In this respect, the process differences in the two types of instruction do seem to have made a difference. In the Category Task, the target words were embedded in sentences (e.g., "Look. The peacock has beautiful feathers."). In other words, the learners had to process the target words in complete sentences in order to achieve the task goals. Learners have been shown to perform better on tests which resemble the type of instruction they received (Beretta & Davies, 1985). In the PPP lessons, the teacher predominantly used the target words in an isolated manner. In the TBLT classroom, on the other hand, the participants needed to comprehend words in context, which may explain why these learners achieved higher scores than the PPP learners in this task.

Why did the TBLT group perform better than the PPP group for adjectives in all four tests?

The key difference in the test results for the adjectives is that whereas the PPP group did not demonstrate durable gains in the free productive use of adjectives (i.e., on the Same-or-Different Task post-test 2), the TBLT group did. Furthermore, the TBLT group outscored not just the control group but also the PPP group on all four tests. In short, the TBLT instruction was clearly superior in enabling the learners to acquire adjectives, and this was evident in both controlled and free production.

It needs to be recalled that while the nouns were introduced systematically in the teacher's instructions in the TBLT class, the adjectives were only introduced when the learners experienced difficulties in identifying the referents of the nouns (i.e., they figured only reactively). In other words, not only did the TBLT result in acquisition of the noun items that were introduced in the pre-planned instructions, but also in the acquisition of the adjectives that only arose incidentally in the interactions generated by the tasks. This supports one of the essential claims about the facilitative effects of incidental learning in task-based teaching (Willis & Willis, 2007).

The results cannot be explained in terms of frequency of exposure (Palmberg, 1987) or the claimed superiority of production-based instruction (Mondria & Wiersma, 2004). For both nouns and adjectives, both the PPP and TBLT groups were exposed to similar amounts of input. However, since the PPP group had more opportunities to produce both word types, this cannot explain why the TBLT group performed as well as the PPP group in the two production tests, and also demonstrated greater acquisition of adjectives. To explain the results it is necessary to take a closer look at the difference in the process features of the two types of instruction.

The process features involving the use of the adjectives were quite different in the two types of instruction. In the PPP instruction, the exposure to adjectives, as much as to nouns, was pre-planned. The students were requested to produce the adjectives and they never initiated the use of adjectives themselves. When the learners chose to produce adjectives, they just borrowed them from the teacher's utterances. In contrast, in the TBLT instruction, the adjectives were introduced reactively when the teacher used them to help the learners identify the referent of a noun in one of her instructions. As a result, the adjectives were contextually embedded. Later, the learners began to use adjectives themselves as in Excerpt 6.4.

Excerpt 6.4
1. T: please take the ostrich to the zoo.
2. S1: <u>green?</u>
3. T: not green.
4. S1: <u>blue?</u>
5. T: no.
6. S1: <u>gold?</u>
7. T: gold? no. the ostrich is big.

(TBLT: Lesson 5)

In this sequence the learners failed to understand '*ostrich*' and began to negotiate its meaning using a number of adjectives which ultimately enabled them to identify the correct referent of the noun. These differences can explain the results for the adjectives. It would seem that the TBLT instruction provided learners with a communicative reason for both comprehending and producing the adjectives whereas the PPP instruction did not. In the case of the adjectives, therefore, Jiang's (2000) claim that learners need to experience the contextualized use of new L2 words in order to develop a full representation is supported. In short, the TBLT instruction provided the learners with a much richer learning environment.

Another process difference concerned the opportunity for student-initiated use of the adjectives. This never occurred in the PPP group, but as Excerpt 6.4 shows it was quite common in the TBLT group. To further examine the causal effects of the TBLT learners' 'self-initiated' production of the adjectives on their acquisition, a simple linear regression was carried out (see Appendix B). The number of 'self-initiated' tokens produced by individual learners in this group (see Table 6.10, p. 120) was the independent variable, and the scores of the two tests the dependent variables. The results showed that on the Same-or-Different Task the effect was approaching significance on post-test 1 and reached significance on post-test 2. For the Discrete-item test, the effects were significant on both post-tests. In other words, those learners who self-initiated the production of adjectives acquired them more efficiently.

Vocabulary acquisition and task-induced involvement load

The overall difference between the two groups probably may further be explained by 'task-induced involvement load' (Laufer & Hulstijn, 2001) (see Chapter 3). Laufer and Hulstijn claimed that vocabulary learning is dependent on the levels of 'need' (i.e., does the vocabulary-learning activity require learners to process the target items to complete the task?), 'search' (i.e., does the learner have to search for the relevant lexical form to express or comprehend the meaning?), and 'evaluation' (i.e., does the learner have to evaluate the appropriateness of the word choice). According to Laufer and Hulstijn, the effectiveness of vocabulary instruction depends less on the medium of the instruction than on the extent to which the activities involve 'need', 'search', and 'evaluation'.

Table 6.12 evaluates the 'need,' 'search', and 'evaluation' of the use of the target words in the two groups. A minus (–) indicates an absence of an involvement factor, a plus (+) indicates that the factor is present to a moderate degree, and a double plus (++) marks the strong presence of an involvement factor (see Laufer & Hulstijn, 2001).

Table 6.12. 'Need' 'Search' and 'Evaluation' in PPP and TBLT

	PPP		TBLT			
	Nouns and adjectives		Nouns		Adjectives	
Need	+	Production was necessary to complete the activities.	+	Comprehension of the nouns was necessary to complete the tasks.	+	Comprehension of the adjectives was useful to complete the tasks.
					+	The use of the adjectives was motivated by the tasks.
Search	–	The pictorial image of the words (word meaning) was provided.	+	Learners engaged or observed self-initiated repair.	+	The activity required inferring the meaning of the adjectives.
Evaluation	+	Positive and negative feedback on production was provided.	+	The activity required choosing the correct noun card.	+	Feedback on the noun choices was provided.
			+	Feedback on the noun choices was provided.	++	The activity required finding the appropriate adjectives to repair the problems.

Note: –: an absence of an involvement factor
+:moderate presence of an involvement factor
++: strong presence of an involvement factor

Both the PPP and the TBLT activities involved 'need', which was externally imposed by instructional requirements. In the PPP activities the learners were required to say the oral form of the words depicted on the cards; in the TBLT activities the learners were required to comprehend the meaning of the nouns and adjectives in the teacher's utterances in order to complete the tasks; moreover, these activities generated learner-initiated production of the adjectives while they were negotiating the meaning of the target nouns.

The opportunity for 'search', which refers to "the attempt to find the meaning of an unknown L2 word or trying to find the L2 word form expressing a concept" (Laufer & Hulstijn, 2001, p. 14), was different in the two groups. In PPP, the meanings of the target words were provided in the learners' L1 at the beginning of each lesson. The learners were then repeatedly asked to produce the words shown on the picture cards. Therefore, the PPP activities did not require any 'search' for the meanings of the target words. In contrast, the TBLT instruction resulted in the learners having to negotiate the meaning of the nouns to complete the tasks, which can be seen as a form of 'search'. Additionally, the learners in this group needed to infer or discover the meaning of the adjectives in order to perform the tasks successfully, since these meanings were not directly taught.

The levels of 'evaluation' also appeared to be different in the PPP and TBLT groups. 'Evaluation' entails "a comparison of a given word with other words, a specific meaning of a word with its other meanings, or combining the word with other words in order to assess whether a word does or does not fit its context" (Laufer & Hulstijn, 2001, p. 14). The PPP activities required 'evaluation' to some extent, but only when learners responded to the teacher's positive or negative feedback on their production. In the TBLT group, learners were required to choose the appropriate noun cards from the collection of picture cards, and to evaluate their task performance (i.e., whether or not they had chosen the correct card) when they received feedback. The TBLT learners needed to engage in 'evaluation' because they were required to determine the meaning of an adjective when the teacher responded to their failure to comprehend by elaborating on an instruction (e.g., T: "*the peacock is blue*") or through the interaction initiated by other students (e.g., S: "*blue?*", T: "*yes*"). When a learner produced an adjective in the process of negotiating meaning, he or she needed to select the appropriate adjective in order to negotiate effectively. This can be considered as a form of 'strong evaluation' rather than 'moderate evaluation' (Laufer & Hulstijn, 2001, p. 15), as it required generative choice rather than selective choice.

Conclusion

This part of the study compared the impact of PPP and TBLT on the acquisition of vocabulary by investigating both the process features of the instruction and the learning outcomes. Although both types of instruction proved to be effective for the acquisition of nouns, the TBLT instruction was found to be more effective for the acquisition of adjectives. Only the TBLT learners were able to use the adjectives in free production. Key differences between the process features of the TBLT and PPP instruction were proposed as an explanation for the difference in learning outcomes. That is, only the TBLT instruction was characterized by (1) contextualized input, (2) the occurrence of self-initiated repair, and (3) student-initiated production.

It is of course possible that the results would have been different if PPP had been operationalized differently (e.g., by providing more explicit corrective feedback rather than recasts). Nevertheless, the PPP instruction used in this study strongly resembles the way in which this approach is operationalized in many classrooms. Clearly, though, there is a need for further research comparing PPP and input-based instruction with beginner-level learners.

One of the main implications of the study is that input-based tasks constitute an effective way of introducing TBLT to beginner learners, as proposed by Ellis (2001). Even though the instruction did not require the production of the target items, the learners chose to use the L2 while performing the tasks. There is also some evidence that those learners who engaged more actively learned more words. The study extends Ellis' research by indicating which process features arising from the implementation of listen-and-do tasks are important for young children's learning.

CHAPTER 7

Incidental acquisition of grammatical features in PPP and TBLT

This chapter presents the results of the study related to the third research question:

> Which instructional approach (TBLT or PPP) is more effective in facilitating the incidental acquisition of grammatical features?

I investigated how the incidental acquisition of two grammatical features – plural *-s* and copula *be* – took place in the two teaching contexts. As we saw in the previous chapter, vocabulary learning took place intentionally in the PPP group and incidentally in the TBLT group. However, both groups were frequently exposed to the two grammatical features, which were not deliberately taught and thus could only be acquired incidentally. I wanted to investigate whether any incidental grammar acquisition occurred in either group and, if so, whether there was any difference between the two groups in how much was acquired. I was also interested in examining the classroom processes related to the incidental acquisition of grammatical features.

In neither the PPP nor the TBLT lessons were the target structures explicitly taught to the learners. However, the instructional materials were designed in such a way as to expose learners to singular and plural nouns. Additionally, the learners were naturally exposed to utterances that contained copula *be* in the interactions that took place. Chapter 4 presents a more detailed explanation of the materials used in the study.

Three tests (the multiple-choice listening test, the Wug Test, and the Same-or-Different Task) measured the acquisition of plural *-s*, and two tests (the Tell-and-Do Task and the Picture Description) measured acquisition of copula *be*. These tests were conducted as a pre-test (one week before the treatment), post-test 1 (one week after the treatment), and post-test 2 (five weeks after the treatment).

The test results showed that incidental acquisition took place but only in the TBLT group and only for receptive knowledge of plural *-s*. There was no evidence of any incidental acquisition by the PPP group. As Figure 7.1 shows, only the multiple-choice listening test showed any significant difference between the groups: the TBLT group improved their scores for plural *-s* after the instructional treatment while the PPP and control groups did not. In the four production tests for the plural *-s* and the copula *be*, none of the groups improved significantly and there were no significant differences between the three groups. However, a few of the learners in the TBLT group showed evidence of acquiring the structures.

Tests	Features	Measured aspects		Results
Multiple-choice listening	Plural *-s*	Comprehension	Discrete-item	Only TBLT group improved.
Wug test		Production	Discrete-item	None of the groups improved. (Only two in the TBLT group produced the form for both 'old' and 'new' items.)
Same-or-Different Task			Task-based	
Picture Description test	Copula *be*	Production	Discrete-item	None of the groups improved. (Only one in the TBLT group produced 'is' but overused it for plural items.)
Tell-and-do Task			Task-based	

Figure 7.1. Overview of the statistical results for the five tests

Now I will report the results in detail and discuss the findings. I will examine the results for plural *-s* and for the copula *be* separately.

Results for plural *-s*

Data analysis

The acquisition of plural *-s* was measured by two discrete-point tests (the multiple-choice listening test and the Wug Test) and one task-based test (the Same-or-Different Task) (see Chapter 4 for details). In order to differentiate between the possible occurrence of 'item learning' (i.e., learners remembering the specific items they had been exposed to) and 'system-learning' (i.e., the internalisation of a 'rule' that was successfully applied to new exemplars of the target feature), the test scores were divided into 'old items' (eight items) and 'new items'(six items) (Robinson, 2005), and expressed as percentages. As the Same-or-Different Task measured the learner's production of the plural *-s* in their spontaneous production during the performance of the task, the scores were transformed into percentages using obligatory occasion analysis (Brown, 1973). The correct number of morphemes supplied was divided by the total number of the obligatory occasions for the use of the target structure.

The scores for the three tests were further classified to show whether plural *-s* was 'acquired' or 'not acquired', using 80% as the criterion level (Jia, 2003). The number of the students in the two experimental groups (TBLT and PPP) who had 'acquired' plural *-s* was then compared. Figure 7.2 summarises how each of the 5 tests were scored and analysed.

Tests	Classifications for analysis	Scoring	Further analysis
Multiple-choice listening test	1. 'old' items (n = 8) 2. 'new' items (n = 6)	Percentage scores	Number of 'acquired' students (80%)
Wug test		Percentage scores	
Same-or-Different Task		Obligatory scores	

Figure 7.2. Scoring and data analysis for the tests

Test results

Table 7.1 shows the descriptive statistics of the three tests measuring plural *-s*. For the multiple-choice listening test, the TBLT group increased its scores across the three repeated tests while the PPP group and the control group stayed at virtually the same level for both the 'old' and 'new' items. For the two production tests, only the TBLT

Table 7.1. Descriptive statistics of the three tests measuring the plural *-s*

		Pre-test		Post-test 1		Post-test 2	
	Group	Mean	SD	Mean	SD	Mean	SD
Multiple-choice listening test							
Old items	PPP (n = 15)	36.67	29.68	43.33	17.59	40.00	24.64
	TBLT (n = 15)	36.67	15.20	86.67	27.76	90.00	22.76
	Control (n = 15)	35.00	26.39	40.00	24.64	33.33	26.16
New items	PPP (n = 15)	48.89	21.35	52.22	18.76	51.11	27.79
	TBLT (n = 15)	52.22	15.27	75.54	24.28	79.98	18.04
	Control (n = 15)	48.89	23.13	51.11	14.76	54.45	13.34
Wug test							
Old items	PPP (n = 15)	0.00	0.00	0.00	0.00	0.00	0.00
	TBLT (n = 15)	0.00	0.00	13.33	35.19	13.33	35.19
	Control (n = 15)	0.00	0.00	0.00	0.00	0.00	0.00
New items	PPP (n = 15)	0.00	0.00	0.00	0.00	0.00	0.00
	TBLT (n = 15)	0.00	0.00	12.50	33.07	11.67	31.15
	Control (n = 15)	0.00	0.00	0.00	0.00	0.00	0.00
Same-or-Different Task							
Old items	PPP (n = 15)	0.00	0.00	0.00	0.00	0.00	0.00
	TBLT (n = 15)	0.00	0.00	6.87	18.40	7.33	19.44
	Control (n = 15)	0.00	0.00	0.00	0.00	0.00	0.00
New items	PPP (n = 15)	0.00	0.00	0.00	0.00	0.00	0.00
	TBLT (n = 15)	0.00	0.00	1.33	5.16	1.33	5.16
	Control (n = 15)	0.00	0.00	0.00	0.00	0.00	0.00

group demonstrated any acquisition on either of the post-tests. The students in both the PPP and the control groups scored zero in both production tests at all times.

The statistical results for the comparative tests are shown in Appendix C. For the multiple-choice listening test, there were no significant differences between the TBLT and PPP groups on the pre-test for either old or new items with marginal effect sizes. However, the TBLT group outperformed the PPP group on both post-tests for both old and new items. The medium to large effect sizes indicated that the instruction received by the two groups had very different effects on their development of receptive knowledge of plural *-s*. No statistical comparisons were attempted for the Wug Test and the Same-or-Different Task as the PPP group scored zero on all these tests.

Table 7.2 shows the number of learners who 'acquired' plural *-s* in the three tests (i.e., achieved the 80% criterion level). It should be noted that none of the learners reached the criterion level on the listening pre-test.

Table 7.2. Number of learners in the three tests who acquired the two structures

		PPP (n = 15)		TBLT (n = 15)	
Tests		**Post-test 1**	**Post-test 2**	**Post-test 1**	**Post-test 2**
Multiple-choice listening test	Old items	2	3	11	12
	New items	0	0	11	12
Wug Test	Old items	0	0	2	0
	New items	0	0	2	0
Same-or-Different	Old items	0	0	0	0
	New items	0	0	0	0

The results for the multiple-choice listening test show a marked difference between the two groups. In the TBLT group, 11 students on post-test 1 and 12 on post-test 2 reached the 'acquired' level for both 'old' and 'new' items, indicating that most of the TBLT learners acquired receptive knowledge of plural *-s*. On the other hand, only two PPP students reached the 'acquired' level for plural *-s* on post-test 1 and three on post-test 2. None of them demonstrated comprehension of the 'new items', suggesting that they had not internalized a general rule for plural *-s*. The difference between the number of students reaching the 'acquired' level in the TBLT and PPP groups was statistically significant on both post-tests and the effect sizes were large (see Appendix C).

On the Wug post-tests, all the participants in the PPP groups scored zero, as did most of the students in the TBLT group. There were no significant differences between the TBLT and PPP groups on either post-test. However, two students in the TBLT group demonstrated some acquisition of plural *-s*: one obtained 100% for the old items and 75% for the new items, and the other 100% for both old and the new items as shown in Table 7.3.

In the Same-or-Different Task, three participants produced some plural forms on the post-tests, though none met the 'acquired' level. Two of the three participants were in the TBLT group. One of them scored 60% on both post-tests, and the other scored 43% on post-test 1 and 50% on post-test 2 (Table 7.3). The third learner, who was in the PPP group, scored 20% on both post-tests.

Table 7.3. Two TBLT students' scores for plural *-s* in the production tests

	Wug Test				Same-or-Different Task			
	Old items		New items		Old items		New items	
	Post 1	Post 2	Post 1	Post 2	Post 1	Post 2	Post 1	Post 2
Student 1	100	100	75	75	66	66	50	50
Student 2	100	100	100	100	75	75	0	25

To sum up, two students in the TBLT group successfully produced the plural form for both 'old' and 'new' items in the Same-or-Different Task, while in the PPP group only one student produced the form and only for an 'old' item. The overall results suggest that TBLT was more likely to foster the incidental acquisition of plural *-s* than PPP for learners who had no prior knowledge of this feature.

Discussion

It seems that opportunities for output in the PPP lessons did not contribute to acquisition while exposure to input in the TBLT lessons did. Both the PPP and the TBLT learners had very limited opportunities to produce plural forms during the nine lessons. Students produced plural *-s* 36 times in the PPP and 15 in the TBLT lessons. Also, both groups had similar exposure to the plural form (the teacher produced plural *-s* 1,019 times in the PPP and 1,282 in the TBLT lessons). Perhaps the TBLT learners were better able to attend to the input than the PPP learners because they were not required to produce the target items. This may have made it easier for them to notice the plural *-s* morpheme and its function.

A good question to ask is why the TBLT learners were able to acquire plural *-s* to some extent, whereas the PPP learners failed. One possible explanation lies in the primary focus of the two types of instruction. While the TBLT lessons were designed to direct the learners' attention to meaning, the PPP lessons focused mainly on the form of the target vocabulary items. In the PPP lessons, the teacher explicitly asked the students to focus on the vocabulary items, and by implication, diverted their attention away from the grammatical features. Loewen et al. (2009) showed that incidental acquisition of 3rd person *-s* is difficult when the focus is on another grammatical structure. Similarly, the PPP learners may have failed to acquire plural *-s* because they were forced to focus on the form of the target words, and thus did not attend to the difference in meaning between the singular and plural nouns. In other words, the TBLT lessons possibly provided learners more opportunities for a form-focus on the plural *-s* than the PPP lessons.

In order to examine this interpretation, I further analyzed the occurrence of two conversational elements that might indicate focus on form, namely repair and uptake. I identified and counted the number of repair sequences (i.e., occasions where some problem arose in the conversation which the participants attempted to solve; see also Chapter 5) and uptake moves in the two groups. Uptake was identified in two ways: (1) the learners' correction of their own erroneous production following corrective feedback; and (2) the learners' demonstration that they had successfully comprehended input after they had initially failed to comprehend it. I also categorized the uptake moves into either 'self-initiated' (i.e., through self-correction or by asking questions) or 'other-initiated' (i.e., through receiving feedback).

Table 7.4 presents the results of this analysis. In the PPP lessons, repair was attempted 444 times and uptake occurred 36 times. All the repairs were initiated by the teacher. In the TBLT lessons, repair occurred 108 times (15 teacher-initiated and 93 student-initiated) with 88 instances leading to uptake. In other words, although the PPP group received substantially more opportunities for repair, it was predominantly initiated by the teacher, and the proportion of students' successful uptake was only 8.8%. The TBLT students had far less opportunity for repair but it was mostly student-initiated, and 81.5% of it led to successful repair. In other words, the teacher-initiated repair in the PPP did not make the learners attend to the form of the plural morpheme.

Table 7.4. The number of attempted repair and uptake for plural *-s* in the two groups

	Repair attempted			
Group	**Teacher-initiated**	**Student-initiated**	**Total**	**Uptake**
PPP	444	0	444	36 (8.8%)
TBLT	15	93	108	88 (81.5%)

One possible explanation for this is that plural *-s* did not have any functional value in the PPP context. Thus, neither the teacher nor the students focused on the accurate production of this feature. As I illustrated in Chapter 5, in the PPP lessons the teacher tended to direct a turn to another student without making sure that the student who had made an error repaired it. This was because both the teacher and the student were focused on the goal of the lesson – to learn new L2 words – rather than on the plural form.

Excerpt 7.1 illustrates such an example in the PPP lessons.

Excerpt 7.1
1. T: okay, your turn.
2. S: ((turns over one card on the table))
3. T: what are they?
4. S: ((collects the card with another card on the table))
5. T: wait wait (.) what are they? what are they?
6. S: mandarin
7. T: mandarins
8. S: *mandar*[in
9. T: [mandarins, yes. ((looks at the next student)) okay your turn.
(PPP, Lesson 3)

In Chapter 5, I have illustrated that in the TBLT lessons a repair sequence involving plural *-s* occurred when students had a problem distinguishing the plural and singular form of a noun in one of the teacher's instructions. I have reported in Chapter 5 that such repair was initiated either by the teacher or the students. The former occurred when the students failed to respond correctly to the teacher's instructions and the teacher provided some kind of support. The latter occurred when one of the students requested clarification either in their L1 or the L2 (e.g., "Two?"), and the teacher or another student responded to it. In either case, uptake can be said to have taken place if the students subsequently demonstrated comprehension of the instruction.

Excerpt 7.2 illustrates one such example. Responding to S1's clarification request (line 2), the teacher directed the students' attention to the form while focusing on completing the task. While S1 failed to uptake, as shown by her clarification request (line 7), S3 was successful (line 8). The teacher's feedback utterance (line 9) seems to have enabled S3 to confirm his potential hypothesis regarding the plural form. This excerpt shows how the teacher and the students collaboratively negotiated the meaning of the plural noun, and how this led to a successful instance of repair.

Excerpt 7.2
1. T: ok the next. take the crocodiles, crocodiles, to the zoo.
2. S1: (1.0) one? one?
3. T: listen listen. *kiite kiite (=listen, listen)*
4. ((shows the singular flash card)) crocodile (.) ((shows the plural card)) crocodiles (.)
5. so:: ((hiding the card in her hands)) please take the crocodiles to the zoo.
6. S2: ((changes the card in his hand to the other card with a quick move))
7. S1: one?
8. S3: three.
9. T: three yes (.) crocodiles.
(TBLT Lesson 5)

To summarize, although both groups needed to process plural *-s* (i.e., by comprehending it in the TBLT and by producing it in the PPP), the nature of this 'need' was fundamentally different. As the primary focus of the PPP lesson was to learn new vocabulary, repair tended to focus more on the production of the target words than on the plural morpheme. In the TBLT lessons, comprehension of the plural form was required for the learners to complete the tasks successfully. Thus, repair in the TBLT was predominantly initiated by the students and focused on the meaning of plural *-s*. It provided the learners with opportunities to establish a form-meaning connection and led to some of them producing a plural noun.

Another explanation for the results on the tests might be that the meaning of plural *-s* was more salient in the TBLT lessons. In PPP, plural *-s* was redundant, as the below example illustrates. The student in Excerpt 7.3 was able to answer the teacher's display question by simply producing the word ('crocodile') without there being any need to use the plural morpheme. Although the teacher often provided corrective feedback by recasting the students' utterances, the learners often failed to uptake, as this example shows.

Excerpt 7.3
1. T: (pointing the picture card with two crocodiles) what are they?
2. S: crocodile.
3. T: crocodiles.
4. S: …
5. T: okay the next.

Task-based work, on the other hand, created situations where the learners needed to choose either a singular or plural picture card by listening to the teacher's directions. As the following example illustrates, this made the plural morpheme functionally salient. Lines 4 and 6 indicate Students 2 and 3 were not able to comprehend the teacher's directions correctly. The students' questions (lines 4, 6 and 8) led to the teacher's answer (line 9), which enabled all the students in the class to perform the task successfully (line 10).

Excerpt 7.4
1. T: please take the mandarins, mandarins to the supermarket.
2. S1: mandarin.
3. T: right. mandarins.
4. S2: one?
5. T: no.
6. S3: two?
7. T: two?
8. S2: three?
9. T: three, yes. okay? ready? three, two, one, go.
10. Ss: (show the correct card).
11. T: yes, that's right. put the mandarins into the supermarket.

(TBLT-A, Lesson 3)

Schmidt (1994, 2001) proposed that the noticing of exemplars of specific grammatical features in communicative input and interaction constitutes a key condition for the acquisition of those features. Loewen et al. (2009) argued that the extent to which the instruction encourages noticing of a structure can explain the results of their study, which reported no incidental acquisition of 3rd person *-s*, while other studies did. This might also be the case in the present study. Plural *-s* was made salient and noticed in the TBLT lessons, but not in the PPP lessons.

The same explanation can account for the contrasting results of the present study and the Izumi and Bigelow (2000) and Izumi, Bigelow, Fujiwara, and Fearnow (1999) studies. These studies indicated that production-based instruction was more effective in promoting the incidental acquisition of relative clauses than comprehension-based activities. The comprehension group received enhanced input consisting of a reading text with the target structure (relative clauses) highlighted, whereas the production group was required to produce the target structure in a text reconstruction task. Izumi et al. (1999) argued that the output led the learners to undertake a cognitive comparison between the target language form and their interlanguage (IL) form, resulting in the modification of the IL form. In the present study, however, cognitive comparison was more likely to occur in the TBLT, which was input-based, rather than the PPP (production-based) group. There is another difference between the present study and Izumi et al. (1999), who investigated adult ESL learners with relatively high levels of proficiency. Perhaps for beginner learners, such as those in the present study, form-function mapping is best achieved via TBLT; on this kind of measure, PPP may be more effective for more advanced learners.

Another question that arises here is why the TBLT group showed improvement only with regard to their receptive knowledge. The reason probably lies in the fact that production is more difficult than comprehension because, as Paradis (2004) noted, "in comprehension, excitatory impulses are triggered by the environment, whereas in production they must come from within" (p. 118). Similarly, VanPatten (1996) claimed that learners' ability to comprehend form-meaning mappings precedes their ability to demonstrate the same mappings in production (see also Chapter 3). There might not have been sufficient time spent on the tasks for the comprehension knowledge of the plural *-s* to become available for production.

It should be noted, however, that there may be a problem with the construct validity of the two production tests. In the comprehension test, the participants needed to process the plural form in order to achieve the task goal (i.e., identifying the correct picture matching the oral form) whereas in the two production tests, the participants did not need to produce the plural form of the word to satisfy the requirements of either the discrete-item production test (i.e., to produce the word representing the picture) or the Same-or-Different Task (i.e., to identify if the pictures on their sheet were the same as those on the teacher's sheet). The following examples illustrate how the students could complete the task successfully without having to produce the nouns (from TBLT group; Post-test 1):

Excerpt 7.5
1. T: okay, number 2, what do you have?
2. S: ....
3. T: I have two crocodiles.
4. S: (nodding).
5. T: do you have two crocodiles? Two?
6. S: yes.
7. T: okay, then the same.
8. S: (ticking the 'crocodiles' picture).

Excerpt 7.6
1. T: number 19, what do you have?
2. S: (looking at the picture of three persimmons in the student sheet), persimmon.
3. T: persimmon? one persimmon? I have three persimmons.
4. S: three.
5. T: three? the same.
6. S: (ticking the 'persimmons' picture).

In Excerpt 7.5, the learner failed to produce the target word ('crocodiles'), but with the researcher's support (lines 3, 5, and 7) he successfully completed the task (line 8). In Excerpt 7.6, to describe the picture, the student produced the unmarked form of 'persimmon' (line 2), which led the researcher to seek clarification (line 3). However, the student answered with the numerical marker (line 4) without producing the plural form. The researcher's response (line 5) enabled the learner to perform the task successfully (line 6). This student was able to detect if the pictures were the same or different for all 13 plural items on his sheet; for eight of them she produced only the unmarked form of the nouns, and for five of them she did not produce the noun at all.

Table 7.5 shows the TBLT and PPP learners' task achievement scores and mean plural *-s* scores for the Wug test and the Same-or-Different Task on post-test 1.

Table 7.5. Task achievement and mean plural *-s* scores for plural *-s* in the two production tests (post-test 1)

		PPP group		TBLT group	
Tests	Task goal	Task achievement	Mean scores	Task achievement	Mean scores
Wug test	Naming the pictures	100.0	.0	93.3	12.7
Same-or-Different Task	Finding if the picture is the same or not	96.4	1.3	97.9	6.8

In both tests, the learners were able to achieve the task goals without producing the plural form correctly. Previous studies (e.g., Corder, 1981; Wee, 2009) indicate that linguistic features are often omitted when their meaning is redundant and there is no functional need to produce them. This might be another reason why the TBLT learners failed to demonstrate improvement in the production tests. In Loschky and Bley-Vroman's (1993) terms, the tests made the use of plural *-s* "natural" but not "essential" and so it was easily avoided.

Results for copula *be*

Data analysis

The acquisition of copula *be* was measured by two production tests: one task-based test (the Tell-and-Do Task) and one discrete-point test (the Picture Description test) (see Chapter 4 for details). For both tests, two scores were calculated – one based on whether any form of *be* was produced in an obligatory context and the other separately in terms of whether there was subject-verb agreement. The learners' individual scores were further classified as 'acquired' or 'not acquired', using the 80% threshold for both production and agreement measures, and then compared. Figure 7.3 summarizes the scoring methods. The detailed statistical test results are reported in Appendix C.

Tests	Classifications for analysis	Scoring	Further analysis
Tell-and-Do Task	1. suppliance of '*be*' 2. correct use of '*be*'	Raw scores	Number of 'acquired' students (80%)
Picture Description		Raw scores	

Figure 7.3. Scoring and data analysis for the tests

Test results

Table 7.6 shows the descriptive statistics for the two tests. The maximum score possible for both tests is 10. The participants failed to score positively in any of the tests with the exception of one student in the TBLT group. This student's production score was 10 but he obtained only 5 for subject-verb agreement as he overused '*is*'.

Only one student, in the TBLT group, demonstrated some preliminary signs of acquisition of copula *be*; the student produced the contracted copula *-'s* for all 10 testing items, which included five singular and five plural items; however, he did not fully acquire subject-verb agreement. There were no significant differences between the TBLT and PPP groups for the two post-tests.

Table 7.6. Descriptive statistics for the copula *be* tests

	Group	Pre-test		Post-test 1		Post-test 2	
		Mean	SD	Mean	SD	Mean	SD
Tell-and-Do Task							
Production of the copula *be*	PPP ($n = 15$)	0.00	0.00	0.00	0.00	0.00	0.00
	TBLT ($n = 15$)	0.00	0.00	1.00	3.87	1.00	3.87
	Control ($n = 15$)	0.00	0.00	0.00	0.00	0.00	0.00
Subject-verb agreement	PPP ($n = 15$)	0.00	0.00	0.00	0.00	0.00	0.00
	TBLT ($n = 15$)	0.00	0.00	0.33	1.29	0.33	1.29
	Control ($n = 15$)	0.00	0.00	0.00	0.00	0.00	0.00
Picture Description Test							
Production of copula *be*	PPP ($n = 15$)	0.00	0.00	0.00	0.00	0.00	0.00
	TBLT ($n = 15$)	0.00	0.00	1.00	3.87	1.00	3.87
	Control ($n = 15$)	0.00	0.00	0.00	0.00	0.00	0.00
Subject-verb agreement	PPP ($n = 15$)	0.00	0.00	0.00	0.00	0.00	0.00
	TBLT ($n = 15$)	0.00	0.00	0.33	1.29	0.33	1.29
	Control ($n = 15$)	0.00	0.00	0.00	0.00	0.00	0.00

Discussion

The results showed no significant improvement in any of the groups or any differences between the three groups. Only one student in the TBLT group managed to produce '*is*', using it for both plural and singular items, on the production post-tests.

The question that arises, then, is why the TBLT group showed incidental acquisition of the plural *-s* but not of copula *be*. One explanation might lie in the opportunities for learners to be exposed to each form. As illustrated in Table 7.6, copula *be* occurred in various forms in both lessons which might have made learning difficult for learners.

Table 7.7. The number of the copula *be* produced by the teacher

	is	Are	-'s	-'re	Total
PPP	982	561	92	21	1,656
TBLT	605	236	375	18	1,234

A more convincing explanation might be that neither the TBLT nor the PPP lessons made copula *be* salient for learners. The process analysis in Chapter 5 suggested that in the TBLT lessons learners focused their attention on the key content words in the teacher's instructions (e.g., "Take the crocodiles to the zoo") or on her elaborated explanations (e.g., "The crocodiles are big and green"). These were important for task completion, as shown by the fact that the learners frequently repeated these key words. The copula *be* was also redundant in the PPP lessons, in which the main focus for both the teacher and the students was the accurate form of the target words.

Another possible explanation might lie in the intrinsic difficulty of the two features involved. Copula *be* is semantically redundant while the plural *-s* is semantically significant. It is widely recognized (George, 1972; VanPatten 1989) that in the early stages of language acquisition learners have difficulties attending to forms which do not contribute to the meaning of the input (i.e., which are redundant).

The results could also be explained by the types of tests used in this part of analysis. The learners' knowledge of the copula *be* was measured only by production tests. A comprehension test was not possible due to the semantic redundancy of the target structure. A grammaticality judgment was not deemed suitable for the very young learners in this study. The two production tests for the copula *be* raise the same validity issue as the production tests for plural *-s*. The participants did not need to produce copula *be* to meet the test requirements for the Picture Description Test or for the Tell-and-Do Task. The following example shows a typical performance where a learner successfully achieved the task goal without producing copula *be* in the Tell-and-Do Task:

Excerpt 7.7
1. S: Crocodile.
2. T: Crocodile? Okay.
3. S: Green.
4. T: Green, okay (colouring the crocodile picture with green).

Table 7.8 shows the learners' task/test achievement scores and the mean test scores for production of the copula *be*. The maximum score possible was 10 for each test. For the Tell-and-Do Task, the learner obtained one point when the teacher coloured the picture correctly following the learner's oral instructions. For the Picture Description test, a learner was awarded a point if she or he described the picture in English irrespective of grammatical accuracy (e.g., by saying "Crocodile green" instead of "The crocodile is

Table 7.8. Learners' task achievement and test scores for the tests for the copula *be*

		PPP group		TBLT group	
Tests	Task goal	Task achievement	Mean scores	Task achievement	Mean scores
Tell and do task	Directing the teacher to colour the picture	47.3	.0	52.7	6.7
Picture Description test	Describing the pictures	94.0	.0	90.7	6.7

green"). The table indicates that the learners were able to achieve the task goals without producing the target features on the test. This might be one reason why no one showed any acquisition of the copula *be*.

Conclusion

In this chapter I reported the results of the study investigating whether any incidental acquisition of plural *-s* and copula *be* took place in the two teaching contexts. The results showed that incidental acquisition did take place, but only in the TBLT group, and the acquisition was only evident in the comprehension test. Three possible factors have been proposed to explain the results. The first factor is the intrinsic difficulty of the target features. Plural *-s* is semantically salient while copula *be* (like 3rd person *-s*) is semantically redundant. The second factor is the type of instruction. The TBLT lessons created the need for the learners to distinguish the plural and singular forms, who therefore had opportunities to establish form-meaning connections for plural *-s*. This did not occur in the PPP lessons, and might explain why only the TBLT learners showed any acquisition of this feature. However, most of the learners in the TBLT group only developed receptive knowledge of plural *-s*. Repair and uptake indicated learners' engagement in learning the language that they were exposed to in the two teaching approaches. As the analysis of the classroom interactions showed, repair in the TBLT lessons only occurred when the learners had problems comprehending the input. Although the TBLT learners occasionally repeated (incorrectly) the teacher's plural nouns, none of them received any corrective feedback. This might be why most of the TBLT group failed to develop knowledge of plural *-s*. The third factor is the extent to which the two types of instruction made the target feature salient. The plural form was more salient in the TBLT interactions than in the PPP interactions, possibly explaining the differences in the results of this study and those of Izumi et al. (1999).

The issue of test validity was also a concern. Specifically, the production tests for both of the grammatical features did not require the learners to produce the target features to achieve the task goals, which is perhaps why so few students produced them. Finally, this study provides further evidence of individual differences in second language acquisition. Only one student managed to produce copula *be*, i.e., one of the three students who demonstrated production ability for the plural form. Further research is needed on this issue, as no data for individual differences factors were obtained in this study.

In the next chapter, I will re-examine the theoretical issues raised in Chapter 3 by drawing on the findings of the current study reported in Chapters 5, 6, and 7).

CHAPTER 8

Theoretical implications of the study

This chapter focuses on how the findings of the study reported in previous chapters inform the theoretical issues addressed in Chapter 3. One of fundamental theoretical differences between PPP and TBLT is that the former aims at intentional L2 learning while the latter aims at incidental L2 learning. However, as with any kind of instruction, incidental learning of features apart from the target of the instruction can occur in both types. The study compared the two types of instruction by examining (1) intentional learning in PPP and incidental learning in TBLT, and (2) incidental learning in both PPP and TBLT. Both vocabulary and grammar acquisition were investigated. I also examined the process features of the instruction, reported in Chapter 5.

I would now like to consider in what ways the study has contributed to our theoretical understandings of the learning that takes place within distinct instructional approaches, as well as the possible methodological implications of this study for other method comparisons, and to make associated suggestions for future research. In the following chapter I will examine the pedagogical implications of the findings of my study.

Incidental and intentional vocabulary learning

The main goal of this study was to examine the relative effects of intentional learning (in PPP) and incidental learning (in TBLT) on the learning of new vocabulary items. Both types of instruction targeted 24 nouns and 12 adjectives. Four task-based and discrete point tests (i.e., the Same-or-Different Task, the discrete-item production test, the Category Task, and the multiple-choice listening test) measured both receptive and productive knowledge of 36 target words. The test results differed for nouns and adjectives. For nouns, both PPP and TBLT were effective in enabling the learners to acquire both receptive and productive knowledge; the two groups did not differ in the acquisition of the target nouns with the exception of the Category Task, where the TBLT group achieved significantly higher scores than the PPP group. As far as adjectives are concerned, TBLT instruction was clearly superior to PPP instruction in terms of both controlled and free production.

The findings of the current study differ from previous studies which have typically compared the incidental learning that occurs through reading with the intentional learning that occurs through production practice (e.g., Hulstijn & Laufer, 2001;

Laufer, 2006). The PPP approach in this study invited a similar intentional learning process to that in previous studies; that is, there was a presentation stage to establish form-meaning connections followed by production practice that required the learners to use the target words. However, the incidental learning through TBLT in this study differed from incidental learning through reading in four ways: (1) the tasks made the comprehension of the target words necessary in order to complete the tasks successfully; (2) the tasks provided feedback on the learners' comprehension; (3) the tasks encouraged negotiation of meaning; and (4) the tasks allowed learners to produce the target adjectives while negotiating for meaning.

Negotiation of meaning and form

An important finding of this part of the study was that the input-based tasks, which did not require the production of the target words, actually led to learner-generated negotiation of meaning. Specifically, this negotiation of meaning occurred when the students voluntarily initiated questions to obtain information about the target nouns from the teacher. Negotiation occurred frequently despite the learners' limited L2 ability (6-year-old beginners). In this respect, the results differed from those of Ellis and Heinbach (1997), who suggested that five-to-six year old children may experience difficulty in negotiating for meaning because of their age. However, a major difference between this study and that of Ellis and Heinbach is the factor of task-repetition. As reported in Shintani (2012), the frequency of the TBLT students' negotiation of meaning increased as the tasks were repeated. In the present study, the learners mostly used adjectives to negotiate, which may explain why the TBLT learners outperformed the PPP learners in the acquisition of adjectives.

Negotiation in the PPP lessons also occurred, but in a very different way. Specifically, it mostly involved 'negotiation of form' (Ellis, 2001, p. 1), whereby the teacher drew attention to form despite the lack of any communication problem; this mostly occurred in IRF exchanges when the teacher recast a learner's utterance following a failure to produce a target word. The results reported in Chapters 6 and 7 showed that such recasting increased the frequency of the target words (nouns and adjectives) and grammatical features (plural *-s*) in the input. However, although this may have contributed to the learning of the target vocabulary, it clearly had no effect on the incidental acquisition of plural *-s*. I argued that negotiation of form was not helpful for acquisition of this particular grammatical feature because the learners were focused on accurate production of the target word and thus failed to pay attention to the corrections involving plural *-s*.

Input-based instruction versus production-based instruction

The current study also demonstrated that, in the case of the young beginner learners, input-based instruction is more effective for vocabulary learning than output-based instruction, specifically of the kind found in PPP. In Chapter 6, I examined the characteristics of L2 input and output occurring in TBLT and PPP lessons and showed that it was the quality, rather than the quantity, of input/output which differed among the two teaching contexts. The TBLT and the PPP groups were exposed to similar amounts of input, but the PPP group had greater opportunities for output than the TBLT group. However, interaction that occurred in the TBLT lesson was very different from that in the PPP lessons. TBLT provided meaningful input because the words were contextualized in the teacher's utterances, which were often modified to make them comprehensible to the learners. In other words, the TBLT instruction afforded input and interaction that made it possible for learners to infer the meanings of the words. The PPP lessons were characterized by a high frequency of restricted IRF exchanges, whereas the TBLT lessons almost invariably led to negotiation of meaning exchanges, some of which were quite lengthy. Self-initiated learner production also occurred predominantly in the TBLT group. Their production was entirely optional and involved the learners using their own linguistic resources, including the target adjectives. In contrast, the PPP learners' production occurred in response to a teacher elicitation or in the form of repetition of the teacher's utterances. When the TBLT learners initiated use of the target items, they had a functional reason for doing so, and for this reason the mapping of form onto meaning may have become more deeply embedded in their memories than what occurred when the PPP learners produced the words for no functional purpose other than that of fulfilling the discourse role required of them. To sum up, three aspects made the quality of the input and output in the TBLT sessions richer, as was evident from the careful analysis of the transcripts in Chapter 5: (1) meaningful input, (2) negotiation of meaning, and (3) self-initiated production.

Pushed output

While learner production occurred in both the PPP and the TBLT lessons, the quality of the output was different. For instance, while production in the PPP lessons was mostly requested by the teacher, production in the TBLT lessons was embedded in the tasks, which made production necessary for their successful completion. The difference in effectiveness can be explained by examining how the output functioned in each lesson. There are generally four ways in which output is thought to contribute to L2 learning (Swain, 1995; de Bot, 1996): (1) consciousness-raising through 'noticing-the-gap'; (2) hypothesis testing; (3) conscious reflection about L2 forms via 'languaging'; and (4) increasing control over partially acquired linguistic forms and thus enhancing fluency. The output in both the PPP and TBLT lessons might have served the first function. The second function (hypothesis testing) took place differently in the two types of instruction. In the PPP lessons, it occurred through the modified output that learners produced following negative feedback from the teacher. In the TBLT lessons, it took place when the learners initiated questions to negotiate meaning when they could not understand a command. The third function was not evident in either group as the lessons did not require the students to consciously reflect on their utterances. The fourth function was not investigated in the study as the learners were complete beginners and had very limited production ability even by the end of the study. There are two conclusions which can be drawn from the role played by output in the lessons: (1) noticing-the-gap in output is more beneficial for learning when learners are focused on the message, as in the TBLT class, than when they are focused on form in a decontextualized manner, as in the PPP class, because it is more likely to establish a form-meaning mapping; and (2) hypothesis testing is better initiated by the learners than by the teacher as it is more likely to reflect the learner's personal linguistic needs.

Task induced involvement load

As discussed in Chapter 5, the learners in the PPP and the TBLT lessons in the current study manifested different levels of involvement (Laufer & Hulstijn, 2001). Task involvement load (Laufer & Hulstijn, 2001) claims that vocabulary learning can be determined by the levels of involvement according to 'need' (i.e., whether the vocabulary-learning activity requires the target items to complete the task), 'search' (i.e., whether the learner has to search for the relevant lexical form to express or comprehend the meaning), and 'evaluation' (i.e., whether the learner has to evaluate the appropriateness of the word choice) (Laufer & Hulstijn, 2001). The evidence presented in Chapter 5 showed that in the TBLT lessons, processing the adjectives required a greater involvement load than the nouns (see Table 8.1). This may explain why learners in this group acquired more adjectives than those in the PPP group.

Table 8.1. Involvement load of the instruction in studies of incidental vocabulary acquisition

	PPP	TBLT	
	Nouns and adjectives	**Nouns**	**Adjectives**
Need	+	+	+
Search	–	+	+
Evaluation	+	+	++

– absence of an involvement factor
\+ moderate presence of an involvement factor
++ strong presence of an involvement factor

In L2 production, 'search' and 'evaluation' might correspond to two different functions of output: 'noticing' and 'hypothesis testing' (Swain, 1995). In L2 input, 'search' and 'evaluation' constitute different levels of 'noticing' (see Robinson, 1995). In line with Craik and Lockhart's (1972) depth of processing model, a number of researchers have suggested that deeper cognitive processing is facilitative of vocabulary acquisition (Joe, 1998; Stahl & Fairbanks, 1986). The current study suggests that depth of processing might ultimately be of greater importance than whether the instruction is input-based or output-based, or whether the instruction invites intentional or incidental learning.

Skill-specificity

There is some evidence to support the notion of skill-specificity (Anderson, 1993; see Chapter 3). The noun scores for both PPP and TBLT resulted in similar gains in test scores for the skill that the instruction did not involve (i.e., comprehension or production), as well as on the tests for the skill that was addressed through the instruction, suggesting that the effects of the two types of instruction were not skill-specific. However, the PPP group demonstrated higher mean scores than the TBLT group in the production tests but inferior scores in the receptive tests. In addition, the TBLT learners demonstrated a higher level of acquisition than the PPP learners in the category test (i.e., a task-based comprehension test), possibly because the processing required by this test closely matched the processing required by the TBLT instruction. These results point to the skill-specificity of the two types of instruction. Perhaps with larger sample sizes and by controlling other factors such as the need for form-meaning mapping, the results of the other tests would have provided further evidence of skill-specificity in the effects of input and output instruction.

Summary

In this section I have discussed the theoretical implications of the findings of the study related to primary aim of the study. The main conclusions I reached were:

1. Input-based tasks can lead to learner-generated negotiation of meaning while PPP tends to involve negotiation of form.
2. For young, beginner learners, input-based task might be more effective for vocabulary learning than PPP.
3. Noticing-the-gap in output is more beneficial when learners are focused on the message (as in the TBLT lessons) than when they are focused on form in a decontextualized manner (as in the PPP lessons).
4. Where vocabulary is concerned, depth of processing might be of greater importance than whether the instruction is input-based or output-based, or whether the instruction invites intentional or incidental learning.
5. Comprehension and production-based instruction are to some extent skill-specific but both can contribute to development of alternative skills.

Incidental grammar acquisition

The secondary aim of the study was to examine the relative effectiveness of the two types of instruction on the incidental acquisition of two grammatical features: plural *-s* and copula *be*. Incidental learning was operationalized as exposure to the grammatical features while the instruction focused on teaching new vocabulary items. Acquisition was measured by three tests for plural *-s* (the multiple-choice plural *-s* listening test, the Wug Test and the Same-or-Different Task test) and two tests for copula *be* (the Tell-and-Do Task test and the picture description test). The results showed that incidental acquisition did take place, but only in the TBLT group and in the main only for receptive knowledge of plural *-s*. A few participants in the TBLT group demonstrated productive knowledge of plural *-s*, but none demonstrated knowledge of subject-verb agreement for the copula. There was no evidence of any incidental acquisition whatsoever by the PPP group.

Hence the study showed that incidental grammar acquisition can take place in the classroom, but only when the learners need to process the meaning of a grammatical structure in order to complete the tasks. Three possible factors have been proposed to explain the results. The first factor is the intrinsic nature of the target features. The copula *be* (like 3rd person *-s*) is functionally redundant in most contexts; this might explain why neither the current study (for copula *be*) nor Loewen et al. (2009) (for 3rd person *-s*) found any evidence of incidental acquisition of these features. Plural *-s*, on the other hand, is semantically salient unless there is some other marker of plurality present. However, this feature has been shown to be problematic for Japanese learners (e.g., Hakuta, 1978), which might explain why only a few participants in the TBLT group acquired productive knowledge of plural *-s*. Nevertheless, it is clear that the TBLT instruction was more effective than PPP in facilitating the process of acquiring plural *-s* incidentally.

The second factor is the extent to which the two types of instruction made the target feature salient. In the TBLT class, the plural *-s* form was provided in a way that made it semantically important (i.e., the learners sometimes <u>needed</u> to distinguish the singular form from the plural form in order to complete the tasks), while copula *be* was semantically redundant (i.e., the learners did not need to distinguish the form to complete the tasks). In the PPP class, both features were redundant (i.e., the activity simply required the learners to name the target items). This also provides an explanation for why learners in the TBLT group were more successful in learning plural *-s*.

The third factor concerns the processing demands of the two types of instruction. Forcing learners to produce in the L2 might have overloaded the short-term memory and thus have had a deleterious effect on acquisition (Gary, 1978). Arguably production is much more demanding than comprehension as it can create greater anxiety in learners and requires access to the articulatory mechanisms.

Overall, then, the results suggest that providing a functional need to process a grammatical feature is necessary for incidental grammar acquisition to take place for young, beginner learners. The findings echo those of other studies that have shown the importance of creating a functional need for learners to attend to the meaning of a grammatical form when performing tasks (Izumi, 2003; Gass & Torres, 2005). The nature of the conversations in the TBLT lesson created such a need. In Loewen et al. (2009), processing 3rd person *-s* was not required in the instruction and no acquisition was evident. An important factor for promoting incidental grammar acquisition, thus, might be whether or not the instruction requires learners to attend to the form-meaning mapping of the target features; this was the case in the TBLT class but not in the PPP class.

To sum up, the evidence indicates that incidental grammar acquisition is possible, but only when the interaction induces learners to make form-meaning mappings. In the research reported above, it occurred only in the TBLT lessons and only for plural *-s*.

Conversational differences of PPP and TBLT

The part of the study reported in Chapter 5 adopted an internal as opposed to an external perspective on instruction. I chose to include this analysis in my research to address one of the major criticisms of comparative method studies, namely that researchers have often failed to examine what transpired during actual instruction (Ellis, 2008). To this end, conversation analysis (CA) was used to examine what transpired when the two types of instruction were implemented. I also examined quantitatively the opportunities for input and output of the target words and grammatical features in the classroom.

The analyses showed that the conversations in the PPP and the TBLT classrooms had contrasting characteristics. The conversations in the PPP classrooms involved frequent IRF exchanges, teacher-initiated display questions, tight teacher control of turn-taking, frequent turns in chorus, and teacher-initiated medium-oriented repair. In contrast, the conversations in the TBLT classrooms often involved overlapping exchanges, student-initiated referential questions, student control of turn-taking, and student-initiated message-oriented repair. Private speech in the TBLT group involved learner repetitions of some parts of the teacher's utterances, which seemed to help learners focus their attention on the task and to solve problems (DiCamilla & Antón, 2004). Private speech in the PPP group occurred mostly in talk not directly related to the instructional activities, as the learners in this group were narrowly focused on producing the target words. These process differences between the two groups lend support to Seedhouse's (2004) claim that there is a reflexive relationship between the pedagogical focus and the characteristics of classroom conversation.

The analyses of the process features showed that the external (i.e., 'method') differences between the two types of instruction were matched by internal (i.e., 'process') differences in the kinds of talk that occurred in each group. The essential difference between TBLT and PPP in terms of the external perspective is that the former aims to teach language through meaningful communication and the latter through the distinct steps of presentation, practice, and production. The internal perspective revealed that, overall, the interactions in the PPP group corresponded to the kind of pedagogic discourse reported in previous studies. The TBLT lessons, on the other hand, resulted in more naturalistic and meaning-focused interactions. Another external difference between the two types of instruction was that the TBLT sessions involved input-based tasks where L2 output was not required, whereas the PPP lessons were primarily output-based. However, the process analysis indicated that when the TBLT approach was implemented, the learners did in fact engage frequently and voluntarily in output. In this case, therefore, there was not a complete match between the external and internal perspectives. What the analyses did show, however, was that the nature of learner output in the two groups was clearly different: in the PPP classroom it was essentially 'pedagogic' while in the TBLT group classroom it was primarily 'conversational'. The results of the analysis demonstrate the importance of examining the processes that actually arise when the effects of different types of instruction are investigated.

Focus on form in TBLT lessons

The process analyses also attest to the importance of 'focus on form' (i.e., occasions where learner's brief attention is drawn to linguistic elements while his or her overt attention is on meaning; Long, 1991) for L2 learning. The analysis of the TBLT interactions demonstrated that a focus on form did take place in the case of the nouns, adjectives, and plural *-s*, but not in the case of copula *be*. Focus on form for the nouns occurred when the learners requested clarification of the meaning of the nouns used in the teacher's commands. By doing so, the learners had the opportunity for form-meaning mapping of the target nouns. Although the adjectives were not the focus of the tasks (i.e., they only arose incidentally in the teacher's utterances as she worked to make her commands comprehensible), there were some occasions where the students used them in negotiating meaning. As shown in Excerpt 5.6 in Chapter 5, students sometimes requested clarification of the meaning of the adjectives (e.g., "Brown?"), which led to the teacher demonstrating the meaning of the word (e.g., the teacher pointing to a brown object and saying "Brown"). There were frequent opportunities for 'noticing-the-gap' (Swain, 1995) of the adjectives in the TBLT class, and students eagerly produced the adjectives when negotiating. Noticing-the-gap was evident in several excerpts presented in Chapter 5, where learners produced adjectives incorrectly (e.g., "*bato*?" in Excerpt 5.18) or used their L1 (e.g., "*Chairo*?" in Excerpt 5.20), but then, with the help of the teacher, eventually self-repaired the form and produced it correctly. The fact that the TBLT group showed consistent superiority in learning adjectives (Chapter 6) supports Loewen's (2005) finding that producing a linguistic form can enhance learning. There was also evidence to show that focus on form took place for plural *-s*, though not for copula *be*. Focus on form with plural *-s* occurred when the learners needed to distinguish the singular form and plural form of a noun in the teacher's command and when they needed to clarify the form (see Excerpt 7.2 in Chapter 7).

To sum up, focus on form was evident for the nouns, plural *-s*, and adjectives (which showed the greatest opportunities for focus on form) but not for copula *be*. Thus, the results support the claim that focus on form is not only facilitative of, but also necessary for L2 learning.

Research methodology

The study reported in this book points to three main methodological implications for research investigating instructed second language acquisition: (1) the conduct of comparative method studies, (2) the importance of investigating the processes as well as the products of instruction, and (3) the need to guard against test bias.

First, the current study showed that a comparative-method study can avoid the pitfalls typically associated with such research when it is carefully designed. Comparative method research is traditionally 'global' (Ellis, 2012); that is, it examines methods or approaches for teaching an L2 over a long period of time and assesses learning outcomes in terms of general language proficiency or achievement. The current study, however, took a 'local' approach: it investigated two types of instruction (TBLT and PPP) over a relatively short period of time and assessed learning outcomes in terms of the acquisition of specific linguistic features. The methodological problems common in global method comparisons were also avoided by assuring the homogeneity of the two groups of learners and by having the same teacher teach both groups. The current study showed that 'local' method comparative studies can be a useful way of both investigating pedagogical issues and testing SLA theories. I acknowledge, however, that the instructional context I investigated was highly controlled in comparison to other instructional contexts in Japan. Thus, the trade-off for a local approach might be that it is not as ecologically valid, or perhaps generalizable, as a large-scare evaluation of a full-on programme or courses in a naturally existing educational setting.

Second, the current research was a process-product study. By analyzing both the process features (i.e., the characteristics of conversation and nature of the input and output) and the products of the instruction (i.e., learning as measured by tests), the study was able to establish that the two types of instruction were different not just in terms of their external descriptions, but also internally in terms of the interactions that transpired when the instruction was implemented. One criticism of process-product research is that the classroom processes are often analyzed using predetermined coding categories (Gage & Needels, 1989). The current study, however, used conversation analysis to examine the process features in the two classrooms and thus avoided such problems and added to Seedhouse's (2004) analysis of the kinds of interactions found in different instructional contexts. I was able to illustrate how the interactions between the teacher and the students differed in the two types of instruction and affirm the value of using CA to investigate classroom instruction.[1]

Third, the current study demonstrated the importance of using multiple measurements to avoid test bias. Nine tests were used to measure both receptive and productive knowledge of the target words and the two grammatical structures. These included both discrete-point and task-based tests. In this way, I counter-balanced the tests, each of which could be considered biased towards a particular type of instruction, and also investigated whether the instruction resulted in a type of L2 knowledge that is deployable not just in traditional tests but also in communicative language use. As already noted, the results obtained from the tests did reflect the types of instruction to some extent (i.e., the TBLT group did better in the reception tests than the production tests and vice-versa for the PPP group). There was also some evidence that task-based instruction led to better performance in a task-based test – see, for example, the results for the Category Task test, which required the learners to comprehend and understand target nouns in sentences. As Norris and Ortega (2000) and Ellis (2009) have pointed out, instructed SLA research has tended to measure acquisition using relatively decontextualized tests. The current study suggests the importance of including task-based tests when investigating task effects.

Future research

In the current study, the two types of instruction combined two variables – PPP versus TBLT and input-based versus production-based instruction. From a theoretical point of view, it is important to avoid this possible confound by comparing (1) incidental input-based instruction with production-based instruction, and (2) intentional input-based versus production-based instruction, though this was not possible in this study

1. I did not strictly adhere to CA conventions in my study but only to the extent that they enabled me to compare the process features of two types of classrooms – my main purpose. In this respect, my use of CA resembled that of Seedhouse (2004), who had a similar purpose (i.e., distinguishing the interactional features of different instructional contexts).

of beginner-level learners. As I pointed out in Chapter 1, if TBLT is to be feasible for such learners, it probably has to be input-based. Thus, comparing input-based TBLT with production-based PPP had high ecological validity in the context investigated. Arguably, too, investigating classroom processes as well as learning outcomes, and using multiple tests to measure learning outcomes went some way towards mitigating the problem of the confound.

The study raises a number of issues for future investigation related to incidental grammar acquisition. Firstly, it would be desirable to investigate the effects of PPP and TBLT over a longer period of time and embedded within authentic instructional settings. Secondly, more research investigating other linguistic features is needed to understand how the intrinsic difficulty of these features impacts incidental acquisition. Finally, the mediating influence of individual learner factors (such as language aptitude and working memory) on the effects of both PPP and TBLT on L2 acquisition warrants further investigation. It is clear that there was considerable individual variation in how the learners responded to the instruction and what they acquired in both groups (see Shintani & Ellis, 2014, for further evidence of this). However, I was not able to comment on the role played by individual learner factors as I did not attempt to measure them.

As far as generalizability is concerned, I must stress that my study only investigated young beginner learners. It is possible that other types of learners (i.e., older learners or more proficient learners) might have reacted to the two types of instruction differently and produced different results. There is thus a need for studies to be conducted with older learners who are cognitively mature and therefore who might be better equipped to benefit from PPP.

There is also the important question of how teachers and learners subjectively experience TBLT. The focus of my study was on the learning that took place and the classroom processes that arose in my implementation of TBLT. But there are other important issues that I did not address. What difficulties do teachers experience in implementing TBLT? To what extent are students able to orientate to treating language as tool for communicating rather than as an object for study? Do teachers and students recognize the importance of incidental acquisition? There is a need, therefore, for ethno-methodological studies that explore teachers' and students' perspectives and attitudes to TBLT and how these impact on what happens in the classroom and what is learned.

There is also a need to examine how the teacher's and the students' cultural orientation might affect their subjective experience of TBLT and the problems that can arise when TBLT constitutes a major innovation in a particular instructional context. In the next chapter, where I turn to consider the pedagogical implications of my study, I address the difficulties that I foresee in introducing TBLT into elementary schools in Japan.

CHAPTER 9

Pedagogical implications of the study

In Chapter 2, I examined a number of pedagogical issues relating to the implementation of task-based language teaching in English classrooms in Japan. I argued that many of the problems concerning the introduction of TBLT in junior- and senior-high schools do not apply to elementary schools as there is no fixed syllabus that has to be followed at this level. That is, teachers in elementary schools have more freedom in their English teaching than those in the junior- and senior-high schools. I also pointed out, however, that there are a number of difficulties that teachers face with TBLT in elementary schools in Japan, such as the learners' and the teachers' (likely) low level of proficiency in English and the teachers' lack of familiarity with the principles and methodology of TBLT. In this chapter I will re-consider the issues discussed in Chapter 2 in the light of the findings of my research. In doing so, I will argue that implementing TBLT in elementary schools is possible. I will also make some suggestions for how teachers can implement input-based tasks successfully with young, beginner learners. I will conclude this chapter with some possibilities for how input-based tasks can be developed to cater for older, more proficient learners.

Input-based tasks for young, beginner learners

One criticism of TBLT is that it is neither feasible nor appropriate for learners with limited L2 proficiency. Both Swan (2005) and Carless (2007) have claimed this, arguing that PPP is needed for such learners. However, the study reported in this book showed that TBLT can be successfully implemented in an L2 classroom with young, beginner learners by means of input-based tasks and also that, in some respects, it is more effective than PPP. The 6 year-old children with zero competence in English demonstrated successful incidental acquisition of the 32 vocabulary items and also receptive knowledge of the plural *-s* after engaging in the nine lessons. The analysis of the process features of the lessons indicated that the learners were actively engaged in the input-based tasks and, although not required to do so, often produced in the L2 when negotiating for meaning. In short, young children with no experience of L2 learning were able to initiate conversations using their limited L2 resources (and their L1 when necessary) and to conduct 'self-initiated' repair when the input-based task required them to do so. This supports Ortega's (2012) suggestion that input-tasks are an effective way of supporting learners with limited proficiency.

In the following sections, I will discuss a number of important methodological points relating to task design and implementation that arose while conducting my study and which would be useful for teachers of beginners to consider. In doing so, I will address the common but mistaken belief that TBLT is not well-suited for teaching complete beginners.

Designing input-based tasks for young, beginner learners

Use of focused tasks

Tasks can be used to implement a linguistic syllabus by employing focused tasks (i.e., tasks that target pre-planned language items) in the last phase of PPP – what Ellis (2003) called task-supported language teaching. However, as I argued in Chapter 2, using tasks in conjunction with a linguistic syllabus is problematic for three reasons: (1) learners might treat the task as simply a means of practising the target form and thus continue to focus primarily on form rather than meaning; (2) a linguistic syllabus is problematic because it may not match the learners' built-in syllabus (Rutherford, 1988); and (3) it is at times difficult to design focused tasks that target certain grammatical features.

The study I have reported, in particular, substantiates the first claim; the analysis of the interactions resulting from the task used in the production stage of the PPP lessons revealed that both the teacher and the students continued to treat the vocabulary items as objects to be learned. This contrasted with the interactions observed in the TBLT lessons, where the students treated English as a tool for achieving the task outcome. In PPP, it is difficult to make the shift from a primary focus on form to a primary focus on meaning. Thus, I suggest a task-based syllabus is a more satisfactory basis for teaching English in elementary schools in Japan.

However, although teachers do not have to follow a linguistic syllabus in the elementary school, it may still be difficult for them to adopt a task-based syllabus because neither the teachers nor the students are familiar with a task-based approach. Also, currently there are no course books that follow a task-based syllabus. Perhaps then, a more realistic approach is to adopt a task-based approach that adheres to a loose linguistic syllabus where some specific linguistic features (in particular vocabulary) are targeted – as, in fact, do many of the course books for elementary schools authorized by the Ministry of Education Culture Sport Science and Technology (MEXT, 2012). It would be possible to supplement these course books by developing focused tasks designed to create communicative contexts for the use of the linguistic features that figure in each unit of the books. However, for this to work and to avoid the problem of using tasks in task-supported language teaching referred to above, it is crucial to ensure that the task is the central to the lesson.

Choice of linguistic targets in focused tasks

Nouns were chosen as the target items in the tasks used in the study reported in this book. Research has shown that to a large extent the acquisition of nouns precedes that of adjectives or verbs for both L1 and L2 learning by young learners (Ellis, 1994; Yoshida, 1978). The TBLT students succeeded in learning the nouns. In addition, the current study showed that these learners also picked up other linguistic features in the interaction (e.g., the adjectives that appeared in the teacher's utterances) when understanding the meanings of these features was necessary to achieve the task outcome. However, I have reported elsewhere that, not surprisingly, the individual students varied in their ability to 'pick-up' language that arose incidentally as the tasks were performed. Shintani and Ellis (2014) showed that the TBLT students all acquired receptive knowledge of two adjectives (i.e., 'big' and 'small') but differed in whether they acquired productive knowledge. Some of the learners were able to produce these adjectives at an early stage while others relied on their L1 or gestures throughout the nine lessons.

The input-based tasks in this study created learning contexts for both the targeted features (i.e., the nouns) and also for non-targeted features (i.e., the adjectives and one of the grammatical features, plural *-s*). However, they failed to create learning contexts for learning copula *be*. This was because copula *be* is both non-salient in its form and redundant in meaning (see Chapter 7 for the discussion). However, task-based lessons could be devised that would likely foster the acquisition of such redundant features. I would argue that such redundant features can be learned later as they are not important for communicating. What is important is that learners initially develop the ability to use the target language in and for communication. Accuracy in the use of non-salient and redundant features can be attended to later.

Implementing input-based tasks for young, beginner learners

Task repetition with beginners

Task repetition clearly contributed to the success of using the tasks with the young, beginner learners. I have reported elsewhere (Shintani, 2012) how the interactions resulting from the implementation of the tasks differed as they were repeated. I examined five aspects of the nine repeated lessons for the TBLT group: (1) the input provided by the teacher, (2) the learners' voluntary production, (3) the learners' comprehension, (4) language learning, and (5) the learners' motivation to communicate in English. The analyses showed that the learners were able to perform the task more easily over time and their comprehension improved. Those interactions where the students took control in asking questions (negotiating for meaning and form) had a crucial role in the success of the tasks. The learners used the L1 less over time while the range of their 'social speech' in the L2 increased even though the task did not require any production. The students' motivation to engage actively in the tasks remained strong throughout. Their interest in performing the tasks was maintained even though the tasks were repeated nine times. The fact that the students voluntarily used the L2 to communicate with the teacher suggests that the tasks kept them motivated, perhaps because the tasks had a competitive element and also because the children grew in confidence about using the L2 within the tasks over time. In short, the study suggests that repeating a task is an excellent way of building young learners' willingness to communicate in the L2.

The study also showed that although the same 'task' was repeated, the 'activity' that resulted from it was clearly different, as Coughlan and Duff (1994) found in their study of task repetition. Each time one of the input-based tasks was repeated it led to a different 'activity', giving the learners the opportunity to build on their previous performance of the same task and in this way fostered opportunities for learning. However, there are also many aspects that were similar in the activities resulting from the repeated tasks. For example, the tasks always involved the teacher controlling the conversation at the beginning and the end of the sequence while giving students the space to initiate communication by asking questions. Because the students were active participants in the tasks, the 'activity' that occurred was always inherently 'communicative' (i.e., the participants were primarily focused on meaning and oriented towards achieving the non-linguistic outcome of the task).

In Shintani (2012, pp. 50–51) I suggested a number of general principles that can guide teachers when repeating tasks. I reproduce these below.

1. The teacher uses the L1 strategically, especially for task procedures but reduces its use over time as the learners become familiar with the procedures and begin to acquire L2 linguistic resources.
2. The teacher also allows the learners' strategic use of the L1 to achieve the task outcome, but encourages them to reduce it over time.
3. The learners are able to make frequent use of private speech to achieve self-regulation.
4. The learners are allowed to take charge of the way in which in an interaction develops (i.e., take on an initiating role).
5. The learners feel free and are able to negotiate understanding if at first they fail to comprehend the input.
6. The teacher modifies her input over time, gradually using more complex language. This should occur intuitively as a result of the teacher's recognition of the development in the learners' input-processing abilities.

7. The teacher 'pushes' the learners by removing lexical support and thus inducing attention to grammatical markers of meaning.
8. The task has a clear outcome and when implemented the learners are given feedback on whether they have successfully achieved the outcome.

Use of L1 in TBLT with beginners

A common criticism of task-based teaching in school contexts in Japan is that it is difficult to motivate students to communicate in the L2 because they have a shared L1 (Sugita & Takeuchi, 2009). Some argue that students are reluctant to use English in the classroom because of the cultural emphasis on social cohesiveness (Kubota, 1998). Kubota argues that communicating in the L1 helps to maintain classroom harmony which has high cultural value in Japan. In the current study, however, the children in the TBLT group did produce the L2 frequently even though the tasks did not require them to do so. The frequency of their L2 production also increased over the nine lessons (Shintani, 2012). Although the students' utterances consisted mainly of the one-word variety, they were used for distinct communicative purposes (e.g., requesting clarification, confirmation, and assisting peers; see Chapter 5). Clearly, then, the supposed problem of learners' failure to use the L2 did not emerge in the current study. This might have been because the learners were very young – six years old – and thus less concerned about making errors or social conventions. It might also have been because the learners had no experience of formal language classrooms and thus were not oriented to a restrictive focus on using English correctly, as occurred in the PPP lessons. The children were prepared to draw on their limited L2 resources without fear or hesitation.

The L1 (Japanese), however, also played some important roles in the TBLT classroom. In Shintani (2012) I showed that the teacher (myself) frequently used the L1 in the earlier lessons to provide 'meta-talk' when explaining task procedures and supporting the students performing the task. I also used the L1 to provide some 'hints' to help the learners achieve the task outcome or to resolve the students' miscomprehension. Non-linguistic resources such as gestures and objects in the classroom were also frequently used. I did not prohibit the use of the L1 but frequently answered the learners' L1 questions in the L2 (see Excerpt 5.6 in Chapter 5). As the lessons were repeated, L1 use by the teacher and the students reduced but did not disappear. In the later lessons, the students used their L1 when they were unable to solve communicative problems by means of the L2 (e.g., when some procedural issue occurred). The conversations in the nine lessons, thus, showed that both the teacher and the students used both the L1 and the L2 skillfully and collaboratively to achieve the task outcome.

I would argue that in the TBLT lessons classroom harmony (Kubota, 1998) was achieved but in a very different way from the traditional L2 classroom. The students in the TBLT group seemed to gradually accept the classroom 'rule' that they were supposed to use the L2 to communicate while they were working on the tasks, but the use of the L1 was also acceptable if necessary. Clearly, interactions took place between the teacher and the students successfully because both the L1 and the L2 were used effectively. The TBLT lessons in my study lend support to Cook's (2001) claims about the utility of the L1 in the L2 classroom. Teachers should not feel they have to use only the L2 in TBLT lessons.

Marginal production in TBLT

There is another criticism about the quality of the L2 produced by learners in TBLT. Seedhouse (2004) claimed that in a 'task-oriented context' (i.e., where learners are performing a task) there is a tendency towards minimalisation and indexicality in learner language because the learners are focused solely on accomplishing the task. The conversation analysis in Chapter 5 did show that the learners' L2 was often minimal and indexical in nature (e.g., "Blue?" instead of "Is that blue?", "Two?" instead of "Does the card have two items?"). But, of course, that the learners' production was minimal and indexical was expected given that they were complete beginners. However, importantly, it did more than just serve as an effective tool to achieve the task outcome. Crucially, it also enabled the learners to acquire new language. Responding to Seedhouse's criticism, Ellis (2009) argued that minimalisation and indexicality are normal and inevitable in the efforts of beginner learners to communicate, as shown, for example, in work on the pre-basic variety (Klein & Perdue, 1997). Teachers need to recognize that the purpose of tasks is not necessarily the accurate production of the 'ideal' form of the L2 but to provide learners with opportunities to use the L2 as a tool and in the process acquire new language. To achieve this, tasks need to direct the learners' attention to meaning (the task outcome) and to provide opportunities for negotiation of meaning. Teachers need not worry if their students' English is very limited initially. Their ability to speak English will develop gradually over time.

The teacher's role in task-based teaching

As Van den Branden (2009) put it, the teacher is "a crucial interactional partner" (p. 284) in TBLT. I took the roles of "motivator", "organizer", and also "conversational partner" (Van den Branden, 2009) during the lessons. As Samuda (2001) noted, the "central to the role of the teacher in TBLT must be ways of working *with* tasks to guide learners towards the types of language processing believed to support L2 development" (p. 120, emphasis in original). In input-based TBLT, the teacher has overall responsibility for managing the interaction but can hand over temporary control to the learners (whenever this is needed) to achieve the outcome of the task. Perhaps the best metaphor to describe the teacher's role in this kind of teaching is "teacher as navigator." I would now like to describe how I functioned as a navigator in the task-based lessons.

First, I used frequent repetition of the commands to help the learners identify the key words. Second, I encouraged them to guess and, when their guesses were wrong, I responded by providing further clues to help them identify the referent of the nouns. These clues, which often took the form of adjectives that described key attributes of the referents, enriched the input. Third, I allowed the learners to participate in the navigation by requesting clarification using the linguistic resources at their disposal. Fourth, I and the learners used Japanese when they experienced difficulty, but, as time passed, I increasingly used English and encouraged them to do likewise. Fifth, I treated the learners as co-participants in the task by allowing them to take control of the conversation and to assist each other but always in a context where I structured the activity by taking responsibility for opening and closing each sequence. Also, as navigator-in-chief, I always assured that the learners' contributions were directed at achieving the task outcome by providing both positive and negative feedback when needed. Finally, I always made it clear to the learners whether they had been successful in achieving the outcome of a task. My experience in teaching these tasks is that the teacher's role is crucial, not just as a provider of input but as a co-participant who takes responsibility for guiding the learners to the outcome. It was the actions that I took to navigate the tasks that created the contexts for learning to take place.

Swan (2005) claimed that TBLT degrades the role of teachers because it positions them as just managers of students as they perform tasks in small groups. This entirely misrepresents the role of a teacher. As I have described above I found myself engaging in a variety of different roles as I and my students navigated our way through each task.

General issues in English teaching in Japan

I would now like to look at more general issues relating to the introduction of TBLT with young children in a country such as Japan – TBLT in large classrooms, developing the teaching skills needed for TBLT, and teachers' English proficiency.

TBLT in a large classroom

Some might argue that the TBLT in this project was successful because the tasks were conducted in small classrooms (six and nine students in one class), and that it would not be applicable to a larger classroom. Classrooms in elementary schools in Japan typically hold 30 to 40 students taught by one classroom teacher. This has been seen as a hindrance to implementing TBLT in schools (e.g., Hu & McKay, 2012).

I would argue that the kind of tasks used in this study can also be used successfully in large classrooms. The input-based tasks involved a teacher-class participatory structure without relying on group work or pair work. In such tasks, the teacher provides the task commands and the students work individually by identifying the relevant flash cards to demonstrate their comprehension. The task outcome can be evaluated collectively as in the listen-and-do tasks in the current study (i.e., by requesting the students to self-check the outcome with the correct outcome shown by the teacher). As the teacher's commands initiate the interaction, it is easy for the teacher to control the lesson organization.

Input-based tasks can cater to students' different proficiency levels in a large classroom. When production is voluntary and the learners use their own linguistic (or non-linguistic) resources, proficient students might initiate negotiation by using their L2 and less proficient students can also benefit from the negotiation by listening to the interactions between the teacher and their peers. For the same reason, input-based tasks also cater to individual learner differences. For example, learners with higher language anxiety might feel more comfortable if they can simply listen to their peers' negotiation. Production-based tasks should be introduced only after the learners have become able to comfortably negotiate meaning in the L2 when performing input-based tasks, and demonstrate their capability to work in pairs or groups.

Developing teaching skills for TBLT

My personal communications with school teachers in Japan has shown me that many teachers do want to use tasks in their classroom but feel that they do not know how to. The necessary first step is to establish a hands-on resource that provides teachers with the essential information needed to implement tasks. Four aspects should be included: (1) a clear understanding of what a 'task' is, (2) how to design or adapt tasks to ensure they are suitable for their students (task design), (3) how to implement the tasks (task methodology), and (4) how to evaluate whether a task has 'worked'.

Earlier in this chapter I referred to the literature that has examined these aspects (e.g., Ellis, 2003; Baralt et al., 2014), but much of this literature is of a scholarly type, which many teachers will find too difficult to access and interpret for their own practice. Although there have been some attempts by teacher educators in Japan to provide principles and examples of tasks in a book (Matsumura, 2012; Takashima, 2005; Tanaka & Tanaka, 2014), they mostly focus on junior- and senior high-school contexts. There is an urgent need for teacher-friendly guidelines for designing and implementing tasks for elementary school teachers in Japan.

The next step is to provide teachers with opportunities to develop the skills needed to implement tasks. This can be done by providing semester-long task-based training programmes for in-service teachers. Through the experience of designing and implementing the input-based tasks for my own research project, I found that my understanding of how to design and implement tasks improved as I used them in my own classroom. Although I had studied the theories and methodologies of TBLT before conducting this study, it was not easy to move from the traditional approach to TBLT in practice. In the process of preparing and teaching the tasks, I found that a number of small adjustments in their design and implementation were needed to make them suitable for the children. I strongly felt the need for project-based teacher training, where I could work collaboratively with other teachers on the design of the tasks and planning of the task-based lessons.

I would also suggest that such a project-based training course should include work on task evaluation. Ellis (1997) outlined an approach to micro-evaluation, where a teacher systematically examines whether the implemented task matches what it was designed to achieve or, perhaps, achieves unexpected responses that are potentially facilitative of language learning. The evaluation can be done by (1) examining how students respond to the task (e.g., the task outcome and the students' use of language), (2) conducting a student-based evaluation (e.g., administrating a questionnaire), (3) the teacher's own evaluation (e.g., teaching log), and (4) a learning-based evaluation (e.g., assessment of learning using tests). Such micro-evaluations were not included in the current study, but to some extent, it did involve (1) and (4) as I analysed the interactions that took place and also used pre- and post-tests to investigate acquisition. Ideally, teachers should be encouraged to evaluate their own tasks in these ways.

In all three stages (designing, implementing, and evaluating a task) in project-based training, teachers will need feedback and guidance from both an experienced facilitator and their own peers. Carless (2011) pointed out that teachers must be able to "gradually implement ideas of their own choice at a pace that suits them and in a way that matches with the exigencies of their context" (p. 201).

Developing teachers' communicative skills

In Chapter 2, I argued that developing L2 communicative skills is not easy and thus, it is better to focus on teaching skills rather than on teachers' communicative skills. It is also true, however, that lack of confidence in their L2 skills is the major problem preventing teachers from introducing tasks in their classroom (Sugita & Takeuchi, 2009). I would suggest that teachers can develop their own L2 skills through implementing tasks. Input-based tasks require teachers to produce the L2 more flexibly and communicatively than in PPP. The conversation analysis showed that in PPP the conversation was strictly controlled by the teacher, and thus tended to entail the use of a limited set of sentences (e.g., "What's this?", "That's right", "Okay, the next"). On the other hand, in the TBLT lessons the teacher often had to produce the L2 spontaneously because the tasks allowed students to take control over the conversation by negotiating meaning when they needed (see for example, Excerpt 5.9 in Chapter 5). In fact, there were some occasions where I, as a teacher, felt worried about the accuracy of my English when I spontaneously responded to the students' questions. I suspect many teachers will have similar feelings, worried about their failure to use English correctly and the embarrassment this will cause them. However, I came to realise that using tasks provided me as well as the students with opportunities for learning English in a naturalistic way. Tasks provide teachers with the chance to use the L2 as a tool for communicating, which will gradually help them to improve their own L2 communicative skills. Perhaps, though, it might be helpful for teachers to prepare a 'script' that they can fall back on in the task-based classroom. There are a number of books that provide "useful short phrases" for teachers to use in English classrooms (e.g., Fujita, 2011). Input-based tasks also allow for the 'input' to be prepared. Perhaps what is needed is that the teacher recognizes that both the teacher and the students are "L2 learners" at different stages of L2 acquisition.

I believe that the first step of implementing tasks in a school context is that teachers believe that TBLT is possible in their own classroom and the skills and knowledge should be developed as they employ the approach, rather than before they do so.

Moving forward

To conclude this chapter, I would like to consider "what's next?" in implementing task-based teaching for young, beginner learners. How do teachers develop tasks as their students improve their communicative skills in English? I will briefly consider what insights research has shed on how to sequence tasks. Then I will suggest the kinds of tasks that teachers can use as students' proficiency develops and provide some examples.

Sequencing tasks

Teachers embarking on TBLT need to make decisions about the tasks they will use with their students. This means that they have to choose tasks that will be at an appropriate level – that is, neither too easy not too difficult. There is a literature that addresses task complexity, which I consider briefly below, before explaining how I dealt with the issue of task selection.

Robinson (2001, 2005) proposed the Cognition Hypothesis, distinguishing three distinct sets of factors that influence task difficulty: task complexity (factors impacting cognitive demands), task condition (factors impacting interactional demands), and task difficulty (learner factors). Factors relating to task complexity are further classified into 'resource-directing variables' that affect the cognitive demands of a task and 'resource-dispersing variables' that affect the procedural demands made on learners. The former increase the conceptual demands of a task and potentially influence the development of the learners' interlanguage system (Robinson, 2005) while the latter lead to "consolidation and fast real-time access to existing interlanguage resources" (Robinson, 2010, p. 248).

More recently Robinson (2010) has argued that task sequencing should be based only on the cognitive demands that tasks make on learners' language processing by manipulating resource-directing variables. However, while this might be theoretically sound, it is difficult to implement in the actual design of tasks and may not be pedagogically feasible. Baralt et al. (2014) reported a case study examining how in-service trainee teachers attempted to apply the Cognition Hypothesis in the design of a simple-to-complex task sequence. The findings showed that the teachers found it very difficult to apply Robinson's framework and ended up making only "cosmetic changes to what they typically plan for in practice" (p. 205). Baralt et al. reported that some of the teachers felt the training they had received in implementing Robinson's framework "too theoretical".

It would seem, then, that teachers need a simpler framework along with examples of actual tasks based on it. The framework proposed by Ellis (2003) might be more accessible for teachers and thus might work better. He proposed four aspects of task design which determine task difficulty: input, conditions, processes, and outcomes. Drawing on Ellis' framework, it is clear that the input tasks used in my study fall into the 'easy' category. All three listen-and-do tasks were single tasks involving only one step (i.e., choosing an appropriate card). They were one-way information gap tasks (i.e., the teacher had the information but the students did not). Pictorial information was used as a medium and the outcome was closed. The topics of the tasks (e.g., zoo and supermarket) were chosen because both were assumed to be familiar to the participants, and because they involved a here-and-now context (i.e., the students were given cards representing the referents that they placed in a folder and a folder attached to pictures of the supermarket and the zoo). The discourse was dialogic involving short simple sentences and high frequency vocabulary. In other words, the task I designed can be considered 'simple' in terms of the four elements of Ellis' framework (i.e., input, conditions, processes, and outcomes.)

Designing tasks for older, more proficient learners

Teachers can easily increase the complexity of the tasks I used in my study. The complexity of the input, for example, could be increased by including descriptive details about the referents in the commands (e.g., "Please find the <u>tall</u> animal with a <u>long</u> neck") instead of the simple commands used in the study (e.g., "Please find a giraffe"). The task conditions could also be changed. For example the Help the Zoo and Supermarket Task could be used as a two-way task, with the students working in pairs to take turns in giving instructions to each other. In other words, the task would become more of a production task. Ellis and He's (1999) study included both input-both tasks of the listen-and-do type used in my study and also output-based tasks involving the same task materials. The tasks in my study involved a simple information-gap (i.e., identifying the items to take to the zoo or supermarket) but they could be modified to include a reasoning-gap or an opinion gap. Prabhu (1987) suggested that information gap tasks were ideal for beginners but that subsequently reasoning-gap tasks and then opinion-gap tasks could be introduced as the learners' L2 proficiency develops. For example, for a reasoning-gap task students could be given picture cards of different animals (as in the 'Help the Zoo' task) and asked to group the animals in different ways (e.g., size; colour; type of food they eat). For an opinion-gap task, students could be asked to decide where each animal should be located in a plan of a zoo. This task could be made more difficult if the number of animals was greater than the number of cages so that some of the animals had to share the same cage in the plan of the zoo. In such production-based tasks, learners would need to produce copula *-be,* which would lead to the opportunity for noticing the form of the structure.

These suggestions for how to sequence tasks according to complexity apply equally to the kinds of focused tasks I used in my study and to unfocused tasks (i.e., tasks that do not have any specific language features as their target). However, in the case of focused tasks teachers would also need to decide which specific linguistic features to target. As I pointed out above, I chose to target nouns and adjectives (rather than verbs) because the learners were complete beginners in my study. Later, however, it would be necessary to design tasks that involved learners processing verbs, initially in terms of their meanings (e.g., the actions they referred to) and subsequently in terms of grammatical meaning (e.g., distinguishing between verbs referring to present and past time). However, I do not believe it possible to give firm guidelines about when to introduce different grammatical features in focused tasks. Teachers will need to use their own judgment, guided by close observation of their students, to see when specific features show signs of emerging in their speech and writing.

The topic addressed by a task is another factor that can affect the level of difficulty. The topics for the tasks in my study were very concrete (e.g., animals, food, and home appliances). Such topics are well suited to beginners because the referents of the key words can be depicted visually. Clearly though more abstract and challenging topics are needed for more advanced and older learners. It is a good idea, however, to first introduce such topics by means of input-based tasks that can serve as a preparation for the performance of output-put based tasks. I will now illustrate how the kind of tasks I used can be further developed to make them suitable for junior-high school students.

In the first task, individual students read about two girls. They first complete an information-transfer activity by completing a table which summarises the stories and which also serves as a means for checking they have understood them. The students are encouraged to use a dictionary if necessary. The table can be completed in either their L1 (i.e., Japanese) or the L2. Afterwards they work in small groups to decide which girl they should invite to study in Japan, giving their reasons.

Task 1

A. Read these stories about two girls.

1. Felicia
   My name is Felicia, 13 years old. I lived in a small village in Bangui. I love to draw. I used to teach my young sister how to draw. I was inside the house with my parents when the rebels came in with guns. They dumped the dead bodies in front of our house. There were my neighbours. I knew them. We ran away in panic. We were separated and my uncle was killed. For weeks, my family and I hid in the bush along a river, and we finally arrived at the camp in September. When I think about that day, I see images and I start crying. More and more people are arriving here. We are running out of clean water and food. In the future I want to study at a school and become an art teacher.
2. Shylyny
   My name is Shylyny. I'm 15 years old. My dream is to become an accountant or a journalist. I lived with my parents, and three younger brothers 3, 6 and 12 years old. When the typhoon "Haiyan" came, my house was cut into two. I climbed to the ceiling of the house. The last time I looked, my mother was just beside me, but when I looked again she was gone. My 12-year-old brother, Richard, tried to help my mother, but she could not move because her legs were under the broken wall. My mother told my brother to take care of his siblings and to be a good boy. Our father carried the two younger boys to the ceiling, but he disappeared in the water soon after. Then we reach a neighbour's rooftop. Now my grandmother's sister is looking after us. I want to go back to school, and get a good job to look after my younger brothers.

B. Use the stories to complete this table about the two girls.

Name		
Age		
What is her future dream?		
What happened to her?		
What country is she from?		
What is needed now?		
What is needed in the future?		

C. Your school is going to invite one of the two girls to study in Japan for one month. Think which girl you would like to invite and give two reasons for your choice. Later, we will take a vote to see which girl receives the most support.

The first part of the task is input-based (i.e., the students have to read and comprehend the written stories but they do not have to produce the L2). The second part is an opinion-gap task that is output-based. The task outcome is determining which girl in the story should be invited to the school. One advantage of this kind of task is that students can 'borrow' from the language provided in the input-based part when completing the output-part. Such 'borrowing' helps to support learners in performing out-put based tasks (see Prabhu, 1987; Samuda, 2001).

In the second task the students work in groups of three. The same two stories are used in this task but each story is divided into two sections so that each student receives one section. Without showing each other their piece of the story, the students discuss the following topics.

Task 2

A. Your school is going to invite one of the two girls to study in Japan for one month. Discuss the following questions in your group.
   1. Which girl would you like to invite? Why?
   2. What would you do to help the girl?
   3. Imagine you have raised 100,000 yen to help the other child (i.e., the one you did not decide to invite). How would you use the money to help the girl?
B. Your group will now present presents their answers to these questions to the class. One student in each group will present to the answers to one of the questions.
C. After all the groups have presented their answers, the teacher will ask the class to decide what you think is the best way of (a) helping the girl you have chosen and (b) spending the 100,000 yen to help the other child.

Task 2 consists of a two-way information gap activity (the four students possess different information that needs to be shared through communication) and a convergent opinion gap activity (the students in each group need to come to the same conclusion). It is production-based and involves student-student interaction. In this kind of task, the teacher has less control but in the class presentation stage there will be opportunity for the teacher to help scaffold students' production and, where appropriate, focus on form.

Both tasks meet the criteria for a task which I considered in Chapter 2.

1. The task has a clearly defined outcome (i.e., choosing one girl to support).
2. The students need to communicate meaningfully to complete the task (i.e., comprehending the message in Task 1 and producing and comprehending the message in Task 2).
3. The students have to use their own <u>the linguistic and non-linguistic resources</u> (i.e., neither of the tasks provides a model dialogue).
4. The students are evaluated in terms of the task outcome (i.e., reaching a convincing decision for choosing one student).

The tasks have both closed and open outcomes. For example in Task 1 the students have to complete the chart about the two girls. The outcome here is closed. This will enable the teacher to see if they have successfully understood the information about the two girls. However, deciding which girl to invite, how to help her and how to spend the money to help the other girl involve open outcomes. These activities allow greater room for students to conceptualize what they want to say and to formulate their own messages. The two tasks also vary in complexity – Task 1 is clearly simpler than Task 2. Task 1 involves only information transfer and a single decision to be made. Task 2 involves information exchange and several decisions to be made.

Teachers, then, need to decide when and how to switch from an 'easy' to a more 'difficult' task. One way to achieve this goal is to redesign an input-based task as an output-based task. It can be done by encouraging the students to negotiate in the L2 rather than in their L1 or by asking one student to take the teacher's role and provide commands in an input-based task for the other students. These strategies would allow the teacher to keep some control of the conversation and be able to provide feedback on the students' production when necessary. Then, the teacher can modify the one-way information gap task by turning it into a two-way task (e.g., by splitting the information between students) and asking the students to perform the task in pairs or groups. In order to decide when to introduce these variants of the task the teacher would need to observe how the learners to perform in an input-based task to see if there is any evidence of a willingness to communicate. Later the teacher would need to decide when to introduce reason-gap and opinion-gap tasks. When first introduced, reasoning-gap tasks might best be carried out with the whole class so that the teacher could scaffold the reasoning-processes the students need to engage in, as in Prabhu (1987). Later they could be performed in pairs or groups, which would pave the way for opinion-gap tasks where students have to reach agreement on a solution to a problem.

In the case of the two tasks above, I would look for ways of scaffolding the learners' performance of Task 1 – for example, by giving them time to prepare a few sentences for the presentation stage, using their dictionaries if they wanted to. Only when I could see that they were comfortable in performing this kind of task without such scaffolding would I consider moving on to the more difficult Task 2. The students would probably need to complete several Type 1 tasks before they were ready for the more demanding Type 2 task, which requires more independent use of the L2 by the students and has open rather than closed outcomes.

Conclusion

Introducing TBLT in the elementary school will challenge teachers as they face the kinds of problems I discussed in the previous sections. I have suggested ways in which these challenges might be addressed. In order for teachers to move from a traditional to an innovative way of teaching, they will need teaching resources, encouragement, incentives, sufficient time, and a leader to support them. Unfortunately, most of these are not readily available in many elementary schools in Japan, although there are a number of in-service seminars and workshops in Japan aiming at developing the knowledge and the skills needed to implement tasks – my own starting point. For this reason, much will depend on the individual teachers, the efforts they are ready to make and the risks they are prepared to take. I can only say that, for me, making the effort and taking the risks proved exciting and worthwhile.

CHAPTER 10

Conclusion

The study reported in this book was motivated by my dissatisfaction with a traditional instructional approach that relied on explicit language teaching and controlled production practice, and also by my desire to experiment with a task-based approach, not just as a means of teaching new language but also as a means of developing students' communicative ability (i.e., their ability to interact effectively in English). I have shown that TBLT can be successfully implemented by means of input-based tasks with young beginner learners in Japan. The input-based tasks created contexts for using language in a way that is natural for young children, where English is used as a 'tool' for achieving communicative outcomes. It differed from PPP, where the target words became 'objects' to be learned. It was also shown that the TBLT approach employed in this project was at least as effective, and in several aspects more effective, than the PPP approach in developing the learners' vocabulary and grammar knowledge.

Task-based teaching is inherently 'experiential' (Dewey, 1938; Norris, 2009). It aims to create contexts in which learners can experience the target language as a tool for doing things rather than as an object for study. It engages learners in acts of language use that can facilitate incidental language acquisition. Input-based tasks of the listen-and-do kind are indispensable for beginner learners as they enable them to use their existing resources (i.e., their L1 and their ability to infer indexical meaning) in the 'task' of making sense of what they hear. They position young, beginner learners as meaning-makers and allow them to experience interaction in the L2 in conjunction with the teacher. Crucially, they provide opportunities for such learners to initiate turns and to take control of topic development by helping to construct interactional contexts collaboratively.

The TBLT approach I adopted constituted a radical departure from my earlier views about language teaching (e.g., that it was necessary to first teach students "some English" before they could communicate with it). I found support for Hatch's (1978) claim that learners do not need to learn language to communicate but can learn language through communicating. Analysing the process of implementing TBLT made me realize the importance of the teacher's role in TBLT. It showed me that the extent to which a task is effective in promoting learning depends crucially on navigating the activity that results from the task.

TBLT in elementary schools in Japan

My study was in part motivated by my hope that, as English is introduced as a subject into the elementary school curriculum in Japan, this would not lead to teachers falling back on the same approach they had experienced when learning English at school, namely, an approach that relied on explicit language teaching and controlled production practice. I wanted to show that it was possible for English to be treated as a tool for making meaning and accomplishing communicative goals. I wanted to offer an alternative to the focus-on-forms (Long, 1991) approach which dominates in published textbooks for teaching young learners in Japan. Above all I wanted to make English 'real' for the young learners in my classroom by giving them a functional need to use it. After all, this is what young children understand language to be – a means for doing things. To my mind this is how learning a new language should start, especially for young children but arguably for older learners too. Later, maybe, a time will come for dissecting language into its component bits, studying them, and intentionally learning them, although there are advocates of TBLT (e.g., Long, 2015) who would dispute whether this is necessary at any time.

I am not naïve, however. I recognize that there are various issues that need to be considered when implementing TBLT in elementary schools in Japan, such as the learners' limited L2 proficiency and the teachers' lack of confidence. I have argued that an input-based approach is not only a theoretically sound way of starting TBLT for beginner-level learners but also provides a practical solution for how to introduce it in elementary schools in Japan. I have suggested that the use of 'scripts' can help teachers have confidence in performing input-based tasks with children and, importantly, that teaching tasks will not just help to develop students' English proficiency but also the teacher's own proficiency.

However, I do not intend to suggest that I have solved all the problems that teachers will face with attempting to innovate language teaching via TBLT. There are a number of institutional issues that also need to be addressed, such as the lack of teaching resources, incentives for innovation, support from the teachers' school and their peers, and appropriate teacher training opportunities (Ely, 1995). I realize that that preparing for TBLT will be time consuming for hard-pressed teachers. However, I also believe that an innovation in teaching starts with small individual successes by individual teachers. I hope my own experience in introducing TBLT, which I have documented in this book, will encourage teachers to experiment with TBLT.

Ideological issues

I would like to conclude my book with some comments about the debates about English education in Japan. Some educators and politicians argue that language instruction directed at communication skills requires 'adopting' the cultural attitudes and behaviours of the West. Seargeant (2009) pointed out that there is a serious mismatch between government policy which promotes that teaching of communicative English skills in school and the highly structured nature of the educational system in Japan, although, arguably, this is less an issue in the elementary school where teachers have more freedom to choose what and how to teach. At a more general level, some commentators note that there is a persistent unwillingness to learn English in Japan because of its closed cultural history and its strong essentialist view of the national language (Kawai, 2007). These are general points that apply to the teaching of English in Japan, but they are of special relevance to the introduction of English at the elementary level, which has been controversial and has taken place much later than in other East Asian countries.

I do not share these negative views about the teaching and place of English in Japan. Based on my experience of managing a language school in Japan, people do want to acquire communicative ability in English and they believe they can do so without giving up their own identities. They do not consider that learning English is a threat to their own Japanese language. Although English is not normally a medium of communication in Japan, many people have a strongly felt need to learn communicative English skills. Many of the major companies in Japan require 'communicative English skills' as one of the conditions of employment or promotion. The parents of my students sent their children to my private language school because they thought English would be 'useful' for their children in the future. Some parents told me that they didn't want their children to have the same experience as they did (i.e., a limited career because of their lack of English). Of course these parents did not necessarily want their children to become westernized and did not believe that sending them to my school would result in this. They also sent their children to learn traditional cultural skills such as Japanese calligraphy. The adult learners of English I have met in Japan usually do not want to become like a native speaker of English but to develop into good Japanese speakers of English. It is true that there is a conflict between the philosophy of education that underlies the structured Japanese system, and the traditional roles of teacher and students in that system, and the philosophy that underscores TBLT. But educational policy is changing in Japan and there is official support for a more communicative approach to teaching English. Communicative language teaching can be made to work in the Japanese context by adopting a task-based approach. The young children in my research enjoyed 'communicating' in English and demonstrated their command of English in the communicative tasks, albeit in a limited way as they were beginners. Such an approach, I would argue, can also be made to work for older learners.

In the unique social context of Japan, learners will have different purposes for learning English, and these purposes may differ from those of learners in other social contexts (e.g., Kubota, 2009). However, I believe that the task-based approach can be modified to meet these purposes without imposing western norms. Task-based language teaching is not monolithic. It is a highly flexible type of instruction, ideally suited to the kind of children I investigated in my study, but also relevant to older learners in Japan. It draws on what is fundamental about language – that language is a tool for communicating. This is something that all Japanese people, indeed most people around the world, can readily understand.

References

Adams, R., & Newton, J. (2009). TBLT in Asia: Constraints and opportunities. *Asian Journal of English Language Teaching, 19*, 1–17.

Aichi Prefectural Education Center. (2002). *Classroom English: Jyugyo o eigo de okonau tameno hyogen-syu* [The list of expression to conduct lessons in English]. Retrieved from ⟨http://www.apec.aichi-c.ed.jp/shoko/kyouka/h20task/part3all.pdf⟩

Alegría de la Colina, A., & del Pilar García Mayo, M. (2009). Oral interaction in task-based EFL learning: The use of the L1 as a cognitive tool. *IRAL-International Review of Applied Linguistics in Language Teaching, 47*(3–4), 325–345. doi:10.1515/iral.2009.014

Anderson, J. R. (1983). *The architecture of cognition*. Cambridge, MA: Harvard University Press.

Anderson, J. R. (1993). Production systems and the ACT-R theory. In J. R. Anderson & F. S. Bellezza (Eds.), *Rules of the mind* (pp. 1–16). Hilsdale, NJ: Lawrence Erlbaum Associates.

Anthony, E. M. (1963). An approach, method and technique. *English Language Teaching, 17*, 63–67. doi:10.1093/elt/XVII.2.63

Antón, M. (1999). The discourse of a learner-centered classroom: Sociocultural perspective on teacher-learner interaction in the second-language classroom. *The Modern Language Journal, 83*(3), 303–315. doi:10.1111/0026-7902.00024

Antón, M., & DiCamilla, F. J. (1998). Socio-cognitive functions of Ll collaborative interaction in the L2 classroom. *Canadian Modern Language Review, 54*, 314–342. doi:10.3138/cmlr.54.3.314

Asher, J. J. (1972). Children's first language as a model for second language learning. *The Modern Language Journal, 56*(3), 133–139.

Asher, J. J. (1977). *Learning another language through actions*. Los Gatos, CA: Sky Oaks Productions.

Auerbach, E. (1993). Reexamining English only in the ESL classroom. *TESOL Quarterly, 27*(1), 9–32. doi:10.2307/3586949

Baralt, M., Gilabert, R., & Robinson, P. (Eds.). (2014). *Task sequencing and instructed second language learning*. London: Bloomsbury.

Benesse. (2009). *Chugakko eigo ni kansuru kihon chosa (Kyoin chosa)* [Basic research about English in junior high school (Teacher perspectives)]. Tokyo: Benesse.

Beretta, A. (1990). Implementation of the Bangalore Project. *Applied Linguistics, 11*(4), 321–337. doi:10.1093/applin/11.4.321

Beretta, A. (1992). What can be learned from the Bangalore evaluation? In J. C. Alderson & A. Beretta (Eds.), *Evaluating second language education* (pp. 250–273). Cambridge: Cambridge University Press. doi:10.1017/CBO9781139524575.011

Beretta, A., & Davies, A. (1985). Evaluation of the Bangalore Project. *ELT Journal, 39*(2), 121–127. doi:10.1093/elt/39.2.121

Berko, J. (1958). The child's learning of English morphology. *Word, 14*, 150–177.

Berry, M. (1981). Systemic linguistics and discourse analysis: A multi-layered approach to exchange structure. In M. Coulthard & M. Montgomery (Eds.), *Studies in discourse analysis* (pp. 120–145). London: Routledge and Kegan Paul.

Brock, C. A. (1986). The effects of referential questions on ESL classroom discourse. *TESOL Quarterly, 20*, 47–59. doi:10.2307/3586388

Brown, R. (1973). *A first language: The early years*. Cambridge, MA: Harvard University Press.

Brumfit, C. (1984). *Communicative methodology in language teaching: The roles of fluency and accuracy*. Cambridge: Cambridge University Press. doi:10.4159/harvard.9780674732469

Brumfit C. J., & Johnson, K. (1979). *The communicative approach to language teaching*. Oxford: Oxford University Press.

Butler, Y. G. (2004). What level of English proficiency do elementary school teachers need to attain to teach EFL? Case studies from Korea, Taiwan, and Japan. *TESOL Quarterly, 38*(2), 245–278. doi:10.2307/3588380

Butler, Y. G. (2005). *Nihon-no shogakko eigo-o kangaeru- Ajia-no shiten-karano kensho-to teigenn* [English language education in Japanese elementary schools: Analyses and suggestions based on East Asian perspectives]. Tokyo: Sanseido.

Butler, Y. G. (2007). Foreign language education at elementary schools in Japan: Searching for solutions amidst growing diversification. *Current Issues in Language Planning, 8*(2), 129–147. doi:10.2167/cilp115.0

Bygate, M. (1996). Effects of task repetition: Appraising the developing language of learners. In J. Willis & D. Willis (Eds.), *Challenge and change in language teaching* (pp. 136–146). Oxford: Heinemann.

Bygate, M. (2001). Effects of task repetition on the structure and control of oral language. In M. Bygate, P. Skehan, & M. Swain (Eds.), *Researching pedagogic tasks: Second language learning, teaching and testing* (pp. 23–48). Harlow: Longman.

Bygate, M. (2015). Sources, developments and directions of task-based language teaching. *The Language Learning Journal*, 1–20. doi:10.1080/09571736.2015.1039566

Byrnes, H. (1986). *Teaching oral English* (2nd ed.). Harlow: Longman.

Camps, J. (2003). The analysis of oral self-correction as a window into the development of past time reference in Spanish. [Article]. *Foreign Language Annals, 36*(2), 233–242. doi:10.1111/j.1944-9720.2003.tb01473.x

Carless, D. (2002). Implementing task-based learning with young learners. *English Language Teaching Journal, 56*(4), 389–396. doi:10.1093/elt/56.4.389

Carless, D. (2003). Factors in the implementation of task-based teaching in primary schools. *System, 31*(4), 485–500. doi:10.1016/j.system.2003.03.002

Carless, D. (2007). The suitability of task-based approaches for secondary schools: Perspectives from Hong Kong. *System, 35*(4), 595–608. doi:10.1016/j.system.2007.09.003

Carless, D. (2011). *From testing to productive student learning: Implementing formative assessment in Confucian-heritage settings*. New York, NY: Routledge.

Carreira, J. M. (2012). Motivational orientations and psychological needs in EFL learning among elementary school students in Japan. *System, 40*(2), 191–202. doi:10.1016/j.system.2012.02.001

Chaudron, C. (1988). *Second language classroom: Research on teaching and learning*. Cambridge: Cambridge University Press. doi:10.1017/CBO9781139524469

Chen, J. F., Warden, C. A., & Chang, H. T. (2005). Motivators that do not motivate: The case of Chinese EFL learners and the Influence of culture on motivation. *TESOL Quarterly, 39*(4), 609–633. doi:10.2307/3588524

Chun, A. E., Day, R. R., Chenoweth, N. A., & Luppescu, S. (1982). Errors, interaction, and correction: A study of native-nonnative conversations. *TESOL Quarterly, 16*(4), 53–547. doi:10.2307/3586471

Cohen, J. (1988). *Statistical power analysis for the behavioral sciences*. New York, NY: Academic Press.

Conrad, L. (1989). The effects of time-compressed speech on native and EFL listening comprehension. *Studies in Second Language Acquisition, 11*(1), 1–16. doi:10.1017/S0272263100007804

Cook, V. (2001). Using the first language in the classroom. *Canadian Modern Language Review, 57*(3), 402–423. doi:10.3138/cmlr.57.3.402

Corder, S. P. (1981). *Error analysis and interlanguage*. Oxford: Oxford University Press.

Coughlan, P., & Duff, P. (1994). Same task, different activities: analysis of SLA from an activity theory perspective. In J. Lantolf & G. Appel (Eds.), *Vygotskian approaches to second language research* (pp. 173–194). Norwood, NJ: Ablex.
Cox, D. (2005). Can we predict language items for open tasks? In C. Edwards & J. Willis (Eds.), *Teachers exploring tasks in English language teaching* (pp. 171–186). Houndmills: Palgrave Macmillan.
Craik, F. I. M., & Lockhart, R. S. (1972). Levels of processing: A framework for memory research. *Journal of Verbal Learning and Verbal Behavior, 11*(6), 671–684. doi:10.1016/S0022-5371(72)80001-X
Daulton, F. E. (1999). English loanwords in Japanese: The built-in lexicon. *The Internet TESL Journal, 5*(1), 1–5.
de Bot, K. (1996). The psycholinguistics of the Output Hypothesis. *Language Learning, 46*(3), 529–555. doi:10.1111/j.1467-1770.1996.tb01246.x
de la Fuente, M. J. (2002). Negotiation and oral acquisition of L2 vocabulary: The roles of input and output in the receptive and productive acquisition of words. *Studies in Second Language Acquisition, 24*, 81–112. doi:10.1017/S0272263102001043
de la Fuente, M. J. (2006). Classroom L2 vocabulary acquisition: Investigating the role of pedagogical tasks and form-focused instruction. *Language Teaching Research, 10*(3), 263–295. doi:10.1191/1362168806lr196oa
DeKeyser, R. (1998). Beyond focus on form: Cognitive perspective on learning and practicing second language grammar. In C. Doughty & J. Williams (Eds.), *Focus on form in classroom second language acquisition* (pp. 42–63). Cambridge: Cambridge University Press.
DeKeyser, R. (2007). *Practice in a second language: Perspectives from applied linguistics and cognitive psychology.* New York, NY: Cambridge University Press.
DeKeyser, R. M. (2015). Skill Acquisition Theory. In B. VanPatten & J. Williams (Eds.), *Theories in Second Language Acquisition: An Introduction* (pp. 94–112). New York, NY: Routledge.
Dewey, J. (1938). *Experience and education.* New York, NY: Collier Books.
DiCamilla, F. J., & Antón, M. (2004). Private speech: A study of language for thought in the collaborative interaction of language learners. *International Journal of Applied Linguistics, 14*(1), 36–69. doi:10.1111/j.1473-4192.2004.00053.x
Dörnyei, Z. (2001). *Teaching and researching motivation.* Harlow: Longman.
Dörnyei, Z. (2007). *Research methods in applied linguistics: Quantitative, qualitative, and mixed methodologies.* Oxford: Oxford University Press.
Dörnyei, Z., & Kormos, J. (2000). The role of individual and social variables in oral task performance. *Language Teaching Research, 4*(3), 275–300. doi:10.1177/136216880000400305
Doughty, C. (2001). Cognitive underpinnings of focus on form. In P. Robinson (Ed.), *Cognition and second language instruction* (pp. 206–57). Cambridge: Cambridge University Press. doi:10.1017/CBO9781139524780.010
Dupuy, B., & Krashen, S. (1993). Incidental vocabulary acquisition in French as a foreign language. *Applied Language Learning, 4*, 55–63.
Duranti, A., & Goodwin, C. (1992). *Rethinking context: Language as an interactive phenomenon.* Cambridge: Cambridge University Press.
Eckerth, J., & Tavakoli, P. (2012). The effects of word exposure frequency and elaboration of word processing on incidental L2 vocabulary acquisition through reading. *Language Teaching Research, 16*(2), 227–252. doi:10.1177/1362168811431377
Elgort, I., & Nation, P. (2010). Vocabulary learning in a second language: Familiar answers to new questions. In P. Seedhouse, S. Walsh, & C. Jenks (Eds.), *Conceptualising 'learning' in applied linguistics* (pp. 89–104). Houndmills: Palgrave Macmillan.

Ellis, N. (1994). Vocabulary acquisition: The implicit ins and outs of explicit cognitive mediation. In N. Ellis (Ed.), *Implicit and explicit learning of language* (pp. 213–282). London: Academic Press.
Ellis, N. (2002). Frequency effects in language processing: A review with implications for theories of implicit and explicit language acquisition. *Studies in Second Language Acquisition, 24*, 143–188.
Ellis, N. (2006). Selective attention and transfer phenomena in L2 acquisition: Contingency, cue competition, salience, interference, overshadowing, blocking, and perceptual learning *Applied Linguistics, 27*(2), 164–194. doi:10.1093/applin/aml015
Ellis, N. C. (2002). Frequency effects in language processing. *Studies in Second Language Acquisition, 24*(2), 143–188.
Ellis, N., & Beaton, A. (1993). Factors affecting the learning of foreign language vocabulary: Imagery keyword mediators and phonological short-term memory. *The Quarterly Journal of Experimental Psychology, Section A, 46*(3), 533–558. doi:10.1080/14640749308401062
Ellis, R. (1984). Can syntax be taught? A study of the effects of formal instruction on the acquisition of WH questions by children. *Applied Linguistics, 5*(3), 138–155. doi:10.1093/applin/5.2.138
Ellis, R. (1993). The structural syllabus and second language acquisition. *TESOL Quarterly, 27*(1), 91–113. doi:10.2307/3586953
Ellis, R. (1995). Modified oral input and the acquisition of word meanings. *Applied Linguistics, 16*, 409–441. doi:10.1093/applin/16.4.409
Ellis, R. (1997). The empirical evaluation of language teaching materials. *ELT Journal, 51*, 36–42. doi:10.1093/elt/51.1.36
Ellis, R. (2001). Introduction: Investigating form-focused instruction. *Language Learning, 51*(s1), 1–46. doi:10.1111/j.1467-1770.2001.tb00013.x
Ellis, R. (2003). *Task-based language learning and teaching*. Oxford: Oxford University Press.
Ellis, R. (2004). The definition and measurement of L2 explicit knowledge. *Language Learning, 54*(2), 227–275. doi:10.1111/j.1467-9922.2004.00255.x
Ellis, R. (2005). Measuring implicit and explicit knowledge of a second language. *Studies in Second Language Acquisition, 27*, 141–172.
Ellis, R. (2008). *The study of second language acquisition: Second edition*. Oxford: Oxford University Press.
Ellis, R. (2009). Task-based language teaching: sorting out the misunderstandings. *International Journal of Applied Linguistics, 19*(3), 221–246. doi:10.1111/j.1473-4192.2009.00231.x
Ellis, R. (2012). *Language teaching research and language pedagogy*. Chichester: Wiley-Blackwell. doi:10.1002/9781118271643
Ellis, R., & He, X. (1999). The roles of modified input and output in the incidental acquisition of word meanings. *Studies in Second Language Acquisition, 21*, 285–301. doi:10.1017/S0272263199002077
Ellis, R., & Heimbach, R. (1997). Bugs and birds: Children's acquisition of second language vocabulary through interaction. *System, 25*(2), 247–259. doi:10.1016/S0346-251X(97)00012-2
Ellis, R., & Shintani, N. (2014). *Exploring language pedagogy through second language acquisition research*. London: Routledge.
Ellis, R., Basturkmen, H., & Loewen, S. (2001). Learner uptake in communicative ESL lessons. *Language Learning, 51*(2), 281–318. doi:10.1111/1467-9922.00156
Ellis, R., Basturkmen, H., & Loewen, S. (2002). Doing focus-on-form. *System, 30*(4), 419–432. doi:10.1016/S0346-251X(02)00047-7
Ellis, R., Loewen, S., & Erlam, R. (2006). Implicit and explicit corrective feedback and the acquisition of L2 grammar. *Studies in Second Language Acquisition, 28*(2), 339–368.

Ellis, R., Tanaka, Y., & Yamazaki, A. (1994). Classroom interaction, comprehension, and the acquisition of L2 word meanings. *Language Learning, 44*(3), 449–491. doi:10.1111/j.1467-1770.1994.tb01114.x

Ely, D. P. (1990). Conditions that facilitate the implementation of educational technology innovations. *Journal of Research on Computing in Education, 23*(2), 298–305. doi:10.1080/08886504.1990.10781963

Ely, D. P. (1995). *Technology is the answer! But what was the question?* ERIC Document Reproduction Service No. ED 381: 152.

Erlam, R. (2003). Evaluating the relative effectiveness of structured-input and output-based instruction in foreign language learning. *Studies in Second Language Acquisition, 25*, 559–582. doi:10.1017/S027226310300024X

Estaire, S., & Zanon, J. (1994). *Planning class work: A task-based approach.* Oxford: Heinemann.

Færch, C., & Kasper, G. (1986). The role of comprehension in second-language learning. *Applied Linguistics, 7*(3), 257–274. doi:10.1093/applin/7.3.257

Fennelly, M., & Luxton, R. (2011). Are they ready? On the verge of compulsory English, elementary school teachers lack confidence. *The Language Teacher, 35*(2), 19–24.

Fujita, T. (2011). *Sensei no tame no eigo rensyu bukku* [An English practice book for teachers]. Tokyo: ALC.

Gage, N. L., & Needels, M. C. (1989). Process-product research on teaching: A review of criticisms. *The Elementary School Journal, 89*(3), 253–300. doi:10.1086/461577

Gary, J. O. (1978). Why speak if you don't need to? The case for a listening approach to beginning foreign language learning. In W. Ritchie (Ed.), *Second language acquisition research* (pp. 185–200). New York, NY: Academic Press.

Gass, S., & Selinker, L. (2001). *Second language acquisition: An introductory course* (2nd ed.). Mahwah, NJ: Lawrence Erlbaum Associates.

Gass, S., & Torres, M. J. A. (2005). Attention when: an investigation of the ordering effect of input and interaction. *Studies in Second Language Acquisition, 27*(1), 1–31. doi:10.1017/S0272263105050011

Gasser, M., & Smith, L. B. (1998). Learning nouns and adjectives: A connectionist account. *Language and Cognitive Processes, 13*(2), 269–306. doi:10.1080/016909698386537

George, H. (1972). *Common errors in language learning: Insights from English.* Rowley, MA: Newbury House.

Griffiths, R. (1990). Speech rate and NNS comprehension: A preliminary study in time-benefit analysis. *Language Learning, 40*(3), 311–336. doi:10.1111/j.1467-1770.1990.tb00666.x

Hakuta, K. (1978). A report on the development of the grammatical morphemes in a Japanese girl learning English as a second language. In E. Hatch (Ed.), *Second language acquisition* (pp. 132–147). Rowley, MA: Newbury House.

Harley, B. (1989). Functional grammar in French immersion: A classroom experiment. *Applied Linguistics, 19*, 331–359. doi:10.1093/applin/10.3.331

Hatch, E. (1978). Discourse analysis and second language acquisition. In E. Hatch (Ed.), *Second language acquisition* (pp. 402–435). Rowley, MA: Newbury House.

Hauser, E. (2005). Coding 'corrective recasts': The maintenance of meaning and more fundamental problems. *Applied Linguistics, 26*(3), 293–316. doi:10.1093/applin/ami010

Hawkes, M. L. (2012). Using task repetition to direct learner attention and focus on form. *ELT Journal, 66*(3), 327–336. doi:10.1093/elt/ccr059

Housen, A., Pierrard, M., & Van Daele, S. (2005). Structure complexity and the efficacy of explicit grammar instruction. In A. Housen & M. Pierrard (Eds.), *Investigations in instructed second language acquisition* (pp. 235–270). Berlin: Mouton de Gruyter. doi:10.1515/9783110197372.2.235

Hu, G. (2002). Recent important developments in secondary English language teaching in the P.R.China. *Language Culture and Curriculum, 15*(1), 30–49. doi:10.1080/07908310208666631

Hu, G., & McKay, S. L. (2012). English language education in East Asia: Some recent developments. *Journal of Multilingual and Multicultural Development, 33*(4), 345–362. doi:10.1080/01434632.2012.661434

Hulstijn, J. H., & Laufer, B. (2001). Some empirical evidence for the involvement load hypothesis in vocabulary acquisition. *Language Learning, 51*(3), 539–558. doi:10.1111/0023-8333.00164

Hulstijn, J. H., Hollander, M., & Greidanus, T. (1996). Incidental vocabulary learning by advanced foreign language students: The influence of marginal glosses, dictionary use, and reoccurrence of unknown words. *The Modern Language Journal, 80*(3), 327–339. doi:10.1111/j.1540-4781.1996.tb01614.x

Hutchby, I., & Wooffitt, R. (1988). *Conversation analysis.* Cambridge: Polity Press.

Izumi, S. (2003). Comprehension and production processes in second language learning: In search of the psycholinguistic rationale of the output hypothesis. *Applied Linguistics, 24*(2), 168–196. doi:10.1093/applin/24.2.168

Izumi, S., & Bigelow, M. (2000). Does output promote noticing and second language acquisition? *TESOL Quarterly, 34*(2), 239–278. doi:10.2307/3587952

Izumi, S., Bigelow, M., Fujiwara, M., & Fearnow, S. (1999). Testing the output hypothesis: Effects of output on noticing and second language acquisition. *Studies in Second Language Acquisition, 21*(3), 421–452. doi:10.1017/S0272263199003034

Jefferson, G. (2004). Glossary of transcript symbols with an introduction. In G. Lerner (Ed.), *Conversation analysis: Studies from the first generation* (pp. 13–31). Amsterdam: John Benjamins. doi:10.1075/pbns.125.02jef

Jia, G. (2003). The acquisition of the English plural morpheme by native Mandarin Chinese-speaking children. *Journal of Speech, Language, and Hearing Research, 46*(6), 1297–1311. doi:10.1044/1092-4388(2003/101)

Jiang, N. (2000). Lexical representation and development in a second language. *Applied Linguistics, 21*(1), 47–77. doi:10.1093/applin/21.1.47

Jing, H. (2006). Learner resistance in metacognition training? An exploration of mismatches between learner and teacher agendas. *Language Teaching Research, 10*(1), 95–117. doi:10.1177/1362168806001000107

Joe, A. (1998). What effects do text-based tasks promoting generation have on incidental vocabulary acquisition? *Applied Linguistics, 19*(3), 357–377. doi:10.1093/applin/19.3.357

Joshi, R. M. (2009). *International business.* Oxford: Oxford University Press.

Karavas-Doukas, K. (1998). Evaluating the implementation of educational innovations: Lessons from the past. In P. Rea-Dickins & K. P. Germaine (Eds.), *Managing evaluation and innovation in language teaching: Building bridges* (pp. 25–50). Harlow: Longman.

Kawai, Y. (2007). Japanese nationalism and the global spread of English: An analysis of Japanese governmental and public discourses on English. *Language and Intercultural Communication, 7*(1), 37–55. doi:10.2167/laic174.0

Keck, C., Iberri-Shea, G., Tracy-Ventura, N., & Wa-Mbaleka, S. (2006). Investigating the empirical link between task-based interaction and acquisition. *Synthesizing Research on Language Learning and Teaching, 13,* 91–131. doi:10.1075/lllt.13.08kec

Kikuchi, K., & Sakai, H. (2009). Japanese learners' demotivation to study English: A survey study. *JALT Journal, 31*(2), 183–204.

Klein, W., & Perdue, C. (1992). *Utterance structure: Developing grammars again.* Amsterdam: John Benjamins. doi:10.1075/sibil.5

Klein, W., & Perdue, C. (1997). The basic variety (or couldn't natural languages be much simpler?). *Second Language Research, 13*, 301–347. doi:10.1191/026765897666879396

Koike, I., & Tanaka, H. (1995). English in foreign langauge education policy in Japan: Toward the twenty-first century. *World Englishes, 14*(1), 13–25. doi:10.1111/j.1467-971X.1995.tb00336.x

Kormos, J. (1999). Monitoring and self-repair in L2. *Language Learning, 49*(2), 303–342. doi:10.1111/0023-8333.00090

Krashen, S. (1982). *Principles and practice in second language acquisition.* Oxford: Pergamon.

Krashen, S. (1985). *The input hypothesis: Issues and implications.* London: Longman.

Krashen, S. (1998). Comprehensible output? *System, 26*(2), 175–182. doi:10.1016/S0346-251X(98)00002-5

Krashen, S. (2013). Reading and vocabulary acquisition: Supporting evidence and some objections. *Iranian Journal of Language Teaching Research, 1*(1), 27–43.

Kubota, R. (1998). Ideologies of English in Japan. *World Englishes, 17*(3), 295–306. doi:10.1111/1467-971X.00105

Kubota, R. (2009). Rethinking the superiority of the native speaker: Toward a relational understanding of power. In N. M. Doerr (Ed.), *Native speaker concept: Ethnographic investigations of native speaker effects* (pp. 233–248). Berlin: Walter de Gruyter.

Kubota, R. (2011). School curriculum and assessment in Japan: Politics in foreign language education. In Y. Zhao (Ed.), *Handbook of Asian education: A cultural perspective* (pp. 214–230). New York, NY: Routledge.

Kumaravadivelu, B. (2001). Toward a postmethod pedagogy. *TESOL Quarterly, 35*(4), 537–560. doi:10.2307/3588427

Laufer, B. (1998). The development of passive and active vocabulary in a second language: Same or different? *Applied Linguistics, 19*(2), 255–271. doi:10.1093/applin/19.2.255

Laufer, B. (2003). Vocabulary acquisition in a second language: Do learners really acquire most vocabulary by reading? Some empirical evidence *The Canadian modern language review, 59*(4), 567–587. doi:10.3138/cmlr.59.4.567

Laufer, B. (2005). Focus on form in second language vocabulary learning. *EUROSLA Yearbook, 5*, 223–250. doi:10.1075/eurosla.5.11lau

Laufer, B. (2006). Comparing focus on form and focus on formS in second-language vocabulary learning. *The Canadian Modern Language Review, 63*(1), 149–166. doi:10.3138/cmlr.63.1.149

Laufer, B., & Hulstijn, J. (2001). Incidental vocabulary acquisition in a second language: The construct of task-induced involvement. *Applied Linguistics, 22*(1), 1–26. doi:10.1093/applin/22.1.1

Laufer, B., & Rozovski-Roitblat, B. (2011). Incidental vocabulary acquisition: The effects of task type, word occurrence and their combination. *Language Teaching Research, 15*(4), 391–411. doi:10.1177/1362168811412019

Leow, R. P. (1993). To simplify or not to simplify. *Studies in Second Language Acquisition, 15*(3), 333–355. doi:10.1017/S0272263100012146

Levin, L. (1972). *Comparative studies in foreign-language teaching.* Stockholm: Almqvist & Wiksell.

Lightbown, P. (2008). Transfer appropriate processing as a model for classroom second language acquisition. In Z. Han (Ed.,) *Understanding second language process* (pp. 27–44). Clevedon: Multilingual Matters.

Loewen, S. (2005). Incidental focus on form and second language learning. *Studies in Second Language Acquisition, 27*(3), 361–386. doi:10.1017/S0272263105050163

Loewen, S., Erlam, R., & Ellis, R. (2009). The incidental acquisition of third person *-s* as implicit and explicit knowledge. In R. Ellis, S. Loewen, C. Elder, R. Erlam, J. Philip, & H. Reinders (Eds.),

Implicit and explicit knowledge in second language learning, testing and teaching (pp. 262–280). Bristol: Multilingual Matters.

Long, M. H. (1983). Native speaker/non-native speaker conversation and the negotiation of comprehensible input. *Applied Linguistics, 4*(2), 126–141. doi:10.1093/applin/4.2.126

Long, M. H. (1985). A role for instruction in second language acquisition: Task-based language teaching. In K. Hyltenstam & M. Pienemann (Eds.), *Modelling and assessing second language acquisition* (pp. 77–99). Clevedon: Multilingual Matters.

Long, M. H. (1991). Focus on form: A design feature in language teaching methodology. In K. de Bot, R. Ginsberg & C. Kramsch (Eds.), *Foreign language research in cross-cultural perspective* (pp. 39–52). Amsterdam: John Benjamins. doi:10.1075/sibil.2.07lon

Long, M. H. (1996). The role of linguistic environment in second language acquisition. In W. C. Ritchie & T. K. Bhatia (Eds.), *Handbook of second language acquisition* (pp. 413–468). San Diego, CA: Academic Press.

Long, M. H. (2015). *Second language acqisition and task-based language teaching.* Chichester: Wiley Blackwell.

Long, M. H., & Sato, C. J. (1983). Classroom foreigner talk discourse: Forms and functions of teachers' questions. In H. W. Seliger & M. H. Long (Eds.), *Classroom oriented research in second language acquisition* (pp. 268–285). Rowley, MA: Newbury House.

Loschky, L. (1994). Comprehensible input and second language acquisition: What is the relationship? *Studies in Second Language Acquisition, 16*(3), 303–323. doi:10.1017/S0272263100013103

Loschky, L., & Bley-Vroman, R. (1993). Grammar and task-based methodology. In G. Crookes & S. Gass (Eds.), *Tasks and language learning: Integrating theory and practice* (pp. 123–167). Clevedon: Multilingual Matters.

Lynch, T. (1989). Researching teachers: Behaviour and belief. In C. Brumfit & R. Mitchell (Eds), *Research in the language classroom* (pp. 117–127). London: Modern English Publications and the British Council.

Lynch, T., & Maclean, J. (2000). Exploring the benefits of task repetition and recycling for classroom language learning. *Language Teaching Research, 4*(3), 221–250.

Lyster, R. (2001). Negotiation of form, recasts, and explicit correction in relation to error types and learner repair in immersion classrooms. *Language Learning, 51*(1), 265–301. doi:10.1111/j.1467-1770.2001.tb00019.x

Lyster, R. (2004). Differential effects of prompts and recasts in form-focused instruction. *Studies in second language acquisition, 26*(3), 399–432. doi:10.1017/S0272263104263021

Lyster, R. (2007). *Learning and teaching languages through content: A counterbalanced approach.* Amsterdam: John Benjamins. doi:10.1075/lllt.18

Lyster, R., & Ranta, L. (1997). Corrective feedback and learner uptake. *Studies in Second Language Acquisition, 19*(1), 37–66. doi:10.1017/S0272263197001034

Lyster, R., & Saito, K. (2010). Oral feedback in classroom SLA: A meta-analysis. *Studies in Second Language Acquisition, 32*(2), 265–302. Special issue. doi:10.1017/S0272263109990520

Mackey, A. (1999). Input, interaction, and second language development. *Studies in Second Language Acquisition, 21*(4), 557–587. doi:10.1017/S0272263199004027

Mackey, A., & Gass, S. (2005). *Second language research: Methodology and design.* Mahwah, NJ: Lawrence Erlbaum Associates.

Mackey, A., & Goo, J. M. (2007). Interaction research in SLA: A meta-analysis and research synthesis. In A. Mackey (Ed.), *Input, interaction and corrective feedback in L2 learning* (pp. 379–452). Oxford: Oxford University Press.

Markee, N. (2000). *Conversation analysis.* Mahwah, NJ: Lawrence Erlbaum Associates.

Markee, N. (2005). Conversation analysis for second language acquisition. In E. Hinkel (Ed.), *Handbook of research in second language teaching and learning* (pp. 355–374). Mahwah, NJ: Lawrence Erlbaum Associates.

Markee, N. (2008). Toward a learning behavior tracking methodology for CA-for-SLA. *Applied Linguistics, 29*(3), 404–427. doi:10.1093/applin/amm052

Mason, B., & Krashen, S. (1997). Extensive reading in English as a foreign language. *System, 25*(1), 91–102. doi:10.1016/S0346-251X(96)00063-2

Matsumura, A. (2012). *Tasuku wo katsuyou shita eigo jyugyou no dezain* [English lesson designs using tasks]. Tokyo: Taisyukan.

McHoul, A. (1978). The organization of turns at formal talk in the classroom. *Language in Society, 7*(2), 183–213. doi:10.1017/S0047404500005522

Meisel, J. M., Clahsen, H., & Pienemann, M. (1981). On determining developmental stages in natural second language acquisition. *Studies in Second Language Acquisition, 3*(2), 109–135. doi:10.1017/S0272263100004137

Ministry of Education Culture Sport Science and Technology (MEXT). (2005). *Shogakko eigokatsudo jittchi chosa-ni tsuite* [A study of current practices in English activities at elementary schools]. Retrieved from ⟨http://www.mext.go.jp/b_menu/shingi/chukyo/chukyo3/siryo/015/05071201/005/003.htm⟩

Ministry of Education Culture Sport Science and Technology (MEXT). (2006). *Shogakko eigo katsudo jittshi jokyo chosa kekka gaiyou: Heisei 17 nendo* [Summary results of English activities at elementary schools in 2005]. Retrieved from ⟨http://www.mext.go.jp/b_menu/shingi/chukyo/chukyo3/siryo/015/05071201/005/003.htm⟩

Ministry of Education Culture Sport Science and Technology (MEXT). (2008). *Shogakko, chugakko, kotogakko oyobi tokubetu shien gakko no gakusyu shido yoryo to no kaizen ni tuite* [On improving the course of study for primary and secondary schools and schools for students with special needs]. Retrieved from ⟨http://www.mext.go.jp/a_menu/shotou/new-cs/news/20080117.pdf⟩

Ministry of Education Culture Sport Science and Technology (MEXT). (2012). *Hi friends*. Tokyo: Tokyo Shoseki.

Ministry of Education Culture Sports Science and Technology (MEXT). (2011). *Five proposals and specific measures for developing droficiency in English for international communication*. Retrieved from ⟨http://www.mext.go.jp/english/elsec/1319701.htm⟩

Mochizuki, N., & Ortega, L. (2008). Balancing communication and grammar in beginning-level foreign language classrooms: A study of guided planning and relativization. *Language Teaching Research, 12*(1), 11–37. doi:10.1177/1362168807084492

Mondria, J., & Wiersma, B. (2004). Receptive, productive, and receptive + productive L2 vocabulary learning: What difference does it make? In P. Bogaards & B. Laufer (Eds.), *Vocabulary in a second language: Selection, acquisition, and testing* (pp. 79–100). Amsterdam: John Benjamins. doi:10.1075/lllt.10.08mon

Nakata, R., Frazier, K., Hoskins, B., & Graham, C. (2007). *Let's go, level 1*. Oxford: Oxford University Press.

Nassaji, H., & Wells, G. (2000). What's the use of triadic dialogue? An investigation of teacher-student interaction. *Applied Linguistics, 21*(3), 376–406. doi:10.1093/applin/21.3.376

Newman, F. & Holzman, L. (1997). *The end of knowing: A new developmental way of learning*. London: Routledge.

Nitta, R., & Gardner, S. (2005). Consciousness-raising and practice in ELT coursebooks. *ELT Journal, 59*(1), 3–13. doi:10.1093/elt/cci001

Nobuyoshi, J., & Ellis, R. (1993). Focused communication tasks and second language acquisition. *ELT Journal, 47*(3), 203–210. doi:10.1093/elt/47.3.203

Norris, J. M. (2009). Task-based teaching and testing. In M. Long & C. Doughty (Eds.), *Handbook of language teaching* (pp. 578–594). Cambridge: Blackwell. doi:10.1002/9781444315783.ch30

Norris, J. M., & Ortega, L. (2000). Effectiveness of L2 instruction: A research synthesis and quantitative meta-analysis. *Language Learning, 50*(3), 417–528. doi:10.1111/0023-8333.00136

Nunan, D. (2003). The impact of English as a global language on educational policies and practices in the Asia-Pacific region. *TESOL Quarterly, 37*(4), 589–613. doi:10.2307/3588214

Ohta, A. S. (2001). *Second language acquisition processes in the classroom: Learning Japanese*. Mahwah NJ: Lawrence Erlbaum Associates.

Ortega, L. (2012, August). *Task-based language teaching in foreign language contexts: One pragmatist's view.* Unpublished plenary delivered at the JASELE Conference.

Otsu, Y., & Torikai, K. (2002). *Shogakko-de naze eigo?* [Why English at elementary schools?] Iwanami Booklet No. 562. Tokyo: Iwanami.

Palmberg, R. (1987). Patterns of vocabulary development in foreign-language learners. *Studies in Second Language Acquisition, 9*(2), 201–219. doi:10.1017/S0272263100000474

Paradis, M. (2004). *A neurolinguistic theory of bilingualism.* Amsterdam: John Benjamins. doi:10.1075/sibil.18

Parker, K., & Chaudron, C. (1987). The effects of linguistic simplification and elaborative modifications on L2 comprehension. *University of Hawaii Working Papers in ESL*, 6, 107–133.

Pica, T. (1994). Research on negotiation: What does it reveal about second-language learning conditions, processes, and outcomes? *Language Learning, 44*(3), 493–527. doi:10.1111/j.1467-1770.1994.tb01115.x

Pica, T., Holliday, L., Lewis, N., & Morgenthaler, L. (1989). Comprehensible output as an outcome of linguistic demands on the learner. *Studies in Second Language Acquisition, 11*(1), 63–90. doi:10.1017/S027226310000783X

Pienemann, M. (1998). *Language processing and language development: Processability theory.* Amsterdam: John Benjamins. doi:10.1075/sibil.15

Pienemann, M., & Håkansson, G. (1999). A unified approach toward the development of Swedish as L2. *Studies in Second Language Acquisition, 21*(3), 383–420. doi:10.1017/S0272263199003022

Pinter, A. (2005). Task repetition with 10-year-old children. In C. Edwards & J. Willis (Eds.), *Teachers exploring tasks in English language teaching* (pp. 113–126). Houndmills: Palgrave Macmillan.

Pinter, A. (2006). *Teaching young language learners.* Oxford: Oxford University Press.

Prabhu, N. S. (1987). *Second language pedagogy.* Oxford: Oxford University Press.

Ranta, L., & Lyster, R. (2007). A cognitive approach to improving immersion studets' oral language abilities: The awareness-pracetice-feedback sequence. In R. M. DeKeyser (Ed.), *Practice in a second language: Perspectives from applied linguistics and cognitive psychology* (pp. 141–160). Cambridge: Cambridge University Press.

Reeves, J. (2010). Teacher learning by script. *Language Teaching Research, 14*(3), 241–258. doi:10.1177/1362168810365252

Robinson, P. (1995). Attention, memory, and the "noticing" hypothesis. *Language Learning, 45*(2), 283–331. doi:10.1111/j.1467-1770.1995.tb00441.x

Robinson, P. (2001). Task complexity, task difficulty, and task production: Exploring interactions in a componential framework. *Applied Linguistics, 22*(1), 27–57. doi:10.1093/applin/22.1.27

Robinson, P. (2005). Cognitive abilities, chunk-strength, and frequency effects in implicit artificial grammar and incidental L2 learning: Replications of Reber, Walkenfeld, and Hernstadt (1991)

and Knowlton and Squire (1996) and their relevance for SLA. *Studies in Second Language Acquisition, 27*(2), 235–268. doi:10.1017/S0272263105050126

Robinson, P. (2005). Cognitive complexity and task sequencing: Studies in a componential framework for second language task design. *International Review of Applied Linguistics in Language Teaching, 43*(1), 1–32. doi:10.1515/iral.2005.43.1.1

Robinson, P. (2010). Situating and distributing cognition across task demands: The SSARC model of pedagogic task sequencing. In M. Putz & L. Sicola (Eds.), *Cognitive processing in second language acquisition: Inside the learner's mind* (pp. 243–268). Amsterdam: John Benjamins. doi:10.1075/celcr.13.17rob

Rutherford, W. (1988). Grammatical consciousness raising in brief historical perspective. In W. Rutherford & M. Sharwood-Smith (Eds.), *Grammar and second language teaching* (pp. 15–19). New York, NY: Newbury House.

Sacks, H., & Schegloff, E. (1979). Two preferences in the organization of reference to persons in conversation and their interaction. In G. Psathas (Ed.), *Everyday language: studies in ethnomethodology* (pp. 15–21). New Yor, NY: Irvington.

Sacks, H., Schegloff, E. A., & Jefferson, G. (1974). A simplest systematics for the organization of turn-taking for conversation. *Language, 50*(4), 696–735. doi:10.1353/lan.1974.0010

Sacks, H., Schegloff, E., & Jefferson, G. (1995). *Lectures on conversation. Volume II.* Oxford: Blackwell. doi:10.1002/9781444328301

Saito, K., & Lyster, R. (2011). Effects of form-focused instruction and corrective feedback on L2 pronunciation development of /r/ by Japanese learners of English. *Language Learning, 62*(2), 595–633. doi:10.1111/j.1467-9922.2011.00639.x

Sakamoto, M. (2012). Moving towards effective English language teaching in Japan: Issues and challenges. *Journal of Multilingual and Multicultural Development, 33*(4), 409–420. doi:10.1080/01434632.2012.661437

Salaberry, M. R. (1997). The role of input and output practice in second language acquisition. *The Canadian Modern Language Review, 53*(2), 422–451.

Samuda, V. (2001). Guiding relationships between form and meaning during task performance: The role of the teacher. In M. Bygate, P. Skehan & M. Swain (Eds.), *Researching pedagogic tasks: Second language learning teaching, and testing*. London: Longman.

Samuda, V., & Bygate, M. (2008). *Tasks in second language learning.* Houndmills: Palgrave Macmillan.

Schegloff, E. (1991). Conversation analysis and socially shared cognition. In L. B. Resnick, J. M. Levine, & S. D. Teasley (Eds.), *Perspectives on socially shared cognition* (pp. 150–171). Washington, DC: American Psychological Association. doi:10.1037/10096-007

Schegloff, E. (2000). When "others" initiate repair. *Applied Linguistics, 21*(2), 205–243. doi:10.1093/applin/21.2.205

Schegloff, E., Jefferson, G., & Sacks, H. (1977). The preference for self-correction in the organization of repair in conversation. *Language, 53*(2), 361–382. doi:10.1353/lan.1977.0041

Schmidt, R. (1990). The role of consciousness in second language learning. *Applied Linguistics, 11*(2), 129–158. doi:10.1093/applin/11.2.129

Schmidt, R. (1994). Deconstructing consciousness in search of useful definitions for applied linguistics. *AILA Review, 11*, 11–26.

Schmidt, R. (2001). Attention. In P. Robinson (Ed.), *Cognition and second language instruction* (pp. 3–32). Cambridge: Cambridge University Press. doi:10.1017/CBO9781139524780.003

Schmitt, N. (1994). Vocabulary testing: Questions for test development with six examples of tests of vocabulary size and depth. *Thai TESOL Bulletin, 6*(2), 9–16.

Seargeant, P. (2009). *The idea of English in Japan: Ideology and the evolution of a global language.* Clevedon: Multilingual Matters.
Seedhouse, P. (1999). Task-based interaction. *ELT Journal, 53*(3), 149–156. doi:10.1093/elt/53.3.149
Seedhouse, P. (2004). *The interactional architecture of the language classroom: A conversation analysis perspective.* Malden, MA: Blackwell.
Seedhouse, P. (2005). "Task" as research construct. *Language Learning, 55*(3), 533–570. doi:10.1111/j.0023-8333.2005.00314.x
Sharwood-Smith, M. (1986). Comprehension versus acquisition: Two ways of processing input. *Applied Linguistics, 7*(3), 239–256. doi:10.1093/applin/7.3.239
Shehadeh, A. (2001). Self- and other-initiated modified output during task-based interaction. *TESOL Quarterly, 35*(3), 433–457. doi:10.2307/3588030
Shintani, N. (2011). A comparative study of the effects of input-based and production-based instruction on vocabulary acquisition by young EFL learners. *Language Teaching Research, 15*(2), 137–158. doi:10.1177/1362168810388692
Shintani, N. (2012). Repeating input-based tasks with young beginner learners. *RELC Journal, 43*(1), 39–51. doi:10.1177/0033688212439322
Shintani, N., & Ellis, R. (2014). Tracking 'learning behaviours' in the incidental acquisition of two dimensional adjectives by Japanese beginner learners of L2 English. *Language Teaching Research, 18*(4), 521–542. doi:10.1177/1362168813519885
Shintani, N. (2015). The effectiveness of processing instruction on L2 grammar acquisition: A meta-analysis. *Applied Linguistics, 36*(3), 306–325. doi:10.1093/applin/amu067
Sinclair, J. M., & Coulthard, M. (1975). *Towards an analysis of discourse: The English used by teachers and pupils.* Oxford: Oxford University Press.
Skehan, P. (1998). Taks-based instruction. *Annual Review of Applied Linguistics, 18*, 268–286. doi:10.1017/S0267190500003585
Skehan, P. (2012). *Researching tasks; Performance, assessment and pedagogy.* Shanghai: Shanghai Foreign Language Education Press.
Slimani, A. (1989). The role of topicalization in classroom language learning. *System, 17*(2), 223–234. doi:10.1016/0346-251X(89)90035-3
Smith, P. (1970). *A comparison of the audiolingual and cognitive approaches to foreign language instruction: The Pennsylvania Foreign Language Project.* Philadelphia, PA: Center for Curriculum Development.
Stahl, S. A., & Fairbanks, M. M. (1986). The effects of vocabulary instruction: A model-based meta-analysis. *Review of Educational Research, 56*(1), 72–110. doi:10.3102/00346543056001072
Storch, N., & Wigglesworth, G. (2003). Is there a role for the use of the L1 in an L2 setting? *TESOL Quarterly, 37*(4), 760–770. doi:10.2307/3588224
Sugita, M., & Takeuchi, O. (2009). What can teachers do to motivate their students? A classroom research on motivational strategy use in the Japanese EFL context. *Innovation in Language Learning and Teaching, 4*(1), 21–35. doi:10.1080/17501220802450470
Swain, M. (1985). Communicative competence: Some roles of comprehensible input and comprehensible output in its development. In S. Gass & C. Madden (Eds.), *Input in second language acquisition* (pp. 235–256). Rowley, MA: Newbury House.
Swain, M. (1995). Three functions of output in second language learning. In G. Cook & B. Seidelhofer (Eds.), *Principle and practice in applied linguistics: Studies in honor of H.G. Widdowson* (pp. 125–144). Oxford: Oxford University Press.
Swain, M., & Lapkin, S. (2000). Task-based second language learning: the uses of the first language. *Language Teaching Research, 4*(3), 251–274. doi:10.1177/136216880000400304

Swain, M., & Lapkin, S. (1995). Problems in Output and the Cognitive Processes They Generate: A Step Towards Second Language Learning. *Applied Linguistics, 16*(3), 371–391. doi:10.1093/applin/16.3.371
Swain, M., & Lapkin, S. (2008). Lexical learning through a multitask activity: The role of repetition. In T. W. Fortune & D. J. Tedick (Eds.), *Pathways to multilingualism. Evolving perspectives on immersion education* (pp. 119–132). Clevedon: Multilingual Matters.
Swain, M., Kinnear, P., & Steinman, L. (2011). *Sociocultural theory in second language education: An introduction through narratives.* Bristol: Multilingual Matters.
Swan, M. (2005). Legislation by hypothesis: The case of task-based instruction. *Applied Linguistics, 26*(3), 376–401. doi:10.1093/applin/ami013
Taguchi, N., & Kim, Y. (2014). Collaborative dialogue in learning pragmatics: Pragmatic-related episodes as an opportunity for learning request-making. *Applied Linguistics.* Retrieved from ⟨http://applij.oxfordjournals.org/content/early/2014/07/11/applin.amu034.abstract⟩
Takashima, H. (2005). *Bunpou koumoku betsu eigo no tasuku katsudou to tasuku: 34 no jissen to hyouka.* [English task activities and tasks for gramatical structures: 34 practices and evaluations] Tokyo: Taisyukan.
Takimoto, M. (2009). The effects of input-based tasks on the development of learners' pragmatic proficiency. *Applied Linguistics, 30*(1), 1–25. doi:10.1093/applin/amm049
Tanaka, T., & Tanaka, C. (2014). Eigo kyoushi no tame no bunpou shidou dezain. [Grammar teaching design for Enlgish education]. Tokyo: Taishukan.
Tsui, A. B. M., & Tollefson, J. W. (2007). Language policy and the construction of National Cultural identity. In A. B. M. Tsui & J. W. Tollefson (Eds.), *Language, policy, culture, and identity in Asian contexts* (pp. 1–24). Mahwah, NJ: Lawrence Erlbaum Associates.
Ur, P. (1996). *A course in language teaching: Practice and theory.* Cambridge: Cambridge University Press.
Van den Branden, K. (2009). Mediating between predetermined order and complete chaos: The role of the teacher in task-based language education. *IJAL International Journal of Applied Linguistics, 19*(3), 264–285. doi:10.1111/j.1473-4192.2009.00241.x
Van den Branden, K. (1997). Effects of negotiation on language learners' output. *Language Learning, 47*(4), 589–636. doi:10.1111/0023-8333.00023
Van den Branden, K. (Ed.). (2006). *Task-based language education.* Cambridge: Cambridge Applied Linguistics. doi:10.1017/CBO9780511667282
Van Lier, L. (1988). *The classroom and the language learner: Ethnography and second Language classroom research.* London: Longman.
Van Lier, L. (1996). *Interaction in the language curriculum: Awareness, autonomy and authenticity.* London: Longman.
VanPatten, B. (1989). Can learners attend to form and content while processing input? *Hispania, 72*(2), 409–417. doi:10.2307/343165
VanPatten, B. (1996). *Input processing and grammar instruction: Theory and research.* Norwood, NJ: Ablex.
VanPatten, B. (2000). Processing instruction as form-meaning connections: Issues in theory and research. In J. F. Lee & A. Valdman (Eds.), *Form and meaning: Multiple perspectives* (pp. 43–68). Boston, MA: Heinle and Heinle.
VanPatten, B., & Sanz, C. (1995). From input to output: Processing instruction and communicative tasks. In F. Eckman, D. Highland, P. W. Lee, J. Mileham, & R. R. Weber (Eds.), *Second language acquisition theory and pedagogy* (pp. 169–185). Hillsdale, NJ: Lawrence Erlbaum Associates.
Verhoeven, L. T. (1989). Monitoring in children's second language speech. *Second Language Research, 5*(2), 141–155. doi:10.1177/026765838900500203

Vygotsky, L. S. (1978). *Mind in society: The development of higher psychological processes*. Cambridge, MA: Harvard University Press.

Wedell, M. (2009). Developing a capacity to make "English for everyone" worthwhile: Reconsidering outcomes and how to start achieving them. *International Journal of Educational Development, 28*, 628–639. doi:10.1016/j.ijedudev.2007.08.002

Wee, R. (2009). Sources of errors: an interplay of interlingual influence and intralingual factors *European Journal of Social Sciences, 11*(2), 349–359.

Willis, D., & Willis, J. (2007). *Doing task-based teaching*. Oxford: Oxford University Press.

Willis, J. (1996). *A framework for task-based learning*. Harlow: Longman.

Yagi, S., & Igawa, K. (2010). *Shoogakkoo kyooinn ni okeru eigo kyooiku no shishitsu koojo ni kansuru kenkyuu (1): Menkyozyoo kooshin kooshuu no jizen no kadai ishiki tyoosa to jigo hyooka no choosa kekka kara* [Elementary school teachers' professional development for English language education (1): An analysis of the pre/post-survey of a teaching credential renewal course]. *Shitennooji Daigaku Kiyoo, 49*, 167–182.

Yano, Y., Long, M. H., & Ross, S. (1994). The effects of simplified and elaborated texts on foreign language reading comprehension. *Language Learning, 44*(2), 189–219. doi:10.1111/j.1467-1770.1994.tb01100.x

Yoshida, M. (1978). The acquisition of English vocabulary by a Japanese speaking child. In E. M. Hatch (Ed.), *Second language acquisition* (pp. 91–100). New York, NY: Newbury House.

APPENDIX A

Transcription conventions (adapted from Markee, 2008)

Name:	pseudonym of an identified participant
T:	the teacher talking
Ss:	several or all students talking simultaneously
[ ]	overlapped talk
(0.0)	length of silence
(.)	micro-pause
?	rising intonation
!	strong emphasis, with falling intonation
.	a period indicates falling (final) intonation
,	a comma indicates low-rising intonation suggesting continuation
::	noticeably lengthened sound
underlined	marked stress
CAPS	loud volume
((words))	comments by the transcriber
/ /	phonetic transcription
(= *words*)	English translation of the Japanese words

APPENDIX B

Inferential statistics for vocabulary tests

Procedures

The four vocabulary tests were analysed using PASW version 18. Normal distribution was tested using the Kolmogorov-Smirnov test. A series of non-parametric tests were applied (i.e., Kruskal-Wallis test with post-hoc Mann-Whitney U tests and Friedmann Test with post-hoc Wilcoxon Signed Rank tests) for the noun scores in the two production tests as the scores in these tests did not meet the assumption of normality. For all the other test scores, a series of parametric analyses were undertaken (i.e., repeated measures analyses of variance (ANOVA) with pairwise comparisons using Bonferroni adjustments and one-way ANOVAs with pairwise comparisons using Bonferroni adjustments). Table A.1 shows whether a non-parametric or parametric statistical test was used to investigate the scores from the four tests used to measure learning.

Table A.1. Statistical tests for comparative analysis for vocabulary scores

Vocabulary tests	Noun scores	Adjective scores
Same-or-Different task test	Non-parametric	Parametric
Discrete-item production test	Non-parametric	Parametric
Category Task test	Parametric	Parametric
Multiple-choice listening test	Parametric	Parametric

Categorical data were analysed using the chi-square test. The categorical data were analysed using the chi-square test.

Effect sizes for the comparative effects of two variables were estimated using the correlation coefficient effect size *r* because the comparisons involved both parametric and non-parametric tests. Although Cohen's d is generally recommended for parametric test, it has been suggested that *r* should be used for non-parametric tests (Larson-Hall, 2010). To make the comparisons consistent, I decided to use *r* for all the comparisons. To do so, an effect size *d* was first calculated and then converted to *r* using following formulas.

$$d = \frac{\bar{x}_1 - \bar{x}_2}{s}.$$

$$s = \sqrt{\frac{(n_1 - 1)s_1^2 + (n_2 - 1)s_2^2}{n_1 + n_2 - 2}}$$

$$r = \frac{\mathrm{d}}{\sqrt{d^2 + a}}$$

Effect sizes for the categorical variables were estimated using Cohen's *w*. It was defined as:

$$w = \sqrt{\sum_{i=1}^{N} \frac{(p_{0i} - p_{1i})^2}{p_{0i}}}$$

where p_{0i} is the value of the ith cell under H_0 and p_{1i} is the value of the ith cell under H_1.

Test results for nouns (for Table 6.1)

Within-group comparisons

The Same-or-Different Task. The Friedman Test showed that there is no significant difference between the three repeated tests for the control group ($\chi^2 = .667$, $df = 2$, $p > .01$). The Wilcoxon Signed Ranks Test showed that the PPP group significantly improved on post-test 1 from the pre-test ($z = -3.411$, $p < .01$, $r = .80$), and on post-test 2 from the pre-test ($z = -3.417$, $p < .01$, $r = .78$), and the TBLT groups also improved their scores significantly on post-test 1 from the pre-test ($z = -3.411$, $p < .01$, $r = .80$), and on post-test 2 from the pre-test ($z = -3.413$, $p < .01$, $r = .84$). A paired t-test showed that the TBLT group significantly improved from post-test 1 to post-test 2 ($t = 3.413$, $df = 14$, $p < .05$, $r = .23$), but the PPP group did not ($t = 1.429$, $df = 16$, $p = .05$, $r = .08$).

The discrete-item production test. The Friedman Test showed that there is no significant difference between the three repeated tests for the control group ($\chi^2 = 1.400$, $df = 2$, $p > .01$). Wilcoxon Signed Ranks Test showed that the PPP group significantly improved on post-test 1 from the pre-test ($z = -3.474$, $p < .01$, $r = .84$), and on post-test 2 from the pre-test ($z = -3.475$, $p < .01$, $r = .82$), and the TBLT group also improved their scores significantly on post-test 1 from the pre-test ($z = -3.419$, $p < .01$, $r = .86$), and on post-test 2 from the pre-test ($z = -3.419$, $p < .01$, $r = .93$). A paired t-test showed that the TBLT group significantly improved from post-test 1 to post-test 2 ($t = 2.941$, $df = 14$, $p < .05$, $r = .29$), but the PPP group did not ($t = .717$, $df = 16$, $p > .05$, $r = .07$).

The Category Task test. A repeated measures ANOVA for the three groups in the three repeated tests shows there was a significant main effect of the test (F (1.224, 51.424) = 276.747, $p < .01$, partial $\eta^2 = .868$) and a significant interaction effect of the test and the group (F (2.449, 51.424) = 69.304, $p < .01$, partial $\eta^2 = .767$). The sequential Bonferroni adjustment was applied for multiple comparisons, showing that the PPP group and the TBLT group significantly improved their scores from the pre-test to post-test 1 and from the pre-test to post-test 2 but there was no significant improvement between post-test 1 and post-test 2. The control group did not show any significant improvement.

The multiple-choice listening test. A repeated measures ANOVA showed a significant main effect of the test (F (1.369, 57.502) = 194.977, $p < .01$, partial $\eta^2 = .823$) and a significant interaction effect of the test and group (F (2.738, 57.502) = 53.649, $p < .01$, partial $\eta^2 = .719$). The Bonferroni multiple comparisons test showed that both the PPP and the TBLT group significantly improved from the pre-test to post-test 1 and from the pre-test to post-test 2 but there was no significant difference between post-tests 1 and 2. The control group did not show any significant improvement.

Between-group comparison results

The Same-or-Different Task. The Kruskal Wallis Test showed that there was no significant difference between the three groups in the pre-test on the Same-or-Different Task ($\chi^2 = .007$, $df = 2$, $p > .01$). However, there was a significant difference in the three groups in post-test 1 ($\chi^2 = 31.573$, $df = 2$, $p < .01$) and post-test 2 ($\chi^2 = 29.798$, $df = 2$, $p < .01$). The post-hoc Mann-Whitney U showed that there was no significant difference between the PPP and the TBLT groups in post-test 1 (U = 66.500, $p > .01$, $r = .38$) or in post-test 2 (U = 108.500, $p > .01$, $r = .13$) but there were significant differences between the TBLT group and the control group in post-test 1 (U = 1.300, $p < .01$, $r = .80$) and post-test 2 (U = 1.300, $p < .01$, $r = .84$). Also there were significant differences between the PPP group and the control group in post-test 1 (U = .000, $p < .01$, $r = .79$) and post-test 2 (U = .000, $p < .01$, $r = .78$).

The discrete-item production test. The Kruskal Wallis Test showed that there was no significant difference between the three groups in the pre-test ($\chi^2 = .000$, $df = 2$, $p > .01$). However, there was a significant difference in the three groups in post-test 1 ($\chi^2 = 31.040$, $df = 2$, $p < .01$) and post-test 2 ($\chi^2 = 29.967$, $df = 2$, $p < .01$). The post-hoc Mann-Whitney U showed that there was no significant difference between the PPP and the TBLT groups in the post-test 1 (U = 79.500, $p > .01$, $r = .28$) or in the post-test 2 (U = 106.000, $p > .01$, $r = .15$) but there were significant differences between the TBLT group and the control group in post-test 1 (U = .000, $p < .01$, $r = .85$) and post-test 2 (U = .000, $p < .01$, $r = .86$). Also there were significant differences between the PPP group and the control group in post-test 1 (U = .000, $p < .01$, $r = .81$) and post-test 2 (U = .000, $p < .01$, $r = .86$).

The Category Task test. A one-way ANOVA was used for the Category Task test scores. In the pre-test, there was no significant difference among the three groups ($F(2, 42) = 2.623$, $p > .05$). However, there were significant effects in post-test 1 ($F(2, 42) = 74.599$, $p < .05$, partial $\eta^2 = .789$) and post-test 2 ($F(2, 42) = 62.159$, $p < .05$, partial $\eta^2 = .770$). Bonferroni pairwise comparisons test showed that both the PPP and the TBLT groups outperformed the control group in post-tests 1 and 2. Furthermore, the TBLT group outperformed the PPP group in both post-tests 1 and 2.

The multiple-choice listening test. A one-way ANOVA showed there was no significant effect between the three groups in the pre-test ($F(2, 42) = .759$, $p > .05$) but there were significant effects in post-test 1 ($F(2, 42) = 56.788$, $p < .05$, partial $\eta^2 = .688$) and post-test 2 ($F(2, 42) = 57.922$, $p < .05$, partial $\eta^2 = .718$). A Bonferroni pairwise comparisons test showed that both the PPP and the TBLT groups outperformed the control group in both post-tests, but there was no significant difference between the PPP and the TBLT groups in either post-test 1 or 2.

Test Results of adjectives (for Table 6.4)

Within-group comparisons

The Same-or-Different Task test. A repeated measures ANOVA for the three groups in the three repeated tests shows a significant test effect (F (1.485, 62.351) = 44.653, $p < .05$, partial $\eta^2 = .515$). The Bonferroni multiple comparisons showed that the PPP group improved from the pre-test to post-test 1 but there was no significant difference between the pre-test and post-test 2 and between post-tests 1 and 2. The TBLT group improved from the pre-test to post-test 1 and from the pre-test to post-test 2. There was no significant difference between the post-tests 1 and 2. The control group did not show any significant improvement between any of the three tests.

The discrete-item vocabulary production test. A repeated measures ANOVA showed a significant test effect (F (2, 84) = 38.163, $p < .05$, partial $\eta^2 = .476$). The Bonferroni multiple comparisons test showed that both the PPP group and the TBLT group significantly improved both from the pre-test to post-test 1 and from the pre-test to post-test 2, but there was no significant difference between the two post-tests. The control group did not show any significant improvement throughout the testing period.

The Category Task test. A repeated measures ANOVA for the three groups using scores from the three repeated tests shows a significant test effect (F (1.262, 52.990) = 109.946, $p < .05$, partial $\eta^2 = .741$). The post-hoc multiple comparisons showed that both the PPP group and the TBLT group significantly improved their scores both from the pre-test to post-test 1 and from the pre-test to post-test 2,but there was no significant difference between the two post-tests for either group. The control group showed no significant improvement.

The Multiple-choice listening test. A repeated measures ANOVA showed a significant test effect (F (1.720, 72.222) = 188.702, $p < .05$, partial $\eta^2 = .818$). The Bonferroni multiple comparisons test showed that both the PPP group and the TBLT group significantly improved both from the pre-test to post-test 1 and from the pre-test to post-test 2, but there was no significant difference between the two post-tests. The control group did not show any significant improvement.

Between-group comparisons

In order to compare the three groups on acquisition of target adjectives, the test scores for adjectives in post-test 1 and 2 were analysed using One-way ANOVAs.

The Same-or-Different Task. A one-way ANOVA showed there was no significant effect between the three groups in the pre-test ($F(2, 44) = .013, p > .05$) but there were significant effects in post-test 1 ($F(2, 44) = 12.650, p < .05$, partial $\eta^2 = .552$) and post-test 2 ($F(2, 44) = 14.551, p < .05$, partial $\eta^2 = .468$). The Bonferroni pairwise comparisons showed that the TBLT group outperformed the PPP group and the Control group in post-tests 1 and 2. There was no significant difference between the PPP group and the control group in either post-test 1 or 2.

The Discrete-item production test. A one-way ANOVA showed there was no significant effect between the three groups in the pre-test ($F(2, 44) = .325, p > .05$) but there were significant effects in post-test 1 ($F(2, 44) = 11.378, p < .05$, partial $\eta^2 = .318$) and post-test 2 ($F(2, 44) = 26.216, p < .05$, partial $\eta^2 = .348$). The Bonferroni pairwise comparisons showed that both the PPP and the TBLT groups outperformed the control group in both post-tests. Furthermore, the TBLT group outperformed the PPP group in both post-tests.

The Category Task test. A one-way ANOVA showed there was no significant effect between the three groups in the pre-test ($F(2, 44) = .651, p > .05$) but there were significant effects in post-test 1 ($F(2, 44) = 25.557, p < .05$, partial $\eta^2 = .445$) and post-test 2 ($F(2, 44) = 30.699, p < .05$, partial $\eta^2 = .501$). The Bonferroni pairwise comparisons showed that both the PPP and the TBLT groups outperformed the control group in both post-tests. The TBLT group also outperformed the PPP group in both post-tests.

The multiple-choice listening test. A one-way ANOVA showed there was no significant effect between the three groups in the pre-test ($F(2, 44) = .691, p > .05$) but there were significant effects in post-test 1 ($F(2, 44) = 53.212, p < .05$, partial $\eta^2 = .665$) and post-test 2 ($F(2, 44) = 65.833, p < .05$, partial $\eta^2 = .715$). The Bonferroni pairwise comparisons showed that both the PPP and the TBLT groups outperformed the control group in both post-tests. The TBLT group also outperformed the PPP group in both post-tests.

Results for a linear regression. To further examine the causal effects of the TBLT learners' "self-initiated" production of the adjectives on their acquisition, a simple linear regression was carried out. The number of "self-initiated" tokens produced by individual learners in this group was the independent variable and the scores of the two tests the dependent variables. The results showed that in the Same-or-Different Task the effect was approaching significance in Post-test 1 ($R^2 = .254$, $p = .056$) and significant in post-test 2 ($R^2 = .428$, $p = .008$). In the Discrete-item test, the effects were significant in both post-tests ($R^2 = .452$, $p = .006$. for post-test 1 and $R^2 = .445$, $p = .007$. for post-test 2). In other words, the learners who self-initiated the production of adjectives acquired more adjectives.

Test results for process features (for Tables 6.8–6.10)

Frequency of Target Words in Input and Output (for Table 6.8). There were significant differences in teacher's production for both nouns and adjectives (nouns: $\chi^2 = 752.336$, $df = 1$, $p < .01$, $w = .46$; adjectives: $\chi^2 = 205.096$, $df = 1$, $p < .01$, $w = .16$). There were significant differences in students' production for both nouns and adjectives (nouns: $\chi^2 = 2613.838$, $df = 1$, $p > .01$, $w = .96$; adjectives: $\chi^2 = 439.421$, $df = 1$, $p > .01$, $w = .56$). Chi-square tests showed that there were no significant differences between the two groups in terms of input for both nouns and adjectives (nouns: $\chi^2 = .677$, $df = 1$, $p > .01$, $w = .01$; adjectives: $\chi^2 = 1.226$, $df = 1$, $p > .01$, $w = .01$).

Embedded and Isolated Word Production by the Teacher (Table 6.9). Chi-Square tests showed that for both nouns and adjectives there were significant differences between the two groups in the number of the 'embedded' word tokens (nouns: $\chi^2 = 3557.307$, $df = 1$, $p < .01$, $w = .93$, adjectives: $\chi^2 = 1906.128$, $df = 1$, $p < .01$, $w = .95$) and in the 'isolated' tokens (nouns: $\chi^2 = 294.715$, $df = 1$, $p < .01$, $w = .24$, adjectives: $\chi^2 = 895.315$, $df = 1$, $p < .01$, $w = .78$). Cross-tabulation analyses showed a significant difference between the nouns and adjectives in terms of the proportion of 'embedded' and 'isolated' tokens in the TBLT group ($\chi^2 = 528.111$, $df = 1$, $p < .01$, $w = .26$) but no significant differences in the PPP group ($\chi^2 = 1.605$, $df = 1$, $p > .01$, $w = .02$).

Number of requested/optional and self-initiated/borrowed tokens by the students (Table 6.10). Chi-Square tests showed that for both nouns and adjectives there were significant differences between the two groups in the number of the 'self-initiated' tokens (nouns: $\chi^2 = 2.000$, $df = 1$, $p > .01$, $w = .16$, adjectives: $\chi^2 = 254.135$, $df = 1$, $p < .01$, $w = .98$). "Borrowed" tokens (nouns: $\chi^2 = 56.847$, $df = 1$, $p < .01$, $w = .46$, adjectives: $\chi^2 = 1.391$, $df = 1$, $p > .01$, $w = .13$). Cross-tabulation analyses showed a significant difference between the nouns and adjectives in terms of the number of 'self-initiated' and 'borrowed' tokens in the TBLT group ($\chi^2 = 165.308$, $df = 1$, $p < .01$, $w = .68$) but this difference was non-significant in the PPP group ($\chi^2 = .452$, $df = 1$, $p > .01$, $w = .05$).

APPENDIX C

Statistical results for the multiple-choice plural -*s* listening test

Results for test scores

A series of non-parametric analyses (i.e., Friedman Test with post-hoc Wilcoxon Signed Rank tests, and Kruskal-Wallis test with post-hoc Mann-Whitney U tests) were applied for comparative analyses as some of the test scores did not meet the assumption of normality (for pre-test and post-test 2 by the PPP group for the 'old' items, and pre-test by the control group and post-tests 1 and 2 by the PPP group for the 'new' items).

Within-group comparisons

Table C.2 shows the results of the Friedman Test for the three groups.

Table C.2. The Friedman tests for the multiple-choice plural -*s* listening test

	Old items		New items	
Item	χ^2	Asymp.Sig	χ^2	Asymp.Sig
PPP group	1.370	.504	.462	.794
TBLT group	16.930	.000*	14.044	.001*
Cntl. group	1.167	.558	1.590	.452

* The mean difference is significant at the .01 level

As Table C.3 shows, post-hoc Wilcoxon Signed Ranks Tests showed that the TBLT groups improved their scores significantly for the 'old' and the 'new' items from the pre-test to post-test 1 and from the pre-test to post-test 2, but there were no significant differences between the two post-tests.

Table C.3. Wilcoxon signed ranks tests for the multiple-choice plural -*s* listening test

	Pre-Post1		Pre-Post2		Post1-Post2	
Item	Z	Asymp.Sig	Z	Asymp.Sig	Z	Asymp.Sig
Old (8 items)	−3.069	.002*	−3.235	.001*	−.816	.414
New (6 items)	−2.460	.014	−2.916	.004*	−1.511	.131

* The mean difference is significant at the .01 level

Between-group comparisons

Kruskal Wallis Tests (Table C.4) showed significant effects on post-test 1 and post-test 2 both for the 'old' and the 'new' items while there were none in the pre-test.

Table C.4. Kruskal Wallis tests for the multiple-choice plural -*s* listening test

	Pre-test		Post-test 1		Post-test 2	
Item	χ^2	Asymp.Sig	χ^2	Asymp.Sig	χ^2	Asymp.Sig
Old (8 items)	.249	.883	19.335	.000*	22.951	.000*
New (6 items)	.175	.916	11.931	.003*	14.646	.001*

* The mean difference is significant at the .01 level

Post-hoc Mann-Whitney U tests showed that the TBLT group outperformed the PPP group and the control group both for 'old' and 'new' items in post-test 1 and post-test 2 while there were no significant differences between the pre-test scores. No significant differences were found between the PPP and the control groups across the three tests. See Table C.5.

Table C.5. Mann-Whitney U tests for the multiple-choice plural -*s* listening test

		Pre-test		Post-test 1		Post-test 2	
	Item	U	Asymp.Sig	U	Asymp.Sig	U	Asymp.Sig
PPP-TBLT	Old items	112.000	.982	24.000	.000*	17.500	.000*
	New items	105.500	.762	46.500	.005*	43.000	.003*
PPP-Cntl.	Old items	106.000	.778	97.500	.501	96.500	.490
	New items	111.500	.965	109.500	.897	104.500	.731
TBLT-Cntl.	Old items	100.000	.562	26.500	.000*	14.500	.000*
	New items	103.000	.682	38.500	.002*	26.500	.000*

Cntl. = Control group; * = the mean difference is significant at the .01 level

Comparisons between the number of 'acquired' and 'not acquired' students

Within-group comparisons

The differences in the number of 'acquired' students in the three repeated tests for each group were compared using chi-square tests. For the TBLT group, there were significant differences between the pre-test and post-test 1 for the 'old items' (χ^2 = 17.368, df = 1, p < .01) and for the 'new items' (χ^2 = 17.368, df = 1, p < .01), and the pre-test and post-test 2 for the 'old items' (χ^2 =20.000, df = 1, p < .01) and for the 'new items' (χ^2 = 20.000, *df* = 1, $p < .01$). There were no significant differences between the two post-tests for the 'old items' (χ^2 = 3.399, *df* = 1, $p > .01$) or for the 'new items' (χ^2 = 3.399, *df* = 1, $p > .01$). Although some students in the PPP group were categorized as 'acquired' for the 'new' items, the improvement for the group overall was not significant from the pre-test to post-test 1 (χ^2 = 2.143, *df* = 1, $p > .01$) or from the pre-test to post-test 2 (χ^2 = 3.333, *df* = 1, $p > .01$).

Between-group comparisons

The differences among the three groups were also analysed using chi-square tests. The number of 'acquired' students in the TBLT group was higher than the PPP group in post-test 1 (χ^2 =16.425, *df* =1, $p < .01$) and in post-test 2 (χ^2 = 22.941, *df* = 1, $p < .01$), and also higher than the control group in post-test 1 (χ^2 = 20.000, *df* = 1, $p < .01$) and post-test 2 (χ^2 = 22.941, *df* = 1, $p < .01$). There was no significant difference between the PPP group and the control group in post-test 1 (χ^2 = 1.034, *df* = 1, $p > .01$), and none of the participants in either of these groups reached the 'acquired' level in post-test 2.

Index